Supporting Lifelong Learning
Volume 2

Supporting Lifelong Learning, Volume 2: Organizing learning examines the ways in which learning is organized in a diverse range of lifelong learning environments. The contributors recognize that formal institutions are no longer seen as the sole providers of education and consider the learning opportunities that are found in the workplace, social networks and the community. They examine some of the challenges that arise from placing learning at the centre of these diverse settings, and the implications for those supporting learning within them.

This book highlights the collaborative nature of lifelong learning and argues that, if it is to reach its full potential, fundamental changes must be made to existing practices. It will appeal to postgraduate and doctorate level students with an interest in post-school education and training.

This book is one of three Readers prepared for the Open University MA Course: E845 *Supporting Lifelong Learning*. The three separate volumes provide an in-depth examination of lifelong learning from the perspectives of teaching and learning, organizing learning and policy making. They bring together for the first time theories from a diverse range of disciplines that are now central to our understanding of lifelong learning and provide a new and distinctive contribution to the field.

Fiona Reeve is a Lecturer in Lifelong Learning at The Open University.

Marion Cartwright is a Staff Tutor in Education at The Open University.

Richard Edwards is Professor of Education at the University of Stirling.

Supporting Lifelong Learning, Volume 2: Organizing learning

The companion volumes in this series are:

Supporting Lifelong Learning, Volume 1: Perspectives on learning
Edited by Roger Harrison, Fiona Reeve, Ann Hanson and Julia Clarke

Supporting Lifelong Learning, Volume 3: Making policy work
Edited by Richard Edwards, Nod Miller, Nick Small and Alan Tait

All of these Readers are part of a course: *Supporting Lifelong Learning* (E845), that is itself part of the Open University Masters Programme in Education.

The Open University Masters Programme in Education
The Open University Masters Programme in Education is now firmly established as the most popular postgraduate degree for education professionals in Europe, with over 3,000 students registering each year. The Masters Programme in Education is designed particularly for those with experience of teaching, the advisory service, educational administration or allied fields.

Structure of the Masters Programme in Education
The Masters Programme is a modular degree, and students are, therefore, free to select from the programme options that best fit in with their interests and professional goals. Specialist lines in management, applied linguistics and lifelong learning are also available. Study within the Open University's Advanced Diploma can also be counted towards a Masters Degree, and successful study within the Masters Programme entitles students to apply for entry into the Open University Doctorate in Education Programme.

OU-Supported Open Learning
The Masters Programme in Education provides great flexibility. Students study at their own pace, in their own time, anywhere in the European Union. They receive specially prepared study materials, supported by tutorials, thus offering the chance to work with other students.

The Doctorate in Education
The Doctorate in Education is a part-time doctoral degree, combining taught courses, research methods and a dissertation designed to meet the needs of professionals in education and related areas who are seeking to extend and deepen their knowledge and understanding of contemporary educational issues. The Doctorate in Education builds upon successful study within the Open University Masters Programme in Education.

How to apply
If you would like to register for this programme, or simply find out more information about available courses, please write for the *Professional Development in Education* prospectus to the Call Centre, PO Box 724, The Open University, Walton Hall, Milton Keynes, MK7 6ZW, UK (Telephone 0 (0 44) 1908 653231). Details can also be viewed on our web page http://www.open.ac.uk

Supporting Lifelong Learning
Volume 2

Organizing learning

Edited by
Fiona Reeve, Marion Cartwright
and Richard Edwards

The Open
University

London and New York

First published 2002 by RoutledgeFalmer
11 New Fetter Lane, London EC4P 4EE

Simultaneously published in the USA and Canada
by RoutledgeFalmer
29 West 35th Street, New York, NY 10001

RoutledgeFalmer is an imprint of the Taylor & Francis Group

Typeset in Goudy by
Florence Production Ltd, Stoodleigh, Devon
Printed and bound in Great Britain by
St Edmundsbury Press, Bury St Edmunds, Suffolk

British Library Cataloguing in Publication Data
A catalogue record for this book is available from the
British Library

Library of Congress Cataloging in Publication Data
A catalog record for this book has been requested

ISBN 0–415–25928–2(hbk)
ISBN 0–415–25929–0(pbk)

Contents

Illustrations

Figures

Tables

Acknowledgements

We are indebted to the following for allowing us to make use of copyright material:

Chapter 1: Barnett, R. (1999) 'Learning to work and working to learn', in D. Boud and J. Garrick (eds) *Understanding Learning at Work.* London: Routledge.
Reproduced by permission of Taylor & Francis Ltd, 11 New Fetter Lane, London, EC4P 4EE.

Chapter 2: Ashton, D. (1998) 'Skill formation: redirecting the research agenda', in F. Coffield (ed.) *Learning at Work.* Bristol: The Policy Press.
Reproduced by permission of The Policy Press.

Chapter 3: Marsick, V. and Watkins, K. (1999) 'Envisioning new organisations for learning', in D. Boud and J. Garrick (eds) *Understanding Learning at Work.* London: Routledge.
Reproduced by permission of Taylor & Francis Ltd.

Chapter 4: Devos, A. (1996) 'Gender, work and workplace learning', in *Studies in Continuing Education,* 18:2, pp. 110–121.
Reproduced by permission of the University of Technology, Sydney.

Chapter 5: Keep, E. and Rainbird, H. (1999) 'Towards the learning organization' in S. Bach and K. Sisson (eds) *Personnel Management in Britain* (3rd edition). Oxford: Blackwell.
Reproduced by permission of Blackwell Publishers Ltd.

Chapter 6: Eraut, M., Alderton, J., Cole, G. and Senker, P. (1999) 'The impact of the manager on learning in the workplace', in F. Coffield (ed.) *Speaking Truth to Power.* Bristol: The Policy Press.
Reproduced by permission of The Policy Press.

Chapter 7: Kidd, J. (1998) 'Knowledge creation in Japanese manufacturing companies in Italy: reflections upon organizational learning', in *Management Learning*, 29:2, pp. 131–146.
Reproduced by permission of Sage Publications Ltd.

Chapter 8: King, B. (2000) 'Managing institutional change and the pressures for new approaches to teaching and learning', in V. Jukupec and J. Garrick (eds) *Flexible Learning: Human Resource Management*. London: Routledge.
Reproduced by permission of Taylor & Francis Ltd.

Chapter 9: Francis, B. and Humphreys, J. (2000) 'Professional education as a structural barrier to lifelong learning in the NHS', in *Journal of Educational Policy*, 15:3, pp. 281–292.
Reproduced by permission of Taylor & Francis Ltd.

Chapter 10: Wenger, E. (2000) 'Communities of practice and social learning systems', in *Organisations*, 7:2, pp. 225–246.
Reproduced by permission of Sage Publications Ltd.

Chapter 11: Cara, S., Landry, C. and Ranson, S. (1998) 'The learning city in the learning society', in *The Richness of Cities: Urban Policy in a New Landscape*. London: Comedia.
Reproduced by permission of Comedia.

Chapter 12: Mayo, M. (2000) 'Learning for active citizenship: training for and learning from participation in area regeneration', in *Studies in the Education of Adults*, 32:1, pp. 22–35.
Reproduced by permission of NIACE.

While the publishers have made every effort to contact copyright holders of the material used in this volume, they would be grateful to hear from any they were unable to contact.

Introduction

Organizing learning

*Fiona Reeve, Marion Cartwright and
Richard Edwards*

The idea that learning is a central component to organizational efficiency,
effectiveness and competitiveness has become increasingly widespread in
recent years. It is almost as common for employers and trade unionists to be
discussing lifelong learning as it is for educators. While lifelong learning itself
is not a new notion, earlier foci were primarily on its contribution to personal
development, nation-building for post-colonial states and citizenship. While
the role of lifelong learning in relation to work and the economy has always
been an important concern among certain groups, it is only in relatively
recent years that it has become commonplace as a concept.

As the pace of economic change has been perceived to speed up, so the
capacity both of the workforce to learn and of the organization to make
more effective use of what has become known as its human resources has
become a major focus of interest. Initial education is proclaimed as no longer
sufficient for a rapidly changing context marked by globalizing processes and
advances in information and communications technologies. Lifelong learning as an issue has therefore migrated from being primarily a concern of
certain groups of educators to become a focus of research and debate amongst
those concerned with business, management and organizational studies.
Notions of the learning organization, knowledge management, organizational learning, communities of practice and social learning systems are now
found extensively intertwined with certain of the debates surrounding lifelong learning. It is some of those debates that are to be found in this volume.

These ideas have direct relevance for those involved in human resource
development and training and increasingly for other adult educators, since,
with the growing development of the provision of learning opportunities
through quasi-markets, quality audit and performance management, ideas
that might have emerged in subject areas other than education have become
influential in many educational circles as well. Lifelong learning in this
sense is often linked to notions of effectiveness, efficiency, innovation and
productivity, and is heavily influenced by notions of human capital theory

The Introduction was written especially for this volume.

put forward by economists. Here the level of human skills and qualifications are seen as a contributor or even the central contributor to an organization's capacity. The more skilled and qualified a population, the more productive and innovative they will be, thereby contributing to the economic well-being of the workers themselves, their employers and the nation as a whole. In more recent times, it is not only skills and qualifications that have been a focus of workplace learning, but also values and identities, as organizations and even governments attempt to harness or empower people to be motivated towards the goals set for them.

Thus, many of the practices and ideas developed in the commercial domain come to have an impact on public services. They have also extended beyond individual organizations. It is more common now to see discussion of the learning city, the learning region, the learning society, and learning networks. Attempts to forge partnerships and co-ordinate the provision of lifelong learning opportunities within a geographical area are developing. The extent to which this is to increase skills to attract inward investment and/or to support the population to play a more active role in their communities is a matter of debate. Thus, the notion that learning is central to organizations begins to extend into the community as well, with notions of community capacity building as well as individual skill development coming to the fore. The effectiveness of voluntary and campaigning groups can also be argued therefore to be based at least in part on developing the capacities of those involved. Campaigning groups spend a lot of time and energy on educating their members and attempting to educate and persuade the wider community.

We see therefore that there is a continuum of ideas and practices that demonstrates the centrality of lifelong learning to collective endeavours. Organizing that learning therefore becomes a key concern for organizations of whatever sort. There is a blurring of the boundaries over what is relevant to the private, public and voluntary sectors. This text brings together a series of essays that explores that continuum and some of the issues and debates that are to be found in the fields of education and organization studies.

First, we turn to the question of why lifelong learning has become a central feature of concern for organizations and their development. Ronald Barnett argues that the contemporary period is one of supercomplexity, characterized by contestability, challengeability and uncertainty. As such, he argues that work needs to become a form of learning and learning a form of work. This situation is fostered by the globalization of the economy, the rise of the audit state – expecting more from less – and the information technology revolution. As a result, work not simply requires learning, but *demands* it and that learning becomes ever more fraught, challenging and unsettling. Barnett therefore counters those who argue that the vocationalization of learning is a limiting factor on the opportunities available. For him, it is both necessary and a challenge with which to engage.

Barnett points to the centrality of skill formation within organizations as a crucial dimension of lifelong learning. However, this has been an area that has been undervalued in policy and practice by many states and employers alike. Investment in human capital has largely been thought of in terms of the initial and formal provision of education and training, yet research has started to demonstrate the limitations of this view and the importance of less formal processes of skill formation within workplaces. Thus, David Ashton draws upon empirical research of two case studies, one based in the UK, the other a part of a multinational based in South East Asia, to argue that skill formation needs to be conceived as a continuous process in which learning at work is central rather than as a series of discontinuous formal educational or training activities.

Ashton is indicating not only the importance of the workplace in skill formation but also that a lifelong learning approach to researching this is necessary, where the focus is on the learning that people engage in rather than the formal opportunities in which they may participate. He also points to the urgent need for managing learning to be identified and developed as central to workplaces. This is a view shared by Michael Eraut and his colleagues. From their research into informal learning in UK workplaces, they suggest that the notion of the manager as staff developer is too narrow and that they might be more effective in setting a personal example and fostering a culture of informal learning rather than sending people on courses. Here they point to the personality, interpersonal skills, knowledge and learning orientation of managers as crucial to the capacity to manage learning, in particular the informal learning of those around them. They also highlight the inadequacies of notions of management training that focus on standardized outcomes.

Workplace learning has therefore become a central area of interest and there are many attempts to frame the practices in which people engage. One such framing that has emerged over the last two decades is that of the learning organization, an idea explored in the chapter by Victoria Marsick and Karen Watkins. Here they draw upon both their own research and that of others to outline different models of learning in the workplace and the practices and theories of learning associated with them. They suggest four metaphors – machine, open systems, brain/holograph, and chaos/complexity – for understanding workplaces, each of which has different implications for managers, employees and human resource development strategies. They suggest that selective tailoring of the various models to different organizations and sectors of the economy is the best strategy to adopt.

Alongside the concern to develop learning organizations has emerged the separate but related concern for knowledge management. This is about the capacity to make explicit the tacit knowledge that people learn and create in their everyday working practices, in order that this knowledge can be an effective resource for the organization as a whole. One needs to learn the capacities to manage knowledge if one is going to enhance the knowledge management of the organization. Knowledge management therefore does not only point to the need to learn in organizations, but for very specific types of learning.

As with the notion of learning organizations, there are questions about the implications of the notion of knowledge management in relation to different sectors of the economy, different geographical locations and the size of organizations. It has become particularly significant in transnational and multinational organizations operating around the globe. Here it might be felt the bigger and more complex the operations of an organization might be, the more it needs to pay attention to its knowledge management practices and the capacities of those within the organization to manage that knowledge. This is explored in the chapter by John Kidd, based on research into Japanese-owned Italian firms, wherein issues of intercultural conflict become a barrier to effective knowledge management practices.

There is a sense then in which there is a prescriptive dimension to the discussion of learning organizations and knowledge management, something that has been observed of much of the literature. It is aspirational and in certain cases almost proselytizing rather than evaluative or critical. The latter is provided by Ewart Keep and Helen Rainbird. They draw upon the studies of what occurs in UK workplaces to provide a sustained critique of the notion that a learning organization is a common feature of workplace practices. They argue that the development of high levels of organizational learning are hindered by a range of cultural and structural characteristics. These include: the legacy of UK class structures; short-termism; a relatively deregulated labour market that encourages high staff turnover; a tradition of low-trust employer–employee relations; a shareholder model of capitalism; a notion of management as doing/action rather than reflection/analysis.

These are important criticisms. However, it may well be that one of the reasons why the notion of a learning organization has been attractive to some is that it provides a basis, however idealized, to challenge organizations that fail to enhance the learning of those within them. It is also important that in the conclusion to their chapter they point to the centrality of learning for managers if learning is to take root more fully in the organization. This echoes the argument put forward by Ashton and Eraut and his colleagues above.

An even more trenchant critique is provided by Anita Devos. She argues that the uncritical adoption of workplace learning ideas derived from management studies results in issues of gender and power being sidelined. Devos is concerned that approaches to workplace learning result in the continuing discrimination of women, as the 'empowerment' of workers through learning cannot overcome the structural division of labour and the inequalities associated with it. Nor should we forget that in relation to who participates in workplace learning, it is primarily full-time employees and those in higher and management positions. These tend to favour men over women. Thus, the focus on learning as central to organizational effectiveness and efficiency should not blind us to inequalities in the workplace and the role lifelong learning could have in perpetuating rather than helping to overcome them.

The politics of organizations, and the role of lifelong learning within them, is examined by Becky Francis and John Humphreys. In the context of the UK's National Health Service, they argue that professional education provides a structural barrier to lifelong learning. Here the medical profession uses its distinctive professional education to maintain job demarcation and ensure its separateness from the nursing profession. This points to the politics of lifelong learning within organizations, something that is not restricted to professional education, but is equally relevant to all workers. They suggest that opportunities for lifelong learning may be positioned as part of wider organizational strategies that seek to challenge established work practices and job demarcations, usually to introduce greater flexibility into the workplace. Here there is a political dimension to deciding whether lifelong learning is a 'good thing'.

The politics of organizations is also at the heart of the chapter by Bruce King. He draws on the context of Australian higher education to argue that the culture of universities makes it difficult for them to meet contemporary challenges. For King, this can only be addressed through systematic planning at management level, the result being new organizational structures, learning methods, delivery methods, and partnerships and collaboration. A central problem in King's view is the 'resistance' of academic staff to these changes and he suggests that such moves will require the reshaping of academic identities. The adoption by educational institutions of staff development policies and practices – reflecting their own internal commitment to lifelong learning – becomes part of a strategy for organizational change, over which there can be much debate and dispute.

While a number of the chapters allude to the need for learning across organizational boundaries Etienne Wenger develops this further, introducing a model for learning across commercial, public or voluntary organizations. His notion of 'social learning systems' echoes the unbounded quality of lifelong learning itself, offering the potential for learning across different settings, extending even into cyberspace. Here individual communities of practice are connected through 'brokers' and, more structurally, through multiple 'boundary processes'. His model suggests that attempts at organizing lifelong learning should not only focus on individual organizations but also encompass the wider social networks.

For Wenger these wider social networks may be highly dispersed; in contrast the last two chapters explore learning networks that are firmly located in the local community. Stewart Ranson and colleagues explore how learning could be moved to the centre of community life through the development of the 'Learning City'. Such a model demands new levels of co-operation between public authorities, educational providers, businesses and voluntary organizations. Partnership is said to be the key, and crucially the development of an open dialogue that includes rather than excludes community interests. While promoting a highly aspirational model of the learning city they point to the tensions between this vision and the expediencies of implementation, not least of which is the need to balance open structures with organizing effectively. In the final chapter Marjorie Mayo also focuses on learning within the community and in particular on training to facilitate capacity building in area regeneration programmes in the UK. At its best this reflects collaborative arrangements between community groups and educational providers, leading to mutual learning. However, Mayo suggests the overall situation is problematic with specific groups, including minority ethnic communities, being under-resourced.

The chapters in this volume therefore point to the ways in which learning is increasingly seen as a central activity of organizations in the commercial, public and voluntary sectors and within the community more generally. A number of models for how this learning might be supported are explored by the contributors, including 'the learning organization', 'knowledge management', 'social learning systems' and the 'learning city'. The evidence of the chapters suggests that the process of implementation is complex and highly context dependent, resulting in the development not of a single approach but of multiple 'interpretations'. The importance of structural and cultural factors in organizing learning has been alluded to in a number of chapters including those by Keep and Rainbird, King, and Mayo. These can either facilitate support for learning or become significant barriers in themselves. In particular a key theme that emerges from the text is the potential for power relations between individuals or organizations to subvert notions of partnership and mutual learning. A commitment to lifelong learning may therefore require a re-examination of not only the organizational processes that support learning, but also those cultural aspects that may have just as significant an effect.

Chapter 1

Learning to work and working to learn

Ronald Barnett

In this chapter, I shall suggest that, in understanding their relationships in the contemporary era, work and learning can profitably be placed against the background of wider societal and even global shifts. I shall suggest that we live in an age of supercomplexity. That is to say, we live in an age in which our very frameworks for comprehending the world, for acting in it and for relating to each other are entirely problematic. We live in a world characterised by contestability, challengeability, uncertainty and unpredictability.

My argument is that, under conditions of supercomplexity, work has to become learning and learning has to become work. These imperatives – as they have now become – arise out of the fragility of the supercomplex environment in which we are all placed. We cannot escape the conditions of supercomplexity that face us in 'the global age' (Albrow, 1996). As a result, learning in work takes on a new urgency. Equally, learning has itself to be seen as work, as a set of activities that stand, to some extent, outside of individuals and that yield value beyond that of the individuals' efforts. Only through taking work and learning seriously in these ways can we begin to address the age of supercomplexity in which we find ourselves.

Learning and work

What are the relationships between learning and work? Do we learn in order to work more effectively? In other words, is learning prior to effective work? Or do we learn through our work? Does learning occur simultaneously with work? It must be both. But is the learning in the two kinds of situation the same form of learning? The answer that I want to offer in this chapter is twofold: they can be understood as separate activities but they are rapidly converging.

Learning acquired independently of the work situation could be propositional in form; learning acquired within the work situation could be a matter

This is an edited version of an article previously published in D. Boud and J. Garrick (eds), *Understanding Learning at Work*. 1999. Reproduced by permission of Taylor & Francis Ltd.

of knowing how to get by in similar circumstances. Effective work seems to require both kinds of learning: knowing that certain things are the case; and coming to intuit the particular 'form of life' (Wittgenstein, 1978). For example, an accountant simply has to know a great deal of business law, codes of practice and regulations; but he or she has also to acquire much in the way of experiential understanding of what is appropriate professional conduct in engaging with clients in different business milieux.

There is no problem here, then. Each profession has its own mix of factual knowledge, theoretical principles, action understanding, process knowledge, tacit knowledge and communicative competence. The precise mix will be intuited through engagement over time within each profession. The differences will be subtle. Multinational, medium- and small-sized enterprises in different sectors of the economy will have their own styles of communication and interaction, their own attitude to formal knowledge and their own views on the value of research and evaluation. What counts as being effective in particular environments within the world of work may not be spelt out but it will be picked up; the mysteries are revealed even if they are not made explicit.

This is a philosophy of 'it will be all right on the day' and it is increasingly being recognised as being inadequate in the modern age. Three strategies are being developed to address the matter.

First, training and development are taking on a more systematic character through the provision of in-house training schemes (Becher, 1996). Second, professionals are developing their own forms of peer development; often ranging across companies (Gear *et al.*, 1994). For example, in the UK, tax advisers of the major international firms have their own professional association transcending company loyalties. Third, institutions of education, through both face-to-face learning and distance learning, are finding markets in the corporate sector for their services for mid-career training and development.

These three forms of continuing learning, while analytically distinct, spawn hybrid forms of employee development combining formal and informal learning in different degrees. For example, employers are increasingly opening opportunities for personal development, which have no immediate connection with their staff's working environment. As a further example, informal mutual activities that professionals initiate – often in a regional locality – are reinforced by the relevant professional bodies as the latter seek to institute forms of continuing professional development, even, on occasions, requiring evidence of such development in order for individuals to retain their professional status. A yet further example of such hybrid forms of professional development lies in the action learning programmes being promoted by institutions of higher education, which call for professionals in different fields to pool and reflect on their experiences over time and engage in mutual learning circles.

Does all this amount to an incoherent mess or does it represent a proper range of responses to a complex situation? Clearly, the relationships between work and learning are complex; and there is a complexity quite apart from the particular and manifold interests of different kinds of company, of the private and public sectors, of professional bodies and associations, and of state agencies and policies. So a mix of strategies to foster continuing learning through work and beyond would appear to be a proper response. Is that it, then? Complexity of situation requires complexity of response – end of story. Not quite. The complexity facing us in this situation is more problematic than this characterisation.

A supercomplex world

That the world is changing, is even facing exponential rates of change, is part of our modern commonplace understanding. Technologies, economic arrangements, systems, institutions, roles, patterns of work and patterns of consumption are changing with increasing rapidity. The causes of these increasing rates of change are also, to a marked degree, understood. The development of a global economy, with flexible labour markets, networked systems and infrastructures, and international corporations aided now by the information technology revolution, making possible virtually instantaneous flows of information, decisions and capital around the world: these are the main features of the causes of increasing rates of social change.

What, however, is less understood is the deep-seated character of these changes. When we are faced with changes in our technologies, systems and patterns of work, we are also faced with challenges to our basic concepts. Work, communication, identity, self, knowing and even life: the meaning of fundamental concepts such as these is no longer clear in a world of change. As a consequence, the very frameworks that we deploy for making sense of the world in us, between us and around us are dissolving. There is no security available to us; this is an unstable world.

It is a world not just of complexity but of supercomplexity. Complexity is a situation in which a multitude of facts or ideas or possibilities present themselves within a particular domain of activity or understanding. The physicist, the doctor and the company manager are each continually faced with complexity. One of its manifestations is informational overload, whether overload – respectively – of research papers unread, of new drugs to assimilate or data streams on economic performance of the company's activities. With increasing media – fax, e-mail, Internet, mobile phones – such informational overload increases. Increasing information expands one's range of options, so making decision-making more complex. Accordingly, being a professional becomes as much a matter of handling complexity as it is about having first-order expertise as such.

By contrast, supercomplexity is a situation in which different frameworks present themselves, frameworks through which we understand the world and ourselves and our actions within it. In the contemporary era, again such frameworks multiply and are often in conflict with each other. The physicist may start to consider whether he or she is encouraging the use of the Earth's non-replenishable resources. The doctor may reflect as to whether his or her role is increasingly one of counsellor and health adviser, and that the perspectives offered by a background in medical science are insufficient for the widening role. The director of a multinational company may find that local value systems are presenting challenges in communication and that, as a result, both values and communication have to be given attention in themselves rather than treated as taken-for-granted means of action.

Instances such as these are instances of supercomplexity. They present not just additional facts or ideas which can be accommodated within one's basic framework of assumptions and values. Rather, they run against one's basic framework itself. They cannot be accommodated straightforwardly. If situations such as these are to be negotiated with a positive outcome, if presented challenges are seriously to be worked through, then one's basic framework – or part of it, at any rate – has itself to be changed. To say this, of course, is to say that the person concerned, faced with such challenges, has him- or herself to change, for one's basic framework is not entirely separable from the kind of person one is.

To put it another way, through disjunction between the presenting conceptual frameworks (Jarvis, 1992), one is faced with a learning experience, or, at least, the potential for a learning experience. Through such experiences, if met in a positive spirit, one can come to see both the world and oneself in a different way. One can move on effectively, in the light of one's new understanding. Supercomplexity, accordingly, can be not just challenging but disturbing. Having one's dominant presuppositions of the world and oneself challenged – whether beliefs, values or understandings – can be unsettling. But it can also present opportunities for development and learning.

Learning in work

This idea of supercomplexity compels us to take a particular view of the relationship between learning and work. In an age of supercomplexity, work and learning cannot be two distinct sets of activity.

Learning is embedded in work: that much is clear from what I have just said. But even that idea – that learning is embedded in work – has to be re-understood. It is often said that work itself presents opportunities for growth and learning. It does, but by no means always. Much work is built upon a set of routines. This is not just a characteristic of low-skill work. Professionals and others in senior positions in major organisations with near-monopoly situations may feel tacitly that their way of seeing the world, their forms of practising in the world, are secure, and do not require much adjustment. Their work, accordingly, becomes largely a matter of a set of routines that are, in turn, set within the context of frameworks held with some firmness, even dogmatic firmness. Doubtless, this is to be regretted. But it happens. Work is not necessarily a site of learning at the individual level.

On the other hand, learning is necessarily embedded in work at a more general or, as we might put it, a sociological level. Work is increasingly coming under the influence of forces external to itself, which are bound to bring at least change and adaptation, if not learning, in their wake. There are at least three dominant factors at play. First, the spread of markets world-wide: globalisation is the name of this shift and it affects the public sector as much as it affects the private sector. The resultant interconnectedness of economies – now the global economy – means that events and actions have effects, even at a distance. Crashes in the stock market in the Pacific Rim affect small investors, as well as large companies, around the world; international ecological agreements could have unforeseen consequences not just for economies but also for rural communities in tropical rainforests. But such global markets are also seen in the public sectors. Their labour markets – the movement of health workers and academics, for example – are increasingly global in character.

The second dominant force for unforeseen change at work is the state. Governments of whatever hue across the world are wishing to limit public spending and to ensure value for money in the services that they do fund. As a consequence, we have seen the rise of the evaluative state (or the audit state) as it is variously called (Neave, 1990; Power, 1997). The health and education sectors come under ever-proliferating forms of intrusive evaluation, which, in turn, spawn more and more complicated internal quality assurance systems.

In the public sector, markers and standards coincide: for example, professions are increasingly having to be sensitive to international standards of work in their own domains, first, because there is greater international movement of clients, and, second, because standards of professional credentialism are becoming increasingly international in character. Democratic governments also find themselves – sometimes on an international basis – being drawn into themselves developing regulations or standards governing the conduct of affairs in the private sector. (These two factors – markets and audit – often cut across each other, producing tensions in public policies.)

The third major force causing learning to be embedded in work is the information technology revolution. It could be said to be an outcome of the global economy but it has become such a significant feature of the modern world that it deserves to be understood as a major factor in its own right. The significant learning that the information technology revolution is generating lies not in the mastering of the hundreds of techniques for manipulating data that the computer requires, whether numerical, visual, linguistic or aural in character. Rather, the significant learning that the information technology revolution generates lies in the forms of communication that the computer makes possible. The issue is whether, in some respects and in some of its uses, the computer is actually changing our forms of human understanding both of the material world and of the human world.

'Netiquette' is an example of just how we may be dimly aware that such profound changes are occurring. Human communication on a two-dimensional screen affects the character of the information passing between human beings: the result is that the meaning of messages is changed and even, we might say, distorted. Hence 'netiquette' arises in which protocols are developed to lessen the corruption of the information via the computer. It may be said that the computer is in a relatively embryonic form and that the arrival of sound and pictures will restore human communication to its non-digital form. The response misses the point that computers – for example, in three-dimensional design, in the manipulation of chemical compounds, and in the production of mega-databases – are both changing the forms of knowledge production itself and generating opportunities for new forms of intersubjectivity to develop.

These three forces – globalisation, the rise of the audit state and the information technology revolution – are inserting themselves inescapably into work. Individuals may, for a time, ignore them; even companies may do so. But, sooner or later, the press of each of these individually, and all of them collectively, catches up with the recalcitrant. There is no hiding place.

The result is that learning is necessarily embedded in work but, as we might put it, structurally so. Individuals may find themselves in positions where work is relatively routine or they may simply not be inclined to seize every learning opportunity that comes their way. Equally, corporations may be unwilling to learn and to change. But, sooner or later, the world will catch up with them. Whether at the individual or the corporate level, they are likely to find themselves out of kilter: they will be redundant but it will be largely – although not always – a self-imposed redundancy.

The key point is that since change is structural and is an inescapable feature of the world in which we live, so too learning is structural. We might be tempted to say that learning is a necessary feature of work, but, as I have just indicated, this is not the case. Some will avoid it, or a time at least. Rather, we should say that there is an impetus to learn now built into work, and that this impetus is pervasive. Ultimately, the call to learn now embedded in work cannot be ducked.

Work in learning

If learning is structurally embedded in work, work is also embedded in learning. At one level, this is a trivial statement. Learning calls for work – often, indeed, hard work! But the sense in which learning constitutes work deserves explication.

In the first place, the sense of learning being work arises because learning presents personal challenges as well as presenting intellectual challenges.

Learning is unsettling in personal terms: in it, we are dislodged. Our sense of ourselves as individuals with a certain authority, rooted in what we know and understand, is easily shaken if we have to disclose to our peers that we still have much to learn. Learning, we might say, is existentially discomforting, and especially so in a work setting. Learning is typically associated with being young, and being in a state of personal development (or even immaturity). Having publicly, as an adult, to disclose that one is in a state of learning is likely, therefore, to generate mixed messages in relation to one's organisational persona. Self-images of maturity, self-reliance and authority suddenly contrast with those of dependency and of lack of understanding.

In those circumstances, it is not quite clear to whom one is, organisationally, speaking. One is having to admit that work is no longer something over which one has control and command, including one's relationships with other work colleagues. To admit to being a learner is to admit to being uncertain, and in that admission, all too frequently, one is in danger of losing one's authority – or one feels that that is the case. This is particularly so if, in that disclosure, one opens oneself up to a learning situation in which one has to learn a technique or grasp a set of ideas imparted by a more junior colleague. Learning about the Internet from a much more junior colleague and in the company of other more junior colleagues can, for many, be unnerving.

The unnerving is the natural result of roles, work identities and work relationships being built on preconceptions of an equivalence of knowledge and status. In the learning organisation, everyone is a learner, but such a mantra requires a particular kind of organisational culture, one in which its implications are fully understood by everyone. If everyone is a learner, then – potentially, at least – we can all learn from each other all the time. It is this latter step that is rarely made: that we can all learn from each other all the time. At best, the recognition that we are lifelong learners leads merely to the acknowledgement that learning opportunities need to be opened up to individuals. The more radical step in collective understanding – that we can all learn from each other all the time – is much more rarely taken on board. And it is partly the existential challenges to one's personal authority, status and legitimacy that that further step would usher in that prevents it from being seriously tackled.

Learning, then, is work. It is challenging in personal terms, and not just through its adding to one's workload. Extending the point, the earlier distinction between formal and informal learning may appear to be helpful. Formal learning undertaken in the company of others brings elements of self-disclosure and status uncertainty, which less often accompany informal learning. It can appear more as work than as informal learning, where one simply accommodates to new experiences and challenges. But the distinction cannot be completely sustained. Both formal and informal learning constitute work. Both often add to one's workload, and they add to one's existential load. Formal learning can be undertaken privately and allows personal adjustments in one's own time and space; informal learning is often experienced in a group setting, where one's felt clumsiness is all too apparent, particularly to those who 'know' each other.

It follows that learning of any kind can be felt as somewhat alien, having an externality to which one has to accommodate. The degree to which learning is alien is a feature of its load on the individual concerned. And load can be cognitive (having to master new concepts) or operational (having to master new skills) or experiential (having to accommodate to a new set of relationships with the world and with those around one in the work environment).

What, then, does it mean to say that learning is work? Precisely this: that the learning, in a sense, stands outside of oneself. It is a kind of object, an entity in its own right that, in some way, has to be confronted. It contains its own challenges, and perhaps has even come to be configured by 'standards' that have to be attained. In that sense, in its externality, learning takes on characteristics of work. Whatever the opportunities that may be developing for negotiating one's pattern of work in the environment of so-called post-Fordist organisations, work characteristically presents a givenness to which one has to yield.

The challenge that learning presents is not just a matter of willingness or unwillingness. After all, the work that learning represents can be undertaken willingly: witness the professional pianist who practises several hours each day. We sometimes hear people say that 'my work is not really work: I do it happily'. Actually, their happiness is immaterial. People can be happy in their work. The point such a comment is really bringing out is that, where work does not feel like work, it has become part of one's self-identity such that work no longer stands over one, apart from one. The concert pianist may, indeed, say that the practising did not constitute work. The practising incorporates a learning dimension, so it is not being implied that no learning is taking place. What is rather being said is that the practice is so part of one's self-identity as a concert pianist that the demands that it represents come from within the pianist rather than being imposed externally.

Learning is work, then, in the sense that one has to yield to the new experiences that come with learning. The new experiences, if they are worthwhile and if they offer opportunities for learning of any significance, will be complex and will be challenging. They will be challenging because they present demands of understanding, of a capacity to act or of self-reflection. Through the new experience, one is challenged to understand the world in a new way (a new idea or even perspective is presented to one), or to act in the world in a new way (one engages with others around one differently), or one comes to understand oneself in a new light.

Often, learning – especially in a work setting – incorporates a mix of these forms of learning and is, therefore, challenging in multiple ways. That is why it can feel like work: it is challenging in terms of one's knowing, acting and reflecting simultaneously. External features of the world exert their claims on oneself, on one's organising frames for experiencing and for engaging with the world. At the same time, one is being asked to comprehend a new process or product or set of ideas, a new way of dealing with those ideas (e.g. through information technology) and a new way of interacting with others and handling oneself. In the more open networking environment of modern work, ideas may be coming at one from other domains of professional life. Equally, in the global economy, one may have to interrelate to others around the world whose culture one does not know and with whom communication is inevitably problematic. Not surprisingly, learning opportunities may be formally acknowledged as just that, as opportunities, but, inwardly, may be felt as threats. Accordingly, a challenge to those concerned to develop learning organisations is to turn the inward sense of learning as threat into a more publicly visible sense of learning as opportunity.

Work, then, is inherent in learning. Work increasingly – but not universally – provides opportunities for personal change and development; learning opportunities, in other words. But learning of any seriousness and challenge is a form of work: it calls on individuals to yield to the demands of an experience or set of experiences. (These experiences may be more or less organised, or they may arise organically – 'informally' – in work situations.)

Some will feel that the argument has unhelpfully run together the experience of learning with the facticity of work and has produced an equivocation that turns on the notion of work itself. It may be said that, while learning may sometimes be felt to be 'work', inner experience should not be confused with the external institutionalisation of work. The matter is crucial for my argument. Under conditions of supercomplexity, the phenomenology of work and learning, as it were, are merging. Work is becoming learning; that is perhaps relatively uncontentious. But learning is also becoming work through the expanded challenges that supercomplexity presents. Learning is no longer just a matter of inward experience and challenge but is a matter of confronting multiplying expectations, standards and evaluations that stand outside of oneself and that – as with work itself – cannot, to a significant degree, be anticipated in advance.

This intertwining of work and learning itself presents opportunities and challenges, as we have seen. Just as work can be demotivating, overburdensome and even threatening, so too can learning, especially if 'learning' is imposed on individuals and if they are poorly supported – in personal as much as in resource terms – as they are struggling to learn. Learning, therefore, whether it arises intentionally or unintentionally, requires support if it is to be undertaken successfully. This is not to say that all learning requires support; learning is likely to be all the more rapid and meaningful where it is undertaken through an individual's own motivations. But even then, and more generally, learning can often benefit from the presence of a supporting framework, a framework that is designed (e.g. through a system of mentorship) to address the existential anxiety of learning as much as it is designed (e.g. through designated time allowances and, where necessary, financial support) to address the more material aspects of effective learning.

Engaged responsiveness

For all its possible conceptual gain, it might be thought that the past discussion has yielded rather little. Of course, it might be accepted, effective learning requires a supportive framework. Yes, it has to include attention to the more personal and emotional aspects of learning, aspects that are not easily calculable and do not easily lend themselves to a profit-and-loss assessment. But once all that has been put in place, what more is there to be said?

Here, we need to return to the idea of supercomplexity. Supercomplexity, it will be recalled, is that form of complexity in which frameworks for understanding the world are themselves challenged. Whether it is an international oil company being obliged seriously – and not just cosmetically – to take on board ecological features of its activities, or doctors beginning to take seriously the prospect that their main purpose is not to treat disease but to prevent it, or university academics beginning to take seriously the idea that teaching is only occurring if effective learning is taking place: all of these are challenges to frameworks of self-understanding, of one's understanding of the world and of one's relationships to others. Such challenges to fundamental frameworks call for the abandonment of one's primary way of looking at the world, or, at least, for one to take seriously that there can be other, quite different and legitimate ways of viewing the world. The learning challenges that we all face in and through work are increasingly of this supercomplex kind. They require of us not simply that we learn new techniques, or new ideas or new practices. They call upon us to change or at least to widen the very frameworks through which we interpret the world. They demand of us, in effect, that we become different kinds of human being.

Sometimes, perhaps often, we refuse those demands. The challenges to our ways of looking at the world are so considerable that we find it difficult to embrace them. We feel that we cannot become other than we are.

We see, in this idea of supercomplexity, just why learning in work and why work in learning are so pervasive and so problematic, if not to say often threatening. Change becomes daunting because it often calls for fundamental changes in self-conception.

But, as we have just implied, such challenges, and the learning that is caught up in them, are often organisational in character. 'The learning organisation' is a well-worn phrase, but what is perhaps not always understood is that organisational learning has itself to take on a supercomplex dimension. In fact, there are two levels of responsiveness to supercomplexity at work. The first is, indeed, simply that of reactive responsiveness, of trying to cope with supercomplexity. Challenges to a company's frame of reference, its self-understanding and the framework of its structuring operations, are met belatedly, only when they cannot be ducked. Responses are, as a result, *ad hoc* and ill-thought through. Here, organisational learning is a matter of *force majeure*: it occurs when, and only when, it has to do so. The second level of responsiveness is more anticipatory in character. We might be tempted to call such responsiveness either 'strategic' or 'proactive' in character. Both terms have a point but each is somewhat misleading. If the environment within which institutions are having to operate and survive is not only changing but liable to change unpredictably, and in ways that challenge fundamental frames of self-understanding, of an organisation's place in its own market and its relationships with its clients or customers (and, therefore, of its 'mission'), both the ideas of strategy and even of being proactive become problematic. For both rest on the assumption that the future can be in some measure like the past or, at least, where the future can be foretold to some degree. One can develop strategies where the opposed forces are known and can be measured; one can be proactive where it is clear what actions might be fostered. In an age of radical uncertainty, neither of these sets of conditions can be assumed to hold. Accordingly, a different form of responsiveness is required.

Earlier, I suggested the idea of 'anticipatory responsiveness', but even that overplays the matter. For the idea of anticipation is itself problematic under conditions of discontinuous change. But if the future is liable not to be like the past, then we can perhaps develop an organisational responsiveness in which at least that state of affairs is collectively understood. Accordingly, anticipatory responsiveness points us towards not just a readiness to respond to change (for that hardly escapes the position of reactive responsiveness) but, rather, to an engaged responsiveness. This is a form of responsiveness in which the organisation is continually engaging with its environment and in a critical way. For that, it will have multiple frames of reference up its corporate sleeve, or, at the drop of a hat, will be able to generate them.

Organisational learning, then, under conditions of supercomplexity, becomes a matter of generating the capacities for continuing creative insertions into an organisation's environment. It is not suddenly obliged to review its mission, its values, its assumptions, its sense of itself, or its view of its relationships with its clients because these are continually kept under review and new conceptions of each are continually being generated. The organisation becomes literally an organisation that knows how to learn.

Learning and supercomplexity

Learning is inherent in work, and work is inherent in learning. That is a double story, worth understanding, even under conditions of relative stability. But under conditions of supercomplexity, this double story becomes doubly more forceful. Under conditions of supercomplexity, work demands learning; it does not just promote it or encourage it. Correspondingly, under conditions of supercomplexity, learning becomes ever more challenging, fraught and unsettling. It takes on the features of work: it becomes as work.

As we have seen, this story of the interrelationships between learning and work has to be worked out at different levels and in different modes: personal and organisational; formal and informal. The following grid may, accordingly, be a helpful *aide-mémoire* but only if it is interpreted under conditions of supercomplexity.

	Formal	Informal
Organisational		
Personal		

Misrepresented, the grid could simply stamp in forms of learning that are *inappropriate* to conditions of supercomplexity. The static character of such a grid and its demarcation of different modes (formal and informal) and different levels (organisational and personal) of learning retain and are liable to freeze outmoded conceptions of learning. Rather than being understood as dynamic and interrelating systems of learning, such a grid could reinforce conceptions of separateness, which will be inadequate in facing up to conditions of supercomplexity. Supercomplexity – the challenge of multiple, conflicting and ever-emerging frames of understanding and action – requires continual critical reflection and development not in segregated compartments but in ways that are interacting. Supercomplexity repudiates boundaries of learning.

The grid, however, may take on a heuristic value provided that the forms of learning to which it points are not held entirely separate from each other. Total responsiveness is called for: individuals are part of their organisations, and organisations live through the individuals who are attached to them; informal learning is often made effective by formal learning goals or through formal learning situations, while formal learning can only be effective if backed up by informal learning. But, as we have seen, under conditions of supercomplexity, even total responsiveness is insufficient! It is insufficient because the responsive stance is itself insufficient. The responsive stance condemns the learner (individual or organisation) to being always behind the game. What is called for is an engaged responsiveness, in which one is learning through bringing alternative frames of reference to bear on the frames of reference with which one is presented.

We can only live effectively under conditions of supercomplexity if we are engaging with the total environment with which we are presented. In turn, that means that we learn not by responding to supercomplexity but by contributing further to it. We can never get on top of supercomplexity, as it were. Instead, we cope with it by intervening in the world, learning as we are doing so.

We could say that learning under these conditions is necessarily action learning. So it is, but we still have a responsibility to bring to our interventions and to our learning frameworks of interpretation and evaluation. We contest the frames that are presented to us not by resisting them in any facile way but by presenting to them alternative frames. We learn not just by acting and evaluating but additionally by bringing to the party and inserting into the world – through our thinking and our acting – multiple frames of understanding. As for Gorky (1979), life itself remains our best university but only through our best critical, active and creative efforts that we bring to bear in the process.

Conclusion

Work and learning are not synonymous. They are different concepts. Some kinds of work offer little in the way of learning opportunities; some learning would not be called work. But the two concepts overlap. Work can and should offer learning opportunities; much learning is demanding, calling upon the learner to yield to certain standards, and contains the character of work. Whether the overlap between work and learning is slight or extensive, therefore, is a key issue in modern life: in many ways, the challenge here is that of bringing about the greatest overlap between work and learning.

This challenge – of bringing about a greater confluence between work and learning – takes on a particular urgency in a situation in which none of our frames of reference (of thought, action and self-understanding) are reliable. This is the contemporary situation, a situation of supercomplexity, in which all of our frameworks of knowledge and action are unstable. We have to live effectively in a world that is radically uncertain.

In such conditions, conditions of uncertainty, we will survive and prosper only by engaging in a critical way with the world. We combat multiple and conflicting frameworks not by resisting them or by giving into them in any facile way. Instead, we live dangerously with them by bringing to bear yet further possibilities of thought and action, which in turn we subject to critical scrutiny. Under conditions of supercomplexity, therefore, work has to become learning; that much is clear. Work has to be understood as presenting infinite learning opportunities. There is no resting place. All of our frameworks of action, interpretation and self-understanding – whether on an individual or an organisational level – have to be available for perpetual scrutiny. This in itself means that our contemporary situation cannot be a place, or places, of comfort.

But, at the same time, and perhaps less obviously, learning has to become work. It has to become work in the sense of becoming serious. Learning cannot be undertaken lightly. The stakes are too high for that. Not just organisational and personal survival are in question, but so, too, is the fate of whole societies if not of the planet itself. Learning, accordingly, has to become work such that it is undertaken to the most exacting standards. Learning cannot be a matter of self-indulgence. It takes on collective responsibilities, and has to yield a value added far beyond itself. In a situation of supercomplexity, therefore, work has to become learning, and learning has to become work. This is not necessarily an enjoyable state of affairs, but it is the state of affairs in which we find ourselves.

References

Albrow, M. (1996) *The Global Age*, Cambridge: Polity.

Becher, T. (1996) 'The learning professions', *Studies in Higher Education* 21(1): 43–56.

Gear, J., McIntosh, A. and Squires, G. (1994) *Informal Learning in the Professions*, Hull: University of Hull, Department of Adult Education.

Gorky, M. (1979) *My Universities*, London: Penguin.

Jarvis, P. (1992) *Paradoxes of Learning: On Becoming an Individual in Society*, San Francisco: Jossey-Bass.

Neave, G. (1990) 'On preparing for markets: trends in higher education in Western Europe 1988–1990', *European Journal of Education* 25(2): 105–123.

Power, M. (1997) *The Audit Society: Rituals of Verification*, Oxford: Oxford University Press.

Wittgenstein, L. (1978) *Philosophical Investigations*, Oxford: Blackwell.

Chapter 2

Skill formation
Redirecting the research agenda

David Ashton

Introduction

The conventional approach to the analysis of skill formation processes tends to focus on education and formal training as the main components. This is partly a consequence of the dominance of human capital theory with its emphasis on education and training as an investment for the individual, the employer and the society. The analogy with physical investment encourages the view of training as a series of finite activities, the more one invests in education and training the greater the return in terms of earnings, productivity and economic growth. The necessity to provide a convenient measure of this investment leads academics to focus on formal education and training provision, as these can be readily derived from government statistics. Years of schooling and length or frequency of training provide convenient measures of the investments made by individuals, organisations and countries in the process of skill formation. As a result the two tend to become equated.

This is reinforced by public discussion and individuals' perceptions. At a national level, political debate concerning the development of the nation's human resources tends to focus exclusively on education and training: the assumption being that if we can increase investment in education and training we will automatically receive benefits in the form of increased income, productivity and national wealth. At the individual level, findings from research on employees' perception of training suggest that they too tend to equate training with formal training, either on-the-job or off-the-job. Less formal modes of learning, such as informal on-the-job training and self-initiated forms of learning at work are less likely to be perceived by individuals as training (Felstead *et al.*, 1997). It is not surprising that training tends to be perceived by all parties as a series of one-off activities delivered through formal courses. However, this concentration on training in discrete time-bound units in formal institutions as the loci of the process of skill formation is now being challenged from a number of sources.

This is an edited version of an article previously published in F. Coffield (ed.) *Learning at Work*. 1998. Reproduced by permission of The Policy Press.

Michael Eraut (1997) has pointed out how a great deal of learning takes place within the workplace, independently of the provision of formal education and training, and how the discourse about lifetime learning has been dominated by the providers of formal education and training. Meanwhile, outside academia, perhaps the most significant of these challenges comes from the changing practices of employers and changes in the structure of organisations. For example, the globalisation of capital flows and product markets; the success of companies from Japan and the tiger economies in securing substantial parts of world markets for products ranging from ships to electronics and automobiles; the relocation of some labour intensive industries to the low-cost Asian economies. All these have intensified competition in the Western world. Companies have responded by reducing the amount of labour they employ, delayering management and producing flatter organisations. In addition, they have sought to reduce labour costs by outsourcing aspects of the production system and some of their services and increasing the productivity of remaining staff by techniques such as teamworking, multiskilling and enhancing the commitment of employees to the goals of the organisation. In the public sector the programmes of privatisation and the deregulation of sectors such as finance and transport have produced similar pressures with similar effects on the structure of organisations. The result has been that some organisations, but by no means all, have undergone major shifts in their internal structures, which, together with the incessant drive to reduce costs, has had important implications for the process of learning at work.

Organisational change and learning at work

Traditionally, large organisations, such as automobile manufacturers and banks, have organised their training through a centralised training function that delivers a series of programmes from which line managers and employees can choose to participate. The delivery of training and the analysis of the organisation's training needs remain the province of a specialised training function. There, learning takes place in the classroom or workshop under the guidance of a specialist trainer or instructor or through a computer-based training programme designed by a specialist trainer. The training programmes are designed to deliver knowledge and skills ranging from specialised technical skills to organisational procedures and new technology. The individual employee has access to them at a time determined by the central training function and then has to apply the new knowledge/skills in the workplace.

This approach to training is designed to deliver specific skills, to enhance the performance of employees in one particular aspect of their job in organisations where roles are clearly specified and circumscribed. Jobs are clustered in departments or functions, responsibilities are precisely specified and each individual employee occupies a position in a clearly defined hierarchy of authority. Rewards are linked to clearly specified outputs, for example the number of widgets produced or telephone calls handled per unit of time. Training is geared to improving any particular aspect of the employee's behaviour deemed problematic, for example to improve manual dexterity, to enhance technical knowledge of specific product process or service, but other aspects of the employee's behaviour are considered irrelevant to their performance of the job.

As organisation structure changes, moving in the direction of more flexible forms with fewer layers of authority, a greater emphasis on teamwork and multiskilling, this produces what Lawler (1994) terms a move from job-based to competency-based structures. This in turn produces change in the 'training needs' of the individual employee. As responsibility is pushed further down the line with the reduction in the number of hierarchies, and more employees take on managerial responsibilities, their roles are broadened as their responsibilities increase, and cognitive skills become more important. The introduction of teamwork demands new skills in collaboration with colleagues and group working. The broadening of the work role demands that new skills are learned.

A number of studies in different societies (Bertrand and Noyelle, 1989; Kelly, 1989; O'Reilly, 1992; Thompson et al., 1995) have identified similar new skills emerging around three main themes. The first is problem solving: the ability to comprehend the whole process of production, including both technical knowledge and knowledge of the organisation, and to make decisions within that broad framework. The second is teamworking: the ability to work collaboratively in pursuit of a common objective, to share information and communicate effectively, often referred to as social skills. The third is elementary management competencies: the ability to operate in changing conditions; plan time; prioritise; and operate strategically in relation to organisational objectives. These are not skills or competencies that can be readily acquired from one-off courses.

One further consequence of recent organisational changes is that the leaders of an organisation become more concerned with shaping the overall values and behaviour of the employee and less with rewarding or punishing specific aspects of the work performance. Under these circumstances the system of social control within the organisation changes (Townley, 1994). More emphasis is placed on rewarding teamwork and commitment and linking individuals' rewards to the performance of the organisation as a whole. The employer's agenda for training is widened from the traditional concerns of transmitting specific skills and coping with legal obligations, to creating identification with company objectives, implementing organisational change and ensuring adherence to quality standards (Felstead et al., 1997).

Although the evidence is still patchy and unsystematic, the main implications of these changes for the organisation of training are now becoming evident. Training departments are shrinking in size, relative to the parent organisation (American Society for Training and Development, 1996). In some instances the function has been outsourced. This has been accompanied by a decline in the use of off-the-job training courses, both in the UK (Raper *et al.*, 1997) and in the US (Bassi and Cheney, 1996). The responsibilities for training have been given to line managers and training has therefore become more focused on the needs of the line. Concomitant with this there has been an increase in mentoring, coaching and forms of structured on-the-job training (American Society for Training and Development, 1996; Raper *et al.*, 1997). Trainers have been transformed into learning advisers and consultants or performance consultants, whose function is to advise line managers in the delivery of learning at work. Our own research and that in the US (American Society for Training and Development, 1996) has identified a range of new skills required for this role that includes skills in: facilitating the process of learning; systems thinking and understanding; consultancy; and organisational development; and in addition a wider knowledge of business objectives and operational performance. Training is now increasingly seen as part of a process of lifelong learning and becomes part of a longer-term process of skill formation, which encompasses the moulding of attitudes and values as well as the transmission of specific skills.

Case study I

We use the following case study to demonstrate how these changes have reduced the role of formal one-off training courses and refocused attention on skill formation as a continuous process. It illustrates the mechanisms through which the structuring of the learning process has moved away from the training department and become focused on the workplace. The establishment is part of a small, multinational company, engaged in the electronics manufacturing industries, combining some mass production with forms of batch production. In total it has over 4,000 employees in the UK and abroad. It operates in a very competitive market, facing strong competition from European companies. In order to survive it had to move from being production focused to being more responsive to its major customers and more innovative in the market place. This shift in company philosophy to a focus on the customer involved radical changes in the organisational culture and in the system of production.

Increases in productivity had been achieved through the redesign of the production process, for example the eradication of stock; the use of Just-In-Time production; and the introduction of an integrated system of manufacture. Production was operated on the basis of cells with teams responsible for either the whole production process or a significant part. However, success depended on achieving higher levels of commitment on the part of the workforce to the company and its objectives and on a substantial part of the workforce acquiring problem solving, teamwork and management skills as identified above.

Transforming the company culture involved a basic change in the attitude of management toward the workforce. First it had to change its relationships with the unions. The company had three major unions and the first move from the Human Resources Director was to establish a relationship of trust between the company an the unions. This was achieved by opening the company's books to the unions and involving the union leadership and local officials in discussions about the problems facing the company and encouraging them to put forward proposals to overcome them. The unions responded in a positive manner: for example, when confronted with the need to improve productivity the unions suggested running the plant 52 weeks per year to improve productivity and took over responsibility for consulting members in order to minimise any inconvenience to their holiday arrangements. To ensure continued improvements in communication and the maintenance of a trusting relationship, site meetings were held every month with stewards and management representatives. This relationship of trust has underpinned many of the other human resources developments.

Employees' values and attitudes had to change to achieve the flexibility and willingness to operate effectively in teams, with the aim of enhancing company performance. In part this was achieved by the new relationship of trust between unions and employers. This was reinforced by a series of innovations designed to raise employees' awareness of the interdependence of the component parts of the organisation, and the importance of satisfying the customer to ensure the success of the organisation and therefore the security of their jobs. The first of these innovations was to dispense with the old system of teambuilding, which involved sending staff on a two-day outdoor pursuits course at a cost of £6,000 per head, in the hope that teambuilding skills learned there would be transferred to the workplace. This was replaced by a two-day course designed in-house and aimed at demonstrating the problems of running a business. In particular it focused on the problems that each department faced with the aim of improving mutual understanding. In addition, the staff were put through a business game in which they had to compete with other teams in running a business. The aim was to demonstrate the interdependence of the various parts of the business and the importance of satisfying the customer. All staff, manual and non-manual, are currently being put through the course.

However, for the change in attitudes to be sustained through time, the company's commitment to open communication had to be reinforced. This was done through a system of monthly team briefings, the introduction of a company magazine and cross-functional management meetings to improve communication and mutual understanding of the component parts of the business. To involve staff more directly in the decision-making process, they all attended a course on continuous improvement, which has been followed through with regular meetings where decisions on improvements are made in open forum.

The other component was to realign the system of rewards and punishments in accordance with the new emphasis on commitment to the organisation through enhanced performance. Appraisals were introduced for all staff, use was made of relatively simple forms in order to minimise bureaucracy. The function of the appraisal was to identify barriers to improved performance – they were not linked to pay. This technique encouraged more effective upward communications from staff to supervisors. A substantial part of the training process is now devoted to sustaining the changes achieved in values and attitudes.

In the process of achieving this change training activities became focused more on the use of the workplace as a cost-effective means of transmitting the requisite skills for the 'new' organisation. Teamwork exercises were used to focus on team and individual performance and multiskilling was introduced in the form of training across a number of tasks to build in greater flexibility within each team.

Management education was changed. The old off-the-job courses delivered by external providers, which were not seen as linked to the company's needs, were replaced with a system of specialist one-off training sessions on specialist topics directly related to the manager's job, supplemented by enrolment on the UK Open University Effective Manager course, the fees for which are reimbursed on successful completion. For the technical staff, two programmes were run over 18 months. These use a combination of external experts and in-house courses for subjects such as contract law. These are assessed through a written examination, project work and presentation. Staff are paid £500 on successful completion, following which they are expected to demonstrate improved performance and the requisite behaviours before they are considered for promotion. Operatives receive their training on-the-job with most teams having a designated 'trainer' – a person who has successfully performed all the jobs in the team – who is responsible for the training of team members.

Responsible for routine training was taken from the training department and given to the line managers. When new training needs are identified the training department is consulted for advice and help in constructing the course or programme, but the line manager is responsible for delivering the course. Training is now a component part of the business agenda and on the business reviews of line managers.

The effect of these changes has been dramatic. Training is more highly focused on improving company performance and the business objectives, productivity levels have improved and learning is now the responsibility of each manager (although not all managers were equally enthusiastic to acquire these new responsibilities). Training is no longer the exclusive province of the training department. The combined effect of these changes has been that the company has improved its market share from 13 per cent to 26 per cent in six years and reduced working hours from 39 to 37 per week.

There is no evidence from this particular case study that the level of skill formation within the organisation has increased. This may well have been the case, but the important point is that the system of skill formation is now tightly geared to the requirements of the business organisation. No doubt individuals in the past obtained some personal development from the outside courses but this was not closely linked to the requirements of the business. By replacing this and other forms of external courses with training at the workplace, which is tied more closely to improving performance, the company made continuous training an integral part of its activities rather than a series of one-off (frequently externally run) events that had only a tangential relationship to the person's job.

There is a danger with the use of case studies that we can overgeneralise – this example is only used to illustrate a trend. Many organisations have not changed significantly, others contain elements of the old and the new. Where new forms have been introduced, certain elements of the old still persist: smaller centralised training units can coexist with learning consultants. In addition, much training and skill formation remains driven by traditional forces such as legal requirements, organisational procedures, and new technology (Felstead and Green, 1994). This case study simply highlights the direction of the trend.

If, as we have argued, training has become just one component of the skill formation process as learning at work has gained in prominence and employers have become more concerned with shaping values and attitudes as well as job technical skills, what does this mean for the process of learning at work? Recent studies in the US (Darrah, 1996) and in Japan (Koike and Inoki, 1990) have started to explore this issue by focusing on the processes whereby individuals acquire skills in the course of their everyday work activities. Koike argues, on the basis of the Japanese experience, that high levels of skill formation can only be achieved through the use of work-based learning, especially through learning on-the-job. Eraut distinguishes between individual learning, the learning of a group and the learning organisation. We are concerned with the individual and group levels. At the level of group he defines learning capability as

> likely to comprise both overt shared understandings and procedures and tacit knowledge of working together creatively to define, solve and implement solutions to non-routine problems and issues.
>
> (1997: 10)

In building on these studies we are asking the questions, how do individuals experience the process of learning, and how do the groups of which they are a part, as well as the organisation as a whole, shape it? These were questions addressed by the second of the case studies.

Case study 2

The establishment was part of a large, Western, multinational company located in South-east Asia. Semi-structured interviews were conducted with a representative sample of 195 of the 3,000 employees. The company had experienced re-engineering, involving a reduction in the headcount; a delayering of management; and the introduction of a new culture, where the focus was on enhancing efficiency through the adoption of a new way of working, geared to providing a better service to the customer. As the management sought to move the company in the direction of a 'learning organisation', responsibility for training had been devolved down the line, training was co-ordinated through the human resources and development function but the training department had been reduced dramatically in size as the trainers had been transformed into learning consultants. The company was widely recognised as being at the leading edge of developments in training within the region.

The interviews sought to explore all facets of learning at work, and what became evident was the problematic character of the process of learning at work. In order for learning to be effective, knowledge and information have to be shared, individuals have to be provided with the opportunity to apply the knowledge and practise new skills, support has to be provided in the form of effective feedback and, over the long term, the learning acquired has to be rewarded.

Within organisations learning takes place in the context of a variety of relationships with colleagues, superiors and subordinates and central to these relationships is the issue of trust. In the first case study, at the organisational level, building trust was seen as essential in gaining the commitment of the workforce to focus the process of skill formation on the goals of the enterprise. However, at the individual level, this is a problematic process. Although the second case study company had devoted considerable resources to communicating with employees, this was no guarantee of effecting change in individuals' behaviour and attitudes. Much of the communication was mediated by the supervisor or manager and if the relationship with the supervisor or manager is one where the manager is 'fussy', 'doesn't trust us', 'doesn't care', 'shows no interest in staff', there is little impetus for the staff to identify with the organisation or to learn. Even in organisations that have delayered, hierarchy is still a central feature of everyday experience and has a profound effect on the learning process. It was not uncommon that learning was hindered by bosses who did not trust their subordinates and were reluctant to share information and knowledge. As one manager remarked, 'knowledge is power, people are selfish and this is more so at the middle and lower levels'. However, this was not always the case; other managers were careful to bring on their staff – 'staff must understand your style. They share a lot more, including your mistakes. You have to approach them, have a chit-chat.' As with many organisations undergoing change, there were certain groups of managers in both our case study organisations who were reluctant to share knowledge.

Similarly, if the relationship with colleagues is competitive, trust cannot develop and there is little incentive to share experiences and knowledge, to support colleagues in their attempts to develop their skills, or to build the learning capability of the group to which Eraut refers (1997). In some instances this was a case of 'people are willing to share provided they are the right person', or,

> If you know the person there is no difficulty in getting information. You have to do a lot of networking. Bosses might not understand this.

In other instances, where teams were functioning effectively, learning at the group level was taking place and the sharing of knowledge and information among colleagues was not a problem: 'We are in a team, we sink or swim together, so there are no problems in sharing knowledge.' Significantly, in project work where the teams were created for a specific purpose, the sharing of knowledge was least problematic.

When it came to opportunities to apply new knowledge and practice skills, two main issues emerged from the data concerning the factors that influenced this dimension of skill formation. The first was the structural issue of whether senior management grouped tasks in such a way as to provide for individual progression in their learning in the manner outlined by Koike and Inoki (1990), or whether individuals were allocated to different tasks in what appeared to them to be a fairly random process that did not enable them to build up skills progressively during the course of their employment with the company. In the case of management, there was considerable thought put into the development of senior staff to ensure that they acquired the appropriate experience, thus young graduates would report that their job movements within the company had 'broadened their experience', as they moved from technical jobs to supervising subcontractors to jobs involving more managerial skills. However, for those lower down, in clerical jobs, this had not been the case. It appeared to the employees that they were moved around in a fairly random manner, in such a way that the skills acquired in one job were lost when they moved to another where they had to acquire another unrelated set of competencies, thus militating against cumulative learning at the individual level. The more widespread use of teamwork may reduce this as the individual's job movement is likely to be to different jobs within the same workgroup.

The second issue when it came to practising new skills concerned the individual's relationship with their immediate superior. In some instances bosses were reluctant to delegate authority and thereby provide the employee with the opportunity to acquire and practise new skills:

> If the boss has delegated it to you, you should be fully responsible. Some bosses never trust the individual . . . You feel your boss has no confidence in you.

In another instance an employee commented that his boss 'tackles all the difficult stuff himself', the employee was never given the opportunity to extend his knowledge and skills. This is clearly related to the issue of trust but also represents a serious barrier to the process of skill formation.

An individual may have knowledge and opportunity to practise but for learning to continue support is required, either from colleagues or supervisors, depending on the context. Again two major issues emerged from the interviews. The first concerned belief among certain sectors that learning itself was unproblematic, a 'natural' process that occurs of its own accord, that did not require any special support or consideration. This led to a belief in some quarters that new entrants, especially graduates, should not be 'spoon-fed' and that they learn by being 'thrown in at the deep end'. Where this was the case the learner was unlikely to receive further support.

The second issue concerned the lack of knowledge among managers and others about how to support the learning process. The significance of appropriate feedback, especially in the workplace, has been well established by Koike and Inoki (1990). If staff are not provided with feedback on how well they are performing the process of learning becomes haphazard. Some employees had weekly meetings to obtain feedback on their performance. However, although many staff were aware of the importance of receiving feedback so that learning could proceed in anything other than an *ad hoc* manner, the significance of this feedback was not always recognised by those involved in the learning process. As one employee put it, what you require is 'a listening ear, open, not judgmental, able to empathise and give guidance, provide guidelines'. What she did not want from her supervisor was

> someone who argues with you rather than listens to the problem, who shoots you down saying 'You should have done this.' When that happens, you feel depressed and feel the exercise was a waste of time.

Finally, learning can be a rewarding activity in its own right, in that the individual feels a sense of achievement and positive learning experiences enhance self-confidence. However, from the organisation's point of view, if the process of skill formation is to be geared to business objectives, learning that is related to the achievement of these objects requires rewarding and reinforcing. The interesting finding from the interviews was that in the short term the main reward the individuals mentioned was just a 'thank you' or acknowledgement from the superior. Of course, in the longer term this was seen as insufficient in that most of the staff would prefer a concrete reward in the form of progression or promotion.

From the employees' perspective, within this company formal training was an infrequent activity but learning was an everyday occurrence. The company was attempting to move in the direction of a 'learning organisation' but the evidence suggested that this was a problematic process. Employees faced many barriers in their efforts to learn, not because the company deliberately erected them, indeed the company were unaware of them, but because the process of learning is contentious, with the parties involved having different agendas and in many instances not being aware of how to facilitate the process. At each stage in the process – in the sharing of knowledge; in the provision of opportunities for practice; in the support of the learning process; and in the rewarding of it – the process can be easily fractured.

Conclusions

The case for conceptualising skill formation as a continuous process through time in which learning at work is central rather than a series of discontinuous, one-off educational or training activities, derives not only from an academic need to broaden the research agenda but from concrete changes taking place in the workplace. As we have seen, organisational changes are making the process of learning at work more central to the achievement of business objectives. Active involvement in the process is extending beyond trainers to include managers, supervisors and employees, in ways never envisaged before. For trainers, especially those whose role has been transformed into 'learning consultants', and who now find themselves with the new tasks of facilitating the learning process, advising managers on how to identify learning needs and to support the process of learning in the workplace, new skills in consultancy and the management of the learning process are urgently required.

Yet despite these changes, many of those directly involved in the process of learning at work, both managers and individuals, still tend to see learning as relatively unproblematic, a natural occurrence that requires little support. One major implication of this is that we need to develop more adequate theories of learning in the workplace. Conventional theories of 'learning by osmosis' or 'learning by doing' deflect attention from the complexities of the processes we observe. Learning theories derived from experimental observations and studies of the cognitive process abstracted from the realities of the organisational context are of little relevance to the practitioner, or for that matter, the academic struggling to understand the process of learning as embedded in organisational structures.

Eraut has made a useful start on reconceptualising the agenda by drawing our attention to the range of learning that takes place at work and the fact that the process of learning is more specific than merely absorbing information:

> Learning should refer only to significant changes in capability or understanding and exclude the acquisition of further information when it does not contribute to such changes.
>
> (Eraut, 1997)

Such a definition focuses attention more clearly on the central issues at both the individual and group level. However, it also raises the question of whether the changes in attitudes and values necessary for ensuring the commitment of the individual to both the group and the wider organisation should also be a component part of this process of learning. Without that commitment, much of the learning, especially at the group level and above, cannot take place. Other important contributions have been made by Koike in his studies of learning at work (1997), but in focusing on the conditions in Japanese organisations that facilitate the process of skill acquisition, he tends to ignore the conflicts and struggles that are also involved in the process. Nevertheless, these are important contributions that serve to highlight the urgent need for academics to provide a more adequate conceptualisation to guide both theory and practice, and in so doing broaden the research agenda away from its current preoccupation with education and training as the main components of the skill formation process. Practitioners in the field are in urgent need of the help such research could provide.

References

American Society for Training and Development (1996) *Trends that affect corporate learning and performance*, Alexandria: ASTD.

Bassi, L.J. and Cheney, S. (1996) *Restructuring: Results from the 1996 Forum*, Alexandria: ASTD.

Bertrand, O. and Noyelle, T. (1989) *Human resources and corporate strategy: Technological change in banks and insurance companies*, Paris: OECD.

Darrah, C.N. (1996) *Learning and work: An exploration in industrial ethnography*, London: Garland Publishing.

Eraut, M. (1997) 'Perspectives on defining "The Learning Society" ', Paper prepared for the ESRC Learning Society Programme, Brighton: Institute of Education, University of Sussex.

Felstead, A. and Green, F. (1994) 'Training during the recession', *Work, Employment and Society*, vol. 8, no. 2, pp. 199–219.

Felstead, A., Green, F. and Mayhew, K. (1997) *Getting the measure of training: A report on training statistics in Britain*, Leeds: Centre for Industrial Policy and Performance, University of Leeds.

Kelly, M.R. (1989) 'Alternative forms of work organization under programmable automation', in S. Wood (ed.) *The transformation of work*, London: Unwin Hyman.

Koike, K. (1997) *Human resource management*, Tokyo: Japan Institute of Labour.

Koike, K. and Inoki, T. (eds) (1990) *Skill formation in Japan and Southeast Asia*, Tokyo: Tokyo University Press.

Lawler, E.E. (1994) 'From job-based to competence-based organisations', *Journal of Organizational Behaviour*, vol. 15, no. 2, pp. 3–15.

O'Reilly, J. (1992) 'Where do you draw the line? Functional flexibility, training and skill in Britain and France', *Work, Employment and Society*, vol. 6, no. 3, pp. 369–396.

Raper, P., Ashton, D., Felstead, A. and Storey, J. (1997) 'Toward the learning organisation? Explaining current trends in training practice in the UK', *International Journal of Training and Development*, vol. 1, no. 1, pp. 9–21.

Thompson, P., Wallace, T., Flecker, G. and Ahlstraand, R. (1995) 'It ain't what you do, it's the way that you do it: production organisation and skill utilisation in commercial vehicles', *Work, Employment and Society*, vol. 9, no. 4, pp. 719–742.

Townley, B. (1994) *Reframing human resource management: Power, ethics and the subject at work*, London: Sage.

Chapter 3

Envisioning new organisations for learning

Victoria J. Marsick and Karen E. Watkins

It is impossible to understand fully learning in the future workplace of the twenty-first century. The rapidly changing world in which we have been living is giving birth to a host of new ways of understanding work, jobs, organisations, technology and change. Those who design and run organisations in the future will be products of this new era and will bring mindsets to their positions that are in the process of becoming. We cannot predict the exact nature of future shifts, nor whether or when we might again enter a more stable time period.

Much of our work has highlighted the shift away from a compartmentalised, almost assembly-line, approach to learning towards a holistic, integrated vision of a learning organisation. While the logic of the learning organisation may hold up in an ideal world, we recognise that reality is never ideal. In this chapter, we first adopt a historical perspective on this shift. We use several metaphors developed by Morgan (1997) to address the changing nature of organisations and workplace learning. We turn then to a review of current trends, with a focus on the relationship between learning and the development of intellectual capital and knowledge management. We look at the learning organisation in light of these metaphors, and then examine implications for different stakeholders – specifically, managers, employees and HRD professionals. We conclude with reflection and critique on the future of workplace learning.

Metaphors for organising and learning

Training became a field of practice about the time of the Industrial Revolution, although it did not become widespread until the First World War. Prior to the era of training, people frequently learned informally through apprenticeship-like models: 'From first-hand experience, managers at mill companies learned that improving employee skills could result in dramatic increases in

This is an edited version of an article previously published in D. Boud and J. Garrick (eds) *Understanding Learning at Work*. 1999. Reproduced by permission of Taylor & Francis Ltd.

productivity' (Harkins, 1991: 27). Yet it was not for another fifty years or so that training became institutionalised: 'It was the introduction of management training before World War II that opened the door to systematically increasing overall productivity through employee training programs' (ibid.). Harkins point out that Peter Drucker, often considered the father of management in the USA, counted only three university continuing education programmes and two companies in the 1940s that regularly trained managers: Sears Roebuck in the USA and Marks & Spencer in England. Drucker was incorrect of course since many companies were already engaging in managerial training including those in the petroleum industry, government and other major industries (Watkins, 1996). What is significant is that the model of training that was prevalent was that of on-the-job training and classroom-based training.

Training grew more formal for a number of reasons. Organisations became successful by establishing hierarchy, stability and predictability, and uniform standards and practices, Yet managers – who were frequently entrusted with the responsibility for their staff's development – were not very good at helping others learn. Managers were well situated to guide their employees and often held valuable implicit knowledge about performance and desired standards, but their skills were in getting work done rather than in helping employees learn. Trainers gained leverage for organisations by identifying needs and making standards explicit, distilling the best practices of people who successfully met these standards and combining this with external expertise on the topic, and packaging the information systematically to teach it to others.

Trainers in the past were concerned with developing basic skills and knowledge for a generation of people who were not accustomed to pursuing higher education. Today, the workforce is more educated, although demographic trends indicate a growing gap between a relatively smaller number of highly educated, well-prepared workers and a much larger proportion of less educated people who have not had access to the same opportunities, especially in terms of computer literacy. Today's workers are being trained to be proactive problem-solvers, with an emphasis on enhancing behavioural skills, sensitivity to the organisation's culture or way of doing business, and employee values and motivation. The focus is on strategic thinking, knowledge creation and management, and an ability to thrive on constant change.

There are many reasons for these changes in focus, not the least of which are the forces external to organisations that have shaped the way business is conducted, companies structured and training designed. Four metaphors help to understand the forces behind these changes: the machine, organic systems, brain, and chaos/complexity (Morgan, 1997). Table 3.1 lays out these metaphors, as well as implications they hold for design of jobs and organisational structures, and for the systems of learning that flow from them. As will be seen, there is a big difference between the linear machine

Table 3.1 Metaphorical lenses for understanding organising and learning

Metaphor	Nature of work	Organisation's structure	Learning design
Machine	Clearly defined, separate, co-ordinated	Bureaucratic and hierarchical	Instructional systems design: systematic training designed and conducted by experts
Open systems	Interactive with other work, interrelated	Networked	Andragogy: learning is negotiated, self-directed and participatory
Brains/ holograph	Work is self-regulated	More autonomy for individuals; increasing boundary-lessness	Informal and incidental learning: continuous learning that is single and double loop
Chaos/ complexity	Work is self-initiated, subject to random shifts	High level of decentralisation; virtual and knowledge-based structures	Action-based learning; little clear guidance in weighing choices

metaphor and the other three metaphors. The brain and chaos/complexity models incorporate basic elements of the open system model. As well, each succeeding metaphor can be seen as growing from the limitations of the prior metaphor, and either building on or replacing it as a primary organiser. However, we recognise that all of these metaphors can operate simultaneously in different parts of the same organisation for different purposes.

Machine metaphor

In the early Industrial Age, organisations functioned much like machines. Jobs were clearly defined, separated and orchestrated into a whole by a series of hierarchically arranged managers. An icon of this era is Frederick Taylor. His ideas, referred to by the shorthand of Taylorism, included five key principles (Morgan, 1997: 23, Morgan's italics):

1   *Shift all responsibility for the organisation of work from the worker to the manager.* Managers should do all the thinking relating to the planning and design of work, leaving the workers with the tasks of implementation.
2   *Use scientific methods* to determine the most efficient way of doing work. Design the worker's task accordingly, specifying the *precise* way in which the work is to be done.

Table 3.2 Descriptions of models of training/learning

Model	Description
Instructional systems design (Rothwell and Kazanas, 1994 and 1989)	Performance needs of individuals and systems are identified against clearly specified standards; objectives are set to address gaps; learning activities are designed to meet objectives, and gains evaluated against pre-set criteria
Andragogy (Knowles, 1980); self-directed learning (Candy, 1991)	Individuals identify own needs and learning goals in order to maximise their abilities; individual plans are developed that take account of learning-style preferences; learning methods are often participatory and experience based; evaluation is tailored to individual differences as well as organisation's needs
Informal and incidental learning (Marsick and Watkins, 1990; Boud et al., 1993)	Individuals continually learn from their experience through reflection on action in light of prior learning and re-evaluation of prior insights and frames of reference; learning can be focused on tactics/strategies or on underlying assumptions that shape action
Action technologies (Brooks and Watkins, 1994)	Peers join together to use real-life problems or challenges as laboratories for learning; learning includes cycles of problem framing, experimentation, reflection, and reframing; action often leads to individual and systems changes

3   *Select* the best person to perform the job thus designed.
4   *Train* the worker to do the work efficiently.
5   *Monitor* worker performance to ensure that appropriate work procedures are followed and that appropriate results are received.

Uniform training could be designed to ensure that people filled jobs in this machine. Standards were clear, and there was often one best way to solve a problem. For example, Lillian Gilbreth trained managers in her home in the Tayloristic efficiency techniques she and her husband Frank developed (Watkins, 1996). It was more efficient to do most training in the classroom, and then expect that skills could be transferred to similar conditions on the job. 'Training' often implied dependency of the learner on the organisation's official representatives, including the teacher/training who ensured accountability. Instructional systems design (ISD) evolved to help trainers diagnose problems, locate specific deficiencies, and tailor solutions to meet these clear needs. (See Table 3.2 for more detail on ISD.) Today we would look at models of enhanced on-the-job training such as that developed by Jacobs and Jones (1995) as excellent examples of the application of instructional systems design to performance problems – Table 3.2 elaborates.

Open systems metaphor

As we moved into the Information Age, scholars and practitioners began to describe the organisation as an open system that interacted with its environment. Systems are like the human body with its myriad interdependent parts. Another way of thinking about a system is a mobile: if you push one part of the mobile, it affects all the other parts. A key theorist whose work informed this metaphor was Ludwig von Bertalanffy. Morgan (1997: 40–41) summarises key principles of open systems as follows:

1   the modelling of the open system after organisms;
2   the idea of homeostasis or self-regulation towards a steady state;
3   the notion of entropy, that is the tendency to 'deteriorate and run down';
4   the essential focus on interrelationships among structure, function, differentiation and integration;
5   requisite variety, which states that 'internal regulatory mechanisms of a system must be as diverse as the environment with which it is trying to deal';
6   equifinality, that is 'in an open system there may be many different ways of arriving at a given end state';
7   system evolution, that is systems can evolve if they can 'move to more complex forms of differentiation and integration, and greater variety'.

In the open systems model, the learning of one person or work group affects that of others; they are mutually interdependent. Learning does not necessarily take place in classrooms; people frequently learn with one another as they carry out tasks. However, even though employees take more initiative for their learning in the open system, they participate in a series of explicit and implicit negotiations about the nature of their tasks and their learning with others with whom they interact, including the manager and human resource developer. These negotiations are required to maintain desired balance among relationships. The andragogical model of learning, developed by Knowles (1980), is well suited to the systems model because andragogy emphasises a negotiated learning process around goals and outcomes for evaluation, while allowing the learner greater freedom to match pacing and choices of learning methods to individual preferences. (See Table 3.2 for more detail on the andragogical model.) Andragogy is self-directed learning (Candy, 1991), but in practice it also allows for joint modification of plans by learners and institutions.

Brain metaphor

In the 1990s, we moved more towards an understanding of organisations as brain centres that are self-organising, self-monitoring, self-correcting entities.

The brain metaphor involves organic, neural interconnections through which information is processed almost simultaneously. To function like a brain, people must interact more quickly and effectively to identify problems before they become catastrophes and solve them creatively. Morgan (1997: 103) identifies principles of holographic design that characterise organisations as a brain:

1   build the 'whole' into the 'parts'
2   the importance of redundancy
3   requisite variety
4   'minimum specs'
5   learn to learn

The brain image thus suggests that people and organisations be more proactive in scanning their environment, taking corrective action, and learning from the new situation. Learning in a brain-like organisation is more truly a self-directed, self-monitoring, self-correcting continuous process. Not only do people learn to keep up with their own needs; they also learn to help the entire brain-like enterprise flourish. In a very simplistic sense, 'training' is a top-down, expert-centred approach, which is delivered frequently in a classroom, or with the help of technology, to the learner who uses a formal, self-learning package. Continuous learning is a bottom-up, learner-centred approach, which is coterminous with experience; that is, it calls for a model of learning from experience under conditions of very little structured design. Marsick and Watkins (1990) describe this kind of learning as informal or incidental, which is, essentially, learning from experience (Boud et al., 1993). (See Table 3.2 for more detail on the informal and incidental learning model.) In addition, in order to self-regulate, learning must be both single loop and double loop (Argyris and Schön, 1978). Single-loop learning involves changes in tactics and strategies when things do not turn out as desired or predicted. Double-loop learning involves changes in the fundamental way in which problems are understood. Double-loop learning is required for self-regulation because individuals must, at times, change basic directions, which requires reframing basic lenses through which they view the world.

Chaos/complexity metaphor

More recently, scholars have been looking at organisations through the lens of chaos and complexity theory. Examples are drawn from physical phenomena in nature and the galaxy:

> Complex nonlinear systems like ecologies or organisations are characterized by multiple systems of interaction that are both ordered and

> chaotic . . . random disturbances can produce unpredictable events and relationships that reverberate throughout a system, creating novel patterns of change . . . despite all of the unpredictability, coherent order *always* emerges out of the randomness and surface chaos.
>
> (Morgan, 1997: 262)

Wheatley (1992) is well known for her thinking on how chaos theory applies to management. Chaos theorists pay attention to the idea of 'attractors', which are pulls on a system to move in a direction. Systems are often pulled between several strong attractors, which are then responsible for the patterns that emerge. When systems move towards the edge of their equilibrium points, they may encounter alternative 'bifurcation points that are rather like "forks in a road" leading to different futures' (Morgan, 1997: 265).

Chaotic change is enhanced by the simultaneous move in organisations to decentralise so that people and units can more easily respond to flux in their environment. Concomitantly, decentralisation enables people to be pulled by other attractors. People often find themselves mentally free to move from one organisation or cause to another as well, in part because of the change in the psychological contract away from promises of lifelong employment. While on the one hand this freedom is liberating, it also comes with a lessening of links to organisations and to the social norms that have helped people to make sense of random existence. People thus find that they are increasingly being asked to look after themselves. They are told that they are responsible for their own learning, and are pushed towards self-directed learning and self-managed careers. Knowledge can be freely accessed, which provides for rich information, but at the same time, the individual can count on less help from systems in choosing and weighing the ideas that might be of greatest value to an unpredictable future. The organisation is often tied together by knowledge-based design principles rather than by the old hierarchical order; and work is frequently done virtually through the use of technology.

In chaos-based organisations, self-directed learning is still required, but overriding the self-initiation is a push away from prior planning and a pull towards simultaneous action and learning. These learning models also speak to the way in which individual action is shaped by the system's culture and structure. A family of related approaches to learning, based on action research, that fit well in this era are those that have been termed action technologies (Brooks and Watkins, 1994). They include action research, action learning, action science and collaborative enquiry. (See Table 3.2 for more detail on the action-based learning model.) All of these designs involve learners actively in investigating real problems, and in building their learning around these issues in real time. These learning models are inductive and organic; learners discover and meet needs in relationship to the problem they are investigating. They can apply what they learn immediately at work, and they can also take into account in their solutions the rapidly changing work environment. Action-based learning models frequently lead to changes in the system as a whole because learners question collective values, belief systems and ways of organising work in their search for solutions. The action project causes dissonance, which enables unfreezing of old ways. The apparent chaos that often ensues allows new patterns to emerge.

Learning organisations

How can we conceptualise a field that has grown so far beyond its earlier training identity as a teacher who works not in schools but in business, government and industry? It is clear that the short time perspective of short-term training courses is inadequate. The dawning acknowledgement that organisational changes of processes, culture or structure create accompanying learning demands has meant that the field must encompass more than training. The 1990s saw the articulation of new models of workplace learning that emphasised the integration of learning into workplace practices and processes.

The concept of a learning organisation has emerged in recent years to take account of many of these changes (e.g. Field with Ford, 1995; Pedler et al., 1991; Redding and Catalanello, 1994; Senge, 1990; Watkins and Marsick, 1993). The learning organisation has been defined as an organisation that learns continually and has the capacity to transform itself (Pedler et al., 1991; Watkins and Marsick, 1993). The idea of a learning organisation is based on models of organisational learning that have been in the literature for many years (e.g. Argyris and Schön, 1978, 1996; Fiol and Lyles, 1985; Hedberg, 1981; March and Olsen, 1976; Meyer, 1982). It can be argued that all organisations learn, or they would not survive, but learning organisations demand proactive interventions to generate, capture, store, share and use learning at the systems level in order to create innovative products and services.

Many authors agree about what a learning organisation is, although they frequently operationalise core components differently. Most authors focus on learning of the system as a whole, as well as key changes in the way in which work is designed and the organisation is structured in order to allow for free flow of information, knowledge creation and management, and a culture that supports continuous learning (Gephart et al., 1997). Critics of the concept have noted its bias towards idealistic, normative outcomes, the complexity of interventions needed to implement it, and difficulties in measurement of impact (Marsick and Watkins, 1997).

Knowledge management and intellectual capital

Recently, a related vein of literature has emerged on knowledge management and intellectual capital (Edvinnson and Malone, 1997; Nonaka and Takeuchi, 1995; Stewart, 1997). It speaks to the tangible outcomes of the learning organisation: knowledge as a product, its creation and management within the system, and its contribution to knowledge outcomes that are captured through the idea of intellectual capital. Knowledge creation is frequently looked upon in the literature as a hierarchy of increasingly complex levels of integration: data, information, knowledge and wisdom. Data are the raw material out of which people develop information. Information is then woven together to create knowledge, larger meaning chunks that signify patterns and relationships. Wisdom, at the pinnacle of the hierarchy, involves judgements about the value and use of knowledge. Learning – of individuals, and subsequently, of the entire system – is the process that makes the creation and use of knowledge meaningful (Watkins and Callahan, 1998).

Management in several corporations has actively sought to incorporate knowledge creation and exchange as part of its mission to prompt employees to enhance their capacity to produce the most desirable results. Unfortunately, more efforts fail or disappoint than succeed (Lucier and Torsilieri, 1997). One reason for this may be the difficulty in measuring intellectual capital. A measurement approach that is growing in popularity is that of the balanced scorecard – of adding *return on knowledge assets* to the traditional *return on financial assets* to the organisation's yearly accounting metrics.

Measures for intellectual capital grew out of dissatisfaction with conventional economic measures of value. Many of the assets brought to an organisation today reside in intangibles that are the result of knowledge resident in people or systems and products that they create. In the manufacturing age, these intangibles were often identified as 'good will'. In today's knowledge era, intellectual capital is most frequently described as having three components (Stewart, 1997; Edvinnson and Malone, 1997):

1   human capital, that is the people who work in a system themselves with all of their knowledge, experience and capacity to grow and innovate;
2   structural capital, that is what remains behind when people leave the premises: systems, policies, processes, tools or intellectual property that become the property of the system itself; and
3   customer capital, that is the system of relationships that an organisation has with its clients irrespective of the people who work there or the structural capital that is in place.

Strassman (Knowledge Inc., 1996) argues that the number of firms destroying knowledge capital is greater than the number of firms creating it. Re-engineering and downsizing play a critical role in destroying knowledge capital.

The people who possess the accumulated knowledge about a company are the carriers of Knowledge Capital. They are the people who leave the workplace every night and may never return. They possess some-thing for which they have spent untold hours listening and talking while delivering nothing of tangible value to paying customers. Their brains have become the repositories of an accumulation of insights about how 'things work here'.

(ibid.: 4)

Strassman continues, 'Anybody can cut costs by consuming capital.' He explains:

when they downsize they do not calculate what it will do to their Knowledge Capital. What they do, invariably, is slim down, reduce costs and destroy assets in the process. Five years later they wonder why the company is in worse shape than it was before.

(ibid.: 5)

Learning organisations extend capacity to use learning as a strategic tool to generate new knowledge in the form of products, patents, processes and services, and to use technology to capture knowledge.

Applying metaphors to the learning organisation

The idea of the learning organisation can be differently understood by looking at it through the lens of different metaphors as discussed earlier in this chapter. Table 3.3 lays out some broad implications for how three sets of stakeholders might view learning, depending on the predominant lens through which they view this idea. Each lens leads to different decisions regarding what is important and what should be changed.

The machine metaphor actually does not lend itself well to a learning organisation, but it can be used to depict a training organisation in which employees are effectively and efficiently assisted to learn what the organisa-tion wishes them to do best. Some of the better-known organisations before the knowledge era provided for this kind of learning very well. This model is still useful when operations are fairly routine, although under this metaphor, employees can be treated in a dehumanised manner for the specific skill they contribute. Managers in this model can help clearly to identify learning needs, provide incentives and resources for training, and measure success against clear standards. Employees are asked to follow the lead of managers. Therefore, when their best interests are not the same as those of the organisation, employees might join together through collective action to bargain for their rights. Learning is often compartmentalised in this model; neither managers nor employees encouraged learning outside of a clearly defined job description. Hierarchy prevails, so that employees are not given more information than deemed necessary for efficient operation of routine procedures. Curiosity and risk taking are not encouraged or rewarded. The

Table 3.3   Metaphorical lenses: implications for the learning organisation

Lens of learning	Implications for managers	Implications for employees	Implications for HRD
Machine	Provide incentives and resources for training; direct employees to perform to organisation's standards	Improve effectiveness and efficiency as specified; challenge managers through industrial relations	Hire or train employees to fill skill needs; provide instruction to meet defined needs and standards
Open systems	Assist employees in identifying needs and resources; act as coach and mentor; monitor against mutually negotiated goals	Negotiate learning with managers; adjust goals based on feedback; collaborate across boundaries to build knowledge and skills	Identify needed competencies and set up systems for self-directed learning; partner to ensure that needs are met
Brain/ holograph	Model learning; integrate work and learning; provide for job enrichment and rotation; encourage cross-functional teams	Diagnose system's needs; challenge assumptions; initiate/ monitor learning to meet own and system's needs	Design work to integrate learning across functions; provide for variety and continuous learning; build capacity to cross boundaries
Chaos/ complexity	Provide structure and incentives to share knowledge; empower; align vision; act as resource for learning	Build portability of skills and job mobility; experiment and take risks; challenge restrictions and norms	Provide simultaneously for autonomy and for sharing across boundaries; unfreeze status quo

human resource developer in this model needs to hire the right people, and ensure that they gain the knowledge and skills identification to meet the challenges of their jobs. HRD staff are often engaged in contracting for, designing, delivering and evaluating training oriented to transferring expert knowledge and best practices that have been shown to lead to performance according to a desired standard.

The learning organisation concept begins to operate when, minimally, the open systems metaphor prevails. The networked structure common to this model provides incentives for a balanced, negotiated system of learning in which individuals take more initiative for their own learning, and can also get feedback regarding the way in which their actions impact on others in the organisation. In this model, there is more incentive to collaborate across boundaries and to negotiate towards win–win relationships with peers and managers. Arrangements can be developed that provide opportunities for learning, and that allow for mutual building and sharing of knowledge. While individuals take more initiative for learning in the open systems model, those who are designated as having more authority (be they managers or union representatives) are often accorded more responsibility for ensuring that learning goals are set, provided for, resourced and met. While managers are directors under the machine model, they often find themselves playing the role of a facilitator in the open systems model. HRD staff collaborate with managers, employees and collective bargaining units. They create systems that enable everyone more easily to determine knowledge and skill requirements for various roles and functions so that individuals can take the initiative in planning for their learning. Technology often aids in this process through computer-based skill assessments and self-managed learning systems. Technology also allows for the design of effective knowledge creation and management systems.

Under the brain metaphor, the learning organisation concept takes a leap forward. This is the intelligent enterprise that prizes knowledge creation and innovation. In order to be self-monitoring and self-regulating as a system, employees and managers alike seek to ensure that everyone takes an active role in scanning the environment and using this knowledge to improve products and services. Individuals seek out experience in the system as a whole, and are empowered in this model to act more frequently on behalf of the system when decisions fall close to their area of responsibility. Employees are as active as are managers in identifying and meeting learning needs for themselves and the organisational systems. Managers often take on a modelling role. Rather than direct operations, they clear blockages that get in the way of the free flow of information, and seek to involve employees actively in problem framing and reframing. Managers and employees alike are more active to challenge current thinking and assumptions that interfere with a flexible response to the shifting environment. Barriers break down between levels of the hierarchy, and between managers and bargaining units, because interests are more greatly aligned around a common vision. HRD staff actively help managers and employees alike to design work so that learning can also take place, and so that everyone knows as much as possible about the relevant work of others in the system. HRD staff seek to build the capacity of individuals and groups for continuous learning.

The chaos/complexity model may be best suited to the level of experimentation and risk taking that is demanded for the building of intellectual capital in society. However, this model also holds the greatest risks for specific companies and enterprises that may fall short of what is needed to survive in an increasingly competitive environment. New patterns emerge from chaos, but it is hard to predict where they will emerge or who will have developed the skills, knowledge and capacity to take advantage of these new opportunities. This model of learning requires the simultaneous and almost paradoxical nurturing of both autonomy for individuals and concern for linkages across individuals so that the larger system can benefit from what individuals have learned. Managers in this learning model need to provide incentives and opportunities to learn rapidly for both individuals and systems. Empowerment in this model is even stronger than in the brain model, but so too is the need to adjust continually and align the vision to take advantage of what is being learned. Individuals cannot count on the organisation to provide compensation for what they know over time, and, hence, must build portability of knowledge assets. Sacred cows need to be continually challenged if individuals and systems as a whole are to evolve into new forms that can flourish in the future. HRD staff in this model must create structures and advocate for resources so that individuals can meet rapidly changing needs for knowledge and skills. They must also find ways to involve actively representatives of the entire system in learning, decision making and in building a collective knowledge base. HRD staff can serve managers and employees better when they help to unfreeze reliance on the status quo so that space is opened up to experiment and to use learning to change structures, cultures and systems. In this approach, training and education are part of the larger research and development role of the organisation, working to build knowledge capital of a different kind.

The above analysis, of course, assumes that any given organisation falls fairly clearly under the sphere of influence of one or other of these metaphors. In real life, this could well not be the case. Organisations need to develop the capacity to diagnose their learning orientations, and, when necessary, to add to their repertoire of learning responses or to change them. This becomes more complex if we return to our assumption that all of these metaphors can operate simultaneously in different parts of the same organisation for different purposes. In addition, it seems likely that different individuals could hold a viewpoint on learning that might not be shared by the dominant culture. In these cases, the perspectives of different individuals and groups will come into conflict. Schein (1996) points out that in many organisations there are actually three cultures that function in any organisation at any time – that of operators, of engineers and of executives. These differences are not typically recognised, or adequately taken into account, in analysing or addressing issues around the organisation's culture. And, as Field and Ford (1995) point out, in some organisations the conflict of perspectives is suppressed, with a resultant loss of learning. In a learning organisation, with a minimum of an open systems perspective, it should be possible to surface, identify and address conflict constructively and, optimally, to view difference as a catalyst for more effective learning. Nevertheless, it is critical to remember that the lens through which either the organisational culture or the training function views learning is a coherent, but also a limiting, perspective. Diagnosing the prevailing metaphor is one step towards moving beyond its limitations.

Critique of the learning organisation concept

Some take a pessimistic view of the power relations in organisations, and the feasibility of changing these to empower workers to the extent required in a learning organisation. Darrah (1995), for example, analyses workplace training at 'Kramden Computers' to see how the production floor can be viewed as an arena for learning and how training may reify extant social relationships in the workplace. He argues that the function of training may be to 'obscure organisational schisms that can only be addressed through deeper changes in the workplace' (ibid.: 31). He suggests that workplace training and workplace learning are linked and neither is a simple matter of efficient pedagogy. Rather, the organisation of work and the allocation of power deeply influence what is learned. While few would argue with Darrah's assertions, one could counterargue that he is again blaming the victim since trainers are seldom positioned to address these fundamental changes and they, too, are aware of the dilemmas he notes. It is precisely because workplace learning is more than a simple pedagogical interaction that we have seen the emergence of conceptualisations of workplace learning that combine knowledge of pedagogy with knowledge of organisational behaviour and culture.

A broader critique comes from Korten (1995) whose powerfully well-documented critique of corporate greed and power raises the question of individual versus organisational rights. Noting the hold that industrial interests gained over government following the chaos of the US Civil War, President Lincoln said that corporations had become enthroned and corruption and greed would follow that would destroy the Republic. Later, the courts continued to take away the controls citizens had imposed until the case of *Santa Clara County v. Southern Pacific Railroad* in 1886, which ruled that a corporation was a natural person under the US Constitution, which thereby afforded corporations the protection of the Bill of Rights. Korten notes that this was a dramatic victory for corporations since they received the rights of citizens without the responsibility of citizenship. With globalisation, corporations are citizens of no country and responsible only to themselves. Korten suggests that there has been an increasing 'sanctification of greed' and with it less and less concern for the individual and the communities in which corporations reside. Democratic pluralism is lost as is the balance of civic, individual and corporate interests.

Korten argues for corporate social responsibility within corporations. Moreover, he asks human resource developers and managers to use their considerable organisational and group facilitation skills to work with communities to take back their power. Korten argues that the way to transform organisations is to change the balance of power between the vested interests of managers and stockholders, which now makes it unnecessary for them to change at all. Korten's idea of human resource developers and managers is that they are a citizen first and a corporate employee second. His is an arresting and compelling case and also disturbing for professions that have always seen themselves as those who help organisations transform themselves from within.

The idea of the learning organisation has also been questioned as a tool of management that again holds employees responsible for transforming and changing their reluctant organisations (Schied *et al.*, 1997; Welton, 1991). Some labour leaders are envisioning new roles for unions that emphasise partnership, collaboration and consensus building, and they see learning as central to their new focus (Field with Ford, 1995; Scully, 1994). Nonetheless, more organisations have invested in learning organisation experiments focused on the learning and changing of employees than have invested in changing the underlying structures of power and knowledge creation in the organisation.

Other critics have asked: learning for what? If we create organisations that learn faster, better and deeper, and the outcome is to feed corporate profits at the expense of people, societies and the environment, is this not similar to making a more effective gas for the Nazi gas chambers? Again, this is a dramatic form of the question, but the issue is important. Those who raise this question are sensibly asking us to question the validity of a vision of the learning organisation that is only process oriented. What is learned is also significant.

Conclusion

We might well ask where this critique and analysis leads us. How do we reconcile the metaphors of organisation with the learning responses, without falling into the traps the critics identify? One approach implied in this discussion is that organisations must evolve developmentally, starting with the metaphor that now prevails and moving towards one that permits higher-level learning and a more complex learning approach. Another thought is to imagine that the society as a whole is moved by a dominant metaphor. If this were the case, it might be most imperative to align the learning system with the prevailing metaphor. Yet, this seems either too prescriptive or alarmist. An approach more in keeping with our thinking is to seek to create a learning system that incorporates selected elements of each metaphor, tailored to the needs of the industry, the organisation, the division and the individuals who work in this organisational culture.

References

Argyris, C. and Schön, D. (1978) *Organizational Learning: A Theory of Action Perspective*, San Francisco: Jossey-Bass.

Argyris, C. and Schön, D. (1996) *Organizational Learning II: Theory, Method, and Practice*, Reading, MA: Addison-Wesley.

Boud, D., Cohen, R. and Walker, D. (eds) (1993) *Using Experience for Learning*, Buckingham, UK, and Bristol, PA: The Society for Research into Higher Education, and Open University Press.

Brooks, A. and Watkins, K.E. (eds) (1994) *The Emerging Power of Action Inquiry Technologies*, New Directions in Adult and Continuing Education, San Francisco: Jossey-Bass.

Candy, P.C. (1991) *Self-direction for Lifelong Learning: A Comprehensive Guide to Theory and Practice*, San Francisco: Jossey-Bass.

Darrah, C. (1995) 'Workplace training, workplace learning: a case study', *Human Organization* 54(1): 31–41.

Edvinnson, L. and Malone, M. (1997) *Intellectual Capital: Realizing Your Company's True Value by Finding its Hidden Roots*, New York: HarperCollins.

Field, L. with Ford, B. (1995) *Managing Organizational Learning: From Rhetoric to Reality*, Melbourne: Longman.

Fiol, M.C. and Lyles, M.A. (1985) 'Organizational learning', *Academy of Management Review* 10(4): 803–813.

Gephart, M.A., Marsick, V.J. and Van Buren, M.E. (1997) 'Finding common and uncommon ground among learning organization models', in R. Torraco (ed.) *Proceedings of the Fourth Annual Academy of HRD Conference*, Baton Rouge, LA: Academy of Human Resource Development, 547–554.

Harkins, P.J. (1991) 'The changing role of corporate training and development', *Corporate Development in the 90s*, Supplement to *Training*, Minneapolis, MN: Lakewood, 26–29.

Hedberg, B. (1981) 'How organizations learn and unlearn', in P.C. Nystrom and W.H. Starbuck (eds) *Handbook of Organizational Design*, Vol. 1, London: Oxford University Press, 3–27.

Jacobs, R. and Jones, M.J. (1995) *Structured On-the-Job Training: Unleashing Employee Expertise in the Workplace*, San Francisco: Berrett-Koehler.

Knowledge Inc. (1996) 'Leading lights: knowledge strategist Paul Strassmann, Interview', *Knowledge Inc. Executive Report*.

Knowles, M. (1980) *The Modern Practice of Adult Education: From Pedagogy to Andragogy*, second edn, New York: Cambridge Books.

Korten, D. (1995) *When Corporations Rule the World*, San Francisco: Berrett-Koehler.

Lucier, C.E. and Torsilieri, J.D. (1997) 'Why knowledge programs fail: a C.E.O.'s guide to managing learning', *Strategy and Business* No. 9: 14–28.

March, J.G. and Olsen, J.P. (1976) *Ambiguity and Choice in Organizations*, Norway: Universitetsforlaget.

Marsick, V.J. and Watkins, K.E. (1990) *Informal and Incidental Learning in the Workplace*, London: Routledge.

Marsick, V.J. and Watkins, K.E. (1997) 'Organizational learning: review of research', in L.J. Bassi and D. Russ-Eft (eds) *What Works and What Doesn't: Assessment, Development, and Measurement*, Alexandria, VA: American Society for Training & Development, 65–86.

Meyer, A. (1982) 'Adapting to environmental jolts', *Administrative Science Quarterly* 27(4): 515–537.

Morgan, G. (1997) *Images of Organization*, Thousand Oaks, CA: Sage.

Nonaka, I. and Takeuchi, H. (1995) *The Knowledge Creating Company*, New York: Oxford.

Pedler, M., Burgoyne, J. and Boydell, T. (1991) *The Learning Company*, London: McGraw-Hill.

Redding, J. and Catalanello, R. (1994) *Strategic Readiness: The Making of a Learning Organization*, San Francisco: Jossey-Bass.

Rothwell, W. and Kazanas, H. (1994 and 1989) *Human Resource Development – A Strategic Approach*, Amherst, MA: HRD Press.

Schein, E.H. (1996) 'Culture: the missing concept in organization studies', *Administrative Science Quarterly* 41 (June): 229–240.

Schied, F.M., Carter, V.K., Preston, J.A. and Howell, S.L. (1997) 'The HRD factory: an historical inquiry into the production of control in the workplace', in P. Armstrong, N. Miller and M. Zukas (eds) *Crossing Borders, Breaking Boundaries: Research in the Education of Adults, Proceedings of the 27th Annual SCUTREA Conference*, Birkbeck College, University of London, 404–408.

Scully, E. (1994) 'The role of labor unions in the learning organization', Unpublished manuscript.

Senge, P. (1990) *The Fifth Discipline: The Art and Practice of the Learning Organization*, New York: Random House.

Stewart, T. (1997) *Intellectual Capital: The New Wealth of Organizations*, New York: Double Day Currency.

Watkins, K.E. (1996) 'Workplace learning: changing times, changing practices', in F. Spikes (ed.) *Workplace Learning*, New Directions in Adult and Continuing Education Series, San Francisco: Jossey-Bass.

Watkins, K.E. and Callahan, M.W. (1998) 'Return on knowledge assets: investments in educational technology', *Educational Technology* XXXVI(4): 33–40.

Watkins, K.E. and Marsick, V.J. (1993) *Sculpting the Learning Organization*, San Francisco: Jossey-Bass.

Welton, M. (1991) *Toward Development Work: The Workplace as a Learning Environment*, Geelong, Victoria: Deakin University Press.

Wheatley, M. (1992) *Leadership and the New Science*, San Francisco: Berrett-Koehler.

Chapter 4

Gender, work and workplace learning

Anita Devos

In my work as an educator of workplace-based adult educators and in staff development, I have felt increasingly dissatisfied with the dimensions of the debate over learning in the workplace. In my analysis, the mainstream adult education literature in this area has assumed an uncritical position on the nature of work and of work organisation. This is reflected in the lack of attention given to a discussion of power in the workplace as a crucial feature of workplaces and hence the environment for learning, and in the silence in the literature on issues of gender and culture as defining features of the context. Where power inequalities or struggles between groups of people in the workplace – such as workers and managers – are touched on in this material, the conflict tends to be dismissed as a feature of the environment that can be managed through the skilful application of 'technique' by 'change agents' (see, for example, Watkins and Marsick, 1992).

In other words, the presumption is that crucial contradictions and para-doxes, which sometimes manifest themselves in the form of resistance to change, do not represent fundamental differences in people's experiences and understandings of the workplace – based on their gender, class, race, able-bodiedness – but are mere hiccups in the implementation of seamless systems that offer universal benefits to all workers *and* to the organisation itself! The literature works hard to sustain a story according to which every-one stands to gain from economic restructuring – given the 'right' inter-ventions by adult educators – and that any differences can be resolved within the prevailing economic, social and political framework.

The uncritical posture assumed by leading commentators reflects, I suggest, an unholy influence on the mainstream adult education literature exerted by the dominant corporate managerial discourse from which most research, writing and theory-building on the topic has emanated. Witness to this influence is the annotated bibliography by Field with Ford (1994), which

This is an edited version of an article previously published in *Studies in Continuing Education*, 18:2, 1996. Reproduced by permission of the University of Technology, Sydney.

cites 65 references related to organisation learning, overwhelmingly drawn from the management literature.

There is within adult education a tradition that examines organisation learning in a radical framework, asking questions about the social and political and economic context of work, and attempting to challenge power relations (see, amongst others, Hart, 1992; Welton, 1991; Foley, 1994). With the exception of Mechthild Hart's work, however, this work has largely ignored women and been insensitive to the implications of gender for the authors' own goals. The literature fails, in general, to deal adequately with difference other than from a class perspective, working from the presumption of the universal (male) worker. This presumption takes the experience of the white Anglo-Celtic man and represents his experience as universal. The experiences of other men and of women are made invisible, and are not researched, nor considered in the debates.

The challenge for adult educators interested in the potential of learning to transform social relations in the workplace is to make explicit the gendered and cultural assumptions that underpin research and practice in the field of workplace learning and to develop new forms of praxis based on this understanding.

In this paper I do not intend to provide a comprehensive overview or analysis of the literature on workplace learning. Rather, I will review the work of contemporary adult educators, North Americans Victoria Marsick and Karen Watkins, and Australian Laurie Field. I have chosen to focus on their work because of their prominence within the adult education literature on workplace learning, and hence their influence on the professional development of workplace-based adult educators.

My analysis of their work will be informed principally by my reading of feminist theory of the sociology of organisations, and with reference to a critique of the managerial discourse that (predictably) informs management writing on the subject, but with which adult education writings in the field have also become infused. Through this process, I plan to highlight the dilemmas and shortcomings with the current debates over learning in the workplace.

In developing my analysis, I will call on a number of different theoretical traditions and discourses over and above those two referred to above. At the risk of doing none of them justice, I consider such an approach to be productive as it makes some important connections in a complex field of study that, in my view, can only be understood by drawing on a number of discipline perspectives. It is therefore my hope that the ideas developed in the chapter will form the basis for further critique and research in the area, and on the nature of the project with which we are engaged when we seek to intervene in workplaces.

Gender and organisations

> Gender is not just a fancy word for 'women' but a fundamental social structure . . .
>
> (Maroney and Luxton, 1987: 10)

The central argument in my account of gender and organisations is that workplaces and work are organised according to gender, and that an understanding of gender as an organising principle should be central to a debate about work, and about learning in the workplace. This claim is grounded in research conducted over the last twenty or so years, which has illustrated that the ways in which work is organised, skills are defined, and training is designed and delivered, is not gender neutral but reflects a history of struggles over power and control in the workplace (see, for instance, Acker, 1989, 1990; Cockburn, 1983, 1985 and 1991; Game and Pringle, 1983; Jackson, 1991; Pringle, 1988).

This feminist work developed partly in reaction to the tradition of critical, non-feminist, research into organisations and the labour process that had taken shape since the 1970s, stimulated in part by Braverman's book *Labour and Monopoly Capital* (1974). This book broke new ground by challenging the basis of skills categories in industry and questions whose interests they served. Although Braverman and subsequent researchers who emulated his class critique of the labour process focused on questions of control, power and exploitation in organisations, and how these relations might be changed, they nonetheless were insensitive to questions of gender (Acker, 1989). These class-based critiques have been criticised for generalising from studies of men, by men, to arrive at a universal theory of the labour process.

Joan Acker (1990: 139) points to the unproblematic acceptance of the 'male' as 'universal' thus:

> Most of us spend our days in work organisations that are almost always dominated by men. The most powerful organisational positions are almost entirely occupied by men . . . Power at the national and world level is located in all-male enclaves at the pinnacle of large state and economic organisations. These facts are not news, although sociologists paid no attention until feminism came along to point out the problematic nature of the obvious.

It is my assertion that women and gender are also absent from the theoretical and empirical studies on workplace learning, which jeopardises the relevance of much that is written as a useful reference for practice for those educators who ascribe to feminist and emancipatory goals. My purpose here is to make gender problematic for the debates on workplace learning, and to stimulate reappraisal of many of the assumptions on which our views about workplace learning are founded.

One of the obstacles feminists face in bringing to the fore gender is that the dominant discourses of work, and of workplace learning, conceptualise organisations as gender neutral. Or to put it another way . . .

> since men in organisations take their behaviour and perspectives to represent the human, organisational structures and processes are theorised as gender neutral. When it is acknowledged that women and men are affected differently by organisations, it is argued that gendered attitudes and behaviour are brought into (and contaminate) essentially gender-neutral structures. This view of organisations separates structures from the people in them.
>
> (Acker, 1990: 142)

A leading Australian text on organisation learning (Field with Ford, 1995) follows this 'tradition' of describing workplaces in 'non-sexist', or 'sex-free' terms, again implying that the gender of the workforce and the social construction of the work is not salient to a consideration of the workplace. While Field refers very briefly to language difference as an issue in organisations, and discusses unequal status as one of the main barriers to learning, he fails to deal adequately with the forms that 'unequal status' takes. Particularly pertinent to my argument here, he fails to acknowledge the relationship between gender and workplace roles, practices, structures, and language. Furthermore, he does not deal with the complex ways in which sexism, racism and other forms of discrimination based on difference, interact and are reinforced in organisations. Indeed, his book both fails to deal explicitly with the circumstances of women in the workforce, and fails to provide a gender analysis of the evidence and propositions he is considering.

What is the significance of this silence in the literature on questions of gender and difference? In failing to deal with difference, many writers have accepted the premise upon which much literature on work organisation is based, namely the notion of the 'disembodied and universal worker' (Acker, 1990: 149);

> the closest the disembodied worker doing the abstract job comes to a real worker is the male worker whose life centres on his full-time, life-long job, while his wife or another woman takes care of his personal needs and his children.

So we have an abstract worker working in an abstract industry in an abstract occupation doing abstract work. With this level of abstraction, can we seriously begin to theorise about learning in the workplace? I would argue instead we need to base the development of theory about learning on a thorough and feminist analysis of specific workplaces. This work must acknowledge the material inequalities between men and women, and the ways in which gender permeates all facets of the life and practices of organisations.

The current debate over work and family draws attention to the problem of the universal worker, as it highlights the way that work structures and hours of work are based on this outdated notion of the male working life, according to which the man works full-time outside the home, and has a wife at home to cook, clean and raise the kids for him. Joan Acker points out that under industrial capitalism this was only the reality for some men; nonetheless, the myth is pervasive. Eveline's notion (1994: 137) of the 'benchmark' problem is also relevant to our understanding of this debate, according to which 'male' is defined as the norm and unproblematic while women are measured up to the norm, and found deficient.

In developing this argument, I am conscious of the way in which 'the big categories of nation, race, ethnicity and gender disguise differences within the categories and commonalities across their boundaries' (Pettman, 1992: viii). As bell hooks (1994: 63) puts it, 'gender is not the sole factor determining femaleness . . .' – culture, race, able-bodiedness, sexual orientation and class each assume an important role in influencing our experience and understanding of organisations and of the world. Nonetheless, feminist work on the gendered nature of workplace relations offers a critical platform from which to explore the assumptions that underpin most research into workplace learning, and from which to assess the claims of empowerment often associated with workplace learning.

While women's experience of work is by no means uniform, it is nonetheless possible to identify some common features of women's employment experiences. Women in paid employment are overwhelmingly concentrated (numerically) in the sales and personal services, and hospitality industries (O'Donnell and Hall, 1988). Women get paid less than men, work fewer paid hours than men, even when they want to work more, have less access to overaward payments and job-related benefits, such as bonuses, company cars and superannuation, and do most of the housework and child rearing. Occupations and industries in which women are concentrated share certain features in common. They are usually low paid, part-time and casual, and historically have lacked training and career paths (Pocock, 1988).

Workplaces themselves have in turn been influenced and shaped by the sex of the workers employed, and by the history and patterns of interaction of men and women who fulfil certain roles within those workplaces (see, for example, Cynthia Cockburn, 1983, 1985). This applies both in terms of the 'culture' of the workplace (e.g. building sites as male environments hostile to the presence of women), and in terms of the way roles are defined in relation to each other. A classic and familiar example of the latter is the relationship between a boss and a secretary. The relative roles between these two jobs are defined well before any job incumbents take up their duties, with job roles and expectations premised on the presumption that 'boss' is a man and 'secretary' is a woman.

To relate these issues more closely to training and learning, Nancy Jackson (1991) argues that training too becomes the site of struggles for control over knowledge and power at work. At stake are questions of how working knowledge will be organised, whose experience will it validate, and whose interests will it serve. These are essentially the same set of feminist concerns at the core of the struggle for equal pay, and in the debate over the development of competency standards for occupations. The central point made by feminist commentators is that 'skill' is a subjective notion, the definition of which has been closely controlled and guarded to protect the interests of those who have power. In Australian workplaces, those in power are usually white, Anglo-Celtic, full-time employed, industrially well-organised men.

This account of women's experiences in the labour market reflects a history and practice of systemic discrimination against women. Discrimination against women in employment, be it direct or indirect, has a profound impact on women's capacity and freedom to participate in the labour force on an equal footing with men. It therefore also has implications for the development of the workplace as a learning environment that offers opportunities and benefits to women as well as to men.

Understanding workplace learning

There is a growing literature on learning in the workplace, coming from a wide range of disciplines including management, organisation psychology, computer sciences, labour studies, and more recently, adult education. Some of the most often quoted writers include Senge (1990), Argyris and Schön (1978), Field with Ford (1995), Marsick and Watkins (1990) and Watkins and Marsick (1992, 1993).

The term 'workplace learning' is hard to pin down, and is subject to very different meanings, perhaps partly due to the different discipline and political frameworks within which the meanings are construed. Amongst a group of adult education researchers, everyone will nod knowingly when 'workplace learning' is mentioned, yet in my experience at a recent seminar on research into the topic, different people hold quite different private understandings of what the term actually means.

It might be stating the obvious to say that workplace learning is one of the number of terms used to describe learning that is in some way related to the workplace. This could incorporate one or more of the following features depending on the writer, or educator's 'definition-in-use': individuals learning from their experiences at work (informal learning); individuals learning from formal training conducted in their organisations; individuals learning through one-on-one tuition on the job; individuals or groups of people learning incidentally from their experiences at work, through some process the main focus of which was not necessarily learning (or learning of the type intended) (Marsick and Watkins, 1990); a group of people, or a team, learning from their experiences as a group ('group learning' or 'team learning'); and the organisation learning and changing its practices, as a consequence of the collective insight of members of that organisation, particularly following a crisis situation (organisational learning) (Field, 1990; Field with Ford, 1995).

The salient and common feature of all the usages, however, is that learning occurs in a particular context, namely the context of the workplace. Various more critical writers have chosen to emphasise the centrality of context to our understanding of the issues by using terms such as the 'workplace as a learning environment' (Welton, 1991) or the 'educative work environment' (Kornbluh and Greene, 1989). It is our understanding of context, and in particular, the gendered nature of the workplace context, that is the focus of my argument here.

The work of adult educators Victoria Marsick and Karen Watkins is particularly interesting, for a couple of reasons. In their work one can trace the development from thinking about 'training' and 'learning' as synonymous, to recognising the many ways in which people learn in the workplace (see, in particular, Marsick and Watkins, 1990). This includes informal learning that takes place on the job, and the learning dimensions of different forms of working arrangements – such as working in project teams – that are often incidental to the main functions of the teams.

They draw heavily on Carr and Kemmis' work on action research (1986) to develop what they describe as a 'new paradigm for research in the workplace', which they claim is founded on radically different assumptions about the world and how it should be studied (Marsick and Watkins, 1990). Drawing on an essentially interpretive framework for workplace research, their 'new paradigm' reflects a more qualitative and participatory approach to researching and analysing training and learning in organisations than had currency previously. In so doing, Marsick and Watkins have helped to move the debates away from a narrow, instrumentalist approach to the development of new workplace skills and behaviours, towards a more humanist, or interpretive approach consistent with the dominant paradigm in adult education. Their approach endeavours to address the limits of behaviourism when trying to foster reflective abilities and an ability to learn, qualities argued in the rhetoric of organisation change as central to ensuring the survival of contemporary organisations. For these reasons their work has been very popular with workplace-based adult educators, such as industry trainers and human resource development officers, and regularly appears on adult education course reading lists.

A more interesting (but little discussed) feature of their work, however, is the extent to which their thinking about learning in the workplace has been influenced and shaped by the dominant management discourses that operate internationally, and within which many adult educators interested in workplace learning have located themselves. Some of the key texts that have influenced the language we use to describe the 'new workplaces' (even if we haven't actually read them), include Senge's *The Fifth Discipline* (1990), and Drucker's *Post-Capitalist Society* (1993), amongst others. These 'fast capitalist texts', while they differ in detail, 'announce a new enchanted workplace where hierarchy is dead and "partners" engage in meaningful work amidst a collaborative environment of mutual commitment and trust' (Gee and Lankshear, 1995: 5). Gee and Lankshear describe these texts as 'enactive', envisioning a new direction for organisations. Through an analysis of some key words in fast capitalist texts, such as 'empowerment' and 'self-directed learning', they draw attention to many parallels in contemporary debates in education circles with the discourse of contemporary management.

As Gee and Lankshear point out (1995: 11), the language of fast capitalism has very positive connotations, which people feel obliged to embrace, including people who might otherwise have very different interests and purposes. For instance, most people would find it hard to argue that workers should *not* become 'empowered'. Where the adult education literature has largely failed is in critically examining the values and ideologies that lie behind the different uses and contexts in which the terms are used. For example, when Senge speaks of 'empowerment', is he really talking about the same thing as Paolo Freire (1975)?

This critical analysis of the discourse of central texts draws attention to a number of internal contradictions within Marsick and Watkins' work, and raises questions as to whether their framework for workplace learning can deliver on its promises. To illustrate the point, their framework rests on the notion that global and therefore organisational change is inevitable. They argue that the project for contemporary adult educators in organisations in the face of globalisation, new technologies, environmental turbulence and so on is to develop new models for people to understand, function and learn *given* this climate. Neither the direction of change, nor the desirability of the changes, is every subjected to analysis in their work. Their silence on these questions suggests that these matters are not contested, nor at all debatable.

Second, they do not examine how the changes occurring in organisations impact on the humanist objectives that they espouse. On the one hand, we have educational values that place the interests of the adult learner at the centre; on the other, corporate imperatives that in fact determine the direction, pace and method of change. We claim to be engaged in a project of 'empowerment' (whatever we think that means), yet fundamental issues of power, such as who sets the direction of change and whose interests it serves, are not touched.

My third criticism of their work concerns their understanding and application of ideas about critical reflection in the context of learning in organisations. They draw on Jack Mezirow's work on critical reflection (1981) to speak of a process whereby individuals come to understand the forces that shape meaning, and then act on those forces. These ideas have their origins in the work of Jürgen Habermas on knowledge and human interests (1971). In the process of adapting Habermas's theory to contemporary organisational contexts, Marsick and Watkins have redefined Habermas's idea of critical or emancipatory learning. In their framework, emancipatory learning is put to work in the service of adapting the individual to better meet the needs defined by the organisation. The instrumental logic of the organisation takes precedence over other concerns. The three domains of learning in Habermas's framework – namely, the technical, interpretive and emancipatory – are equated in their new paradigm with learning the job, learning the organisation and learning about oneself (Marsick and Watkins, 1995: 177). Within the last of these, critical reflectivity at the individual level replaces the social contextual analysis linked to emancipatory learning, and action (as central to emancipatory learning) is altogether taken out of the equation! Is this really an 'emancipatory' or for that matter 'empowering' project? Their reformulation of Habermas's knowledge framework conflicts with what I regard as the purpose of emancipatory learning, namely as Hart (1992) puts it, to enhance understanding so people can act to change their context in life-enhancing ways. This necessarily involves critical analysis of the context and the forces that shape it, and taking action to transform it. Marsick and Watkins have taken the 'critical' out of 'critical reflection', and instead reduced it to an internalised process, motivated and constrained by organisational requirements and boundaries.

These issues are particularly pertinent to my reading of the debate as they highlight the importance of a critical engagement with the context. This engagement is central to a feminist project in organisations and in society more broadly, as it forms the basis for women and men challenging the social construction of work and work roles, and acting to remove structures and practices that discriminate against women.

The discourse and practice of Total Quality Management (TQM) abounds with similar contradictions. TQM too professes a liberating and empowering ideology of organisations and learning; however, upon closer examination, paradoxes emerge. In his critical analysis of the discourse of TQM, Gee (1994) illustrates how liberation within a TQM framework often stops at the choice of goals, a strange and incomplete form of choice or 'empowerment'. That is, the goals, direction and priorities of the organisation are decided by management with workers rarely 'empowered' by their organisations to turn around and say 'I think it is a really useless life goal to do X' (ibid.: 11)!

While Gee does not specifically develop a gender analysis of the discourse of TQM or the new workplace, his analysis highlights crucial issues in the debate by exposing paradoxes and contradictions between the claims and the reality, by opening the debate about whose interests are being served by change, and by illustrating how language is used to insinuate common interests and to deflect attention away from sources of conflict. This form of analysis adds to a feminist reading of organisations by challenging the proposition that all workers will be offered the opportunity to contribute equally to the formulation of goals, and in turn that all workers will derive benefit from changes proposed.

While the literature offers some descriptions of the environment required to maximise learning opportunities (see, for instance, Field with Ford, 1995), it falls short of embarking on the kind of analysis, critique and theory-building that is necessary to actually set out what action needs to be taken in order to create such an environment. Some commentators might ask whether such a project is indeed possible in capitalist organisations (Foley, 1994). But even to begin to understand the forces at work that can either support or undermine the environment for learning, we must deal directly with issues of power and gender in organisations.

The new forms of 'learning' characterised in the workplace learning literature are qualitatively different to learning in the workplace as we have understood it in the past. In particular, the new forms emphasise group and collective learning as the means to achieving change in organisations. Without doubt, while it is argued employees will derive benefit from change (or at least not lose their jobs), the change is essentially designed to benefit the organisation, with any spin-offs to the workers secondary. Can the interests of workers and the organisations in which they labour be reconciled? While examples may be available that celebrate mutual benefit and growth through organisational change (see, perhaps, Field with Ford, 1994), my investigations into the field, and work experience in industrial relations, workplace reform, affirmative action programmes for women, and human resource management, point to the limitations of much research and writing in the field. For example, who writes the case studies we read? For which audience are they written and for what purpose? How are questions of gender inequality addressed and resolved in the way the organisations are 'transformed'? Have organisational structures, language and social practices that discriminate and exclude been critically examined and challenged? Have organisations in which women predominate been studied? My intention in raising these questions here is to draw attention to the inadequacy from a gender perspective of much of the research to date, and to stimulate discussion on how the field of research and practice might be reframed to incorporate gender analysis.

The implications for workplace-based adult educators

In the current climate, many workplace-based adult educators are trying to make sense of the practical questions they need to deal with as attention moves from the training room and focuses on learning in the workplace. Under pressure from chief executives and line managers to 'create a learning organisation', educators look to the adult education literature for insights and easy answers about how to make it all possible. The fact that the literature fails in this project reflects a broader failure with how the project of workplace learning is conceived.

As attention shifts from a focus on 'training' to a focus on 'learning', we move into the murky and highly contested realm of workplace relations. Our project of 'developing a learning culture', or 'introducing the learning organisation' is not possible without a more careful reading of the labour process and the complex social dynamics of work. This requires us to go beyond earlier critical analyses of work and the labour process to incorporate an analysis of gender as central to our project. In this contested realm, it is no longer possible to pretend to stay out of the politics of work. Part of the project becomes to read and understand what Mechthild Hart (1995) refers to as the 'topography of the world' or in this case, of the organisation. In working out who holds the power and how they continue to do so, we must also decide where we are located in this topography, where we stand in the landscape.

As I have attempted to demonstrate, the conventional adult education literature, such as Marsick and Watkins and Field, presents an overly simplistic and under-theorised framework for understanding and thinking about the issues around learning in the workplace. To develop our critical insight we need to look to other sources, such as the feminist literature on organisations and the labour process, or the critical literacy literature, amongst others.

An understanding of gender as an organising principle provides deep insights into the way organisations work. Its value goes further than just shedding light on what it is like for women in organisations, or members of so-called 'disadvantaged' or 'minority' groups. Instead it offers a critical position from which to develop new understandings about learning starting from a radical approach to redefining the organisation. Such an approach would be characterised (amongst other things) by an entrenched commitment to equality; to an appreciation of difference reflected in organisation policies and practices; a redistribution of opportunities and rewards in the organisation; the recognition and rewarding of the contribution of all those in the organisation; and genuine participation by all workers in decisions that affect their workplace and work. In other words, before we can make real some of the rhetoric about 'empowerment through learning', we have to confront and deal with systemic discrimination and its impact on the potential for learning.

To develop organisations as environments for learning, we need to start therefore by changing organisations. This proposition presupposes a very different type of intervention by the adult educator than one based on a more technical approach to the learning organisation according to which 'learning' is construed as the consequence of a set of activities superimposed on an otherwise unchanged organisation. It also presupposes a commitment on the part of the adult educator that goes beyond the organisation's boundaries and interests to a broader concern with workplace structures and relations that oppress and discriminate against women.

References

Acker, J. (1989) *Doing Comparable Worth: Gender, Class & Pay Equity*. Philadelphia: Temple University Press.

Acker, J. (1990) Hierarchies, jobs and bodies: a theory of gendered organisations. *Gender and Society*, 4, 2, 139–158.

Argyris, C. and Schön, D. (1978) *Organisational Learning: A Theory of Action Perspective*. Reading: Addison-Wesley.

Braverman, H. (1974) *Labour and Monopoly Capital*. New York: Monthly Review Press.

Carr, W. and Kemmis, S. (1986) *Becoming Critical: Education, Knowledge and Action Research*. Geelong: Deakin University Press.

Cockburn, C. (1983) *Brothers: Male Dominance and Technological Change*. London: Pluto Press.

Cockburn, C. (1985) *Machinery of Dominance: Women, Men & Technical Know-How*. London: Pluto Press.

Cockburn, C. (1991) *In the Way of Women: Men's Resistance to Sex Equality in Organisations*. London: Macmillan.

Drucker, P.F. (1993) *Post-Capitalist Society*. New York: Harper.

Elsey, B. (1990) Social theory and liberal adult education perspectives on work, training and human resource development: towards a balanced relationship. *Studies in Continuing Education*, 12, 2, 107–121.

Eveline, J. (1994) The politics of advantage. *Australian Feminist Studies*, 19, 129–154.

Field, L. (1990) *A Study into the learning opportunities in a chemical plant shutdown*. Botany: ICI Botany Operations and Department of Employment, Education and Training. November.

Field, L. with Ford, W. (1994) *Creating the Learning Organisation*. Teaching materials. February. Sydney: UTS.

Field, L. with Ford, W. (1995) *Managing Organisational Learning*. Melbourne: Longman.

Foley, G. (1994) Adult education and capitalist organisation. *Studies in the Education of Adults*, 26, 2, 121–143.

Freire, P. (1975) *Pedagogy of the Oppressed*. New York: Herter and Herter.

Game, A. and Pringle, R. (1983) *Gender at Work*. Sydney: Allen & Unwin.

Garvin, D. (1993). Building a learning organisation. *Harvard Business Review*, July–August, 77–91.

Gee, J. (1994) Quality, science and the lifeworld: the alignment of business and education. *Occasional Papers in Adult Basic Education*, No. 4, February: ALBSAC.

Gee, J. and Lankshear, C. (1995) The new work order: critical language awareness and 'fast capitalism' texts. *Discourse: Studies in the Cultural Politics of Education*, 16, 1, 5–19.

Gunew, S. and Yeatman, A. (1993) *Feminism and the Politics of Difference*. Sydney: Allen & Unwin.

Habermas, J. (1971) *Knowledge and Human Interests*. Boston: Beacon Press.

Hart, M.U. (1992) *Working and Educating for Life: Feminist and International Perspectives on Adult Education*. London: Routledge.

Hart, M.U. (1995) Education and social change. Paper presented at the Social Action and Emancipatory Learning Seminar, UTS. Sydney, September.

Holloway, D.G. (1994) Total Quality Management, the learning organisation and post-compulsory education. *Vocational Aspects of Education*, 46, 2, 117–130.

hooks, bell (1994) *Teaching to Transgress: Education as the Practice of Freedom*. New York: Routledge.

Jackson, N. (1991) *Skills Formation and Gender Relations: The Politics of Who Knows What*. Geelong: Deakin University Press.

Kornbluh, H. and Greene, R. (1989) Learning, empowerment and participative work practices: the educative work environment. In Leymann, H. and Kornbluh, H. (eds) *Socialisation and Learning at Work: A New Approach to Learning Processes in the Workplace and Society*. Avebury: Aldershot, 256–274.

Maroney, H.J. and Luxton, M. (eds) (1987) *Feminism and Political Economy*. Toronto: Methuen.

Marsick, V. (1988) Learning in the workplace: the case for critical reflectivity. *Adult Education Quarterly*, 38, 4, 187–198.

Marsick, V. (ed.) (1987) *Learning in the Workplace*. New York: Croom Helm.

Marsick, V. and Watkins, K. (1990) *Informal and Incidental Learning in the Workplace*. London: Routledge.

Mezirow, J. (1981) A critical theory of adult learning and education. *Adult Education*, 32, 1.

O'Donnell, C. and Hall, P. (1988) *Getting Equal: Labour Market Regulation and Women's Work*. Sydney: Allen & Unwin.

Pettman, J. (1992) *Living in the Margins: Racism, Sexism and Feminism in Australia*. Sydney: Allen & Unwin.

Pocock, B. (1988) *Demanding Skill: Women and Technical Education in Australia*. Sydney: Allen & Unwin.

Pringle, R. (1988) *Secretaries Talk: Sexuality, Power and Work*. London: Verso.

Senge, P. (1990) *The Fifth Discipline: The Art and Practice of the Learning Organisation*. New York: Doubleday.

Watkins, K. (1991) *Facilitating Learning in the Workplace*. Geelong: Deakin University Press.

Watkins, K. and Marsick, V. (1992) Building the learning organisation: a new role for human resource developers. *Studies in Continuing Education*, 14, 2, 115–129.

Watkins, K. and Marsick, V. (1993) *Sculpting the Learning Organisation: The Art and Science of Systemic Change*. San Francisco: Jossey-Bass.

Welton, M. (1991) *Toward Developmental Work: The Workplace as a Learning Environment*. Geelong: Deakin University Press.

Chapter 5

Towards the learning organization?

Ewart Keep and Helen Rainbird

The inadequacies of training and development and the need for reform of the institutional frameworks in the UK have been long-running issues in personnel management as we have previously described in detail (Keep, 1989, 1994; Rainbird, 1994). The ability of organizations to develop the skills and knowledge to do present and future jobs, which roughly translated is what training and development is about, has been critically affected by the wider national vocational and education system. Justifying investment in intangibles such as training and development is not easy at the best of times. It is difficult to prove the benefits and there is always the fear that it will be the employees who will benefit, rather than the organization, because the skills make them a more marketable commodity in a free labour market. The essentially voluntarist approach, coupled with other features, has made things even worse by creating something of a vicious circle that is akin to what economists term 'the prisoner's dilemma'. Organizations tend not to train for fear that other employers, instead of doing their share, will poach employees from them. In the circumstances, with short-term financial results so paramount, it is easy to persuade themselves that training and development are something of a luxury. More pragmatically, if they find they are short of a particular set of skills, they can solve the immediate shortage by recruiting trained workers or alternatively by subcontracting or using temporary workers – all of which are usually easier to justify in a crisis situation than the original investment in training and development. Furthermore, in the case of most occupations, employers in the UK are operating in a relatively low pay economy. This contributes to competitive strategies based on a 'low skills equilibrium' (Finegold and Soskice, 1988) that has been used to characterize the UK economy.

The debate has taken on added urgency in recent years. An increasingly broader band of commentators and policy makers have urged a more general need for greater stress upon skills and knowledge as a source of competitive

This is an edited version of an article previously published in S. Bach and K. Sisson (eds) *Personnel Management in Britain* (3rd edition). 1999. Reproduced by permission of Blackwell Publishers Ltd.

advantage, reflecting a number of interlinking trends said to be driving change in the way organizations in the developed world operate and compete. Thus it is argued that in the global market place organizations in developed countries can no longer compete solely or even mainly on the basis of price. Instead, they must offer a range of customized, tailor-made products and services. Competitive advantage comes from the ability to offer high-quality, personalized service. At the same time, change in product ranges is massive and rapid. Organizations are ceaselessly having to learn to do new things, offer new services and to reorganize fundamentally the way they deliver to their customers, not least because product development lead times and life cycles are apparently becoming ever shorter (the example of personal computers and other consumer electronics is frequently used here). Finally, there is believed to be a massive and sustained shift throughout the developed world towards knowledge-intensive industries and a huge growth in the number of knowledge workers.

In the face of these changes, the only viable response, it is argued, at least for organizations located within the developed world, is to seek long-term competitive advantage via the utilization of the skills and knowledge of their employees. Their skills, viewed collectively, from the organization's core competencies that provide it with features and attributes from which stem its unique competitive advantage. In order to develop and enhance these core organizational competences, organizations need to harness the power of organizational learning, and move from systems, processes and cultures that support individual learning towards higher levels of collective learning and skill acquisition. The aim is to achieve the 'learning organization' defined by Senge (1990: 4) as one 'where people continually expand their capacity to create the results they truly desire, where new and expansive patterns of thinking are nurtured, where collective aspiration is set free, and where people are continually learning to learn together'.

This chapter examines the concept of the 'learning organization' (LO) and explores whether it provides a viable blueprint for producing an integrated approach to training and development with organizations. Whilst it welcomes an approach that emphasizes the social context in which learning takes place as opposed to an emphasis on the individual, it finds the model of the learning organization at odds with the product market strategies of many organizations and weak in its conceptualization of power relations in the workplace. We also point to the absence of an institutional infrastructure in the UK capable of promoting more widespread investment in skills and the adoption of training and development practices that might contribute in some way towards meeting the goals of the learning organization.

This chapter is divided into five sections. We start with an analysis of the textbook model of the learning organization, examining the stages required to achieve this status as well as the theoretical assumptions about the nature of learning and business competition underpinning it. We then turn to the evidence based on individuals' experiences of training and survey evidence from companies and assess the extent to which this provides support for the existence of LOs. The third section discusses how the organizational barriers affect the ability of companies to adopt the model of the LO in their human resource strategies. The fourth section situates the objectives of the LO in the broader societal and economic environment in which companies operate and emphasizes the unsupportive institutional circumstances found in the UK. Finally, we conclude that although there is little evidence of the emergence of LOs or of product market strategies that would require such a commitment to learning there are nevertheless steps that can be made by organizations to create structures that are more conducive to promoting learning.

The basic concept

The LO has been seen by many as a significant development in the conceptualization of learning, skills and knowledge within an organizational setting. Between the late 1980s and the mid-1990s the concept on the LO rose to prominence and a considerable body of literature developed on the topic. The concept of the LO offers an idealized and, at first glance at least, highly attractive model of organizational development. In particular, it provides a broader strategic framework within which skills, training and development policies can be located, thereby providing training and HRM specialists with an approach for selling their wares to senior management. Instead of training and skills being a bolt-on extra, learning moves to centre stage and becomes the chief organizational principle around which business strategy and competitive advantage can be developed.

Put simply, there are said to be three different states of learning within an organization: individuals within an organization learning things; organizational learning – where the organization as an entity starts to develop ways in which it can learn lessons collectively; and the learning organization – where the central organizational goal is systemic learning. The nature of the changes required becomes clearer when we examine the five-stage model of development of a learning organization proposed by Jones and Hendry (1992). The first three stages of the model (Foundation, Formation and Continuation) are taken to represent a state of organizational learning. Stages 4 and 5 (Transformation and Transfiguration) represent progression and transition to becoming a fully blown learning organization (see Table 5.1).

Although the different authors who have analysed the LO have produced varying checklists of criteria that may be taken to characterize an LO, the differences are ones of detail rather than fundamentals, and a broadly representative example is outlined in Table 5.2. For a fuller treatment of these models and a very useful review of the LO literature, see Mabey et al. (1998).

Table 5.1 Stages in the development of a learning organization

Organizational learning

1   Foundation
     Basic skills development, plus equipping learners with habits and enthusiasm to
     learn more. Basic HRD strategies to motivate and build confidence for further
     learning

2   Formation
     Organization encourages and develops skills for self-learning and self-development,
     helps individual learn about the organization and their place in it. Opportunity and
     resources are made available to meet demand for learning

3   Continuation
     The learner and organization are becoming more innovatory, independent and self-
     motivated. HRD promotes learning on an individual basis, with tailor-made learning
     experiences

Step change/Paradigm shift
Learning Organization

4   Transformation
     A complete change in the form, appearance and character/culture of the
     organization. HRM characterized by fairness, openness, flexibility, meritocracy.
     Ethical considerations important in general business management

5   Transfiguration
     People come first and a concern for society's welfare and betterment

     The organization represents a way of life to be cherished because of its values

     Learning is at the centre of activities

     Lack of concern about credentials

     The organization is instructing and controlling itself by means of total involvement
     in the community

     The organization is judged by the extent to which the people who make it up
     control and teach the organization how to learn, rather than vice versa

     No formal appraisals

Source: Adapted from Jones and Hendry (1992).

The LO literature also relies heavily on a number of theoretical models
of individual learning (most notably that developed by Kolb, 1984). The
central question for an LO is how to foster moves from single-loop learning
to the more advanced states of double- and triple-loop learning and how to
manage the collectivization of individual learning through cultural norms
and new forms of organizational structure (such as project teams and quality
improvement groups) (see Pedler, *et al.*, 1991; Jones and Hendry, 1994; and
Swieringa and Wierdsma, 1992 for a detailed treatment of these issues).

A number of comments need to be made about these models. The first
relates to what is perhaps the greatest strength of the concept – its emphasis

Table 5.2 Characteristics of a learning organization

A learning organization:

- capitalizes on uncertainty as a source of growth
- creates new knowledge as a central part of competitive strategy
- embraces change
- encourages accountability at the lowest level
- encourages managers to act as mentors, coaches and learning facilitators
- has a culture of feedback and disclosure
- has a holistic, systemic view of the organization and its systems, processes, and relationships
- has a shared organization-wide vision, purpose and values
- has leaders who encourage risk taking and experimentation
- has systems for sharing knowledge/learning and using it in the business
- is customer driven
- is involved in the community
- links employees' self-development to the development of the organization as a whole
- networks within the business community
- provides frequent opportunities to learn from experience
- avoids bureaucracy and turf wars
- has a high-trust culture
- strives for continuous improvement
- structures, fosters and rewards all types of teams
- uses cross-functional work teams
- views the unexpected as an opportunity to learn

Source: Adapted from Marquardt and Reynolds (1994).

on a systemic approach to learning within an organization. One of the marked counter-trends over the last decade has been an increasing emphasis on shifting more and more responsibility for training and development on to the individual employee, reflecting expectations that, given a process of almost continuous restructuring, the employer is less likely to benefit in the future than in the past. As has been suggested elsewhere (Keep, 1997), this increasing focus on the individual is problematic, not least because it often appears to demand that the individual worker attempt to second guess, without access to reliable information, the demands of the wider economy and of current and future employers.

The LO literature's notion that learning and reflection need to be built into the routines and culture of management activities is also important, because the frequent inability to achieve this goal has been one of the continuing failures of the UK training scene. In marked contrast to the much-vaunted Japanese approach to in-company training and development (Koike, 1997), in UK organizations training all too often continues to be a marginal activity that is regarded as an optional extra rather than as an activity integral to the process of production. The LO concept is useful in posing questions about how organizations can go about building developmental and learning activities into the everyday fabric of what they do.

A less helpful aspect is the language in which some of the literature is couched and its underlying inability to confront the harsh realities that face many organizations. An example would be Jones and Hendry's (1992: 30–31) description of the final stage of development in an LO (Transfiguration), where people come first and the organization is driven by a concern for society's general welfare and betterment, and where the emphasis is on people developing themselves as individuals and being allowed to do what they want to rather than what other people (perhaps their managers) deem appropriate.

The problem with this kind of 'communitarian' vision is that, however attractive it may appear to organizational development specialists, it has at best limited resonance with senior line managers facing the reality of short-term pressures to minimize cost and boost bottom-line performance. 'Transfiguration' is not merely not on their immediate agenda, it has very little to do with what most organizations, certainly in the private sector, but even much of the reformed public sector, are tasked with doing. Within the confines of the Anglo-Saxon model of capitalism, the full-blown LO model looks suspiciously idealistic and perhaps unrealistic. Indeed Scarborough et al. (1998) suggest that one of the reasons for the recent eclipse of the LO concept by models of knowledge management is the former's failure to resonate with the competitive agenda in many organizations.

A related point is the LO concept's underlying assumptions about competitive strategy and organizational architecture. The implicit belief is that competitive advantage comes from customization, ceaseless innovation and high specification, high-quality goods and services delivered by flat, non-hierarchical organizations where workers enjoy considerable empowerment. That LO model sits poorly with Taylorism and Fordism.

As will be argued below, it is open to question if Fordism is dead, at least in large swathes of the UK service sector, or whether the force of Tayloristic systems of job design and work organization is yet spent. At the very least, it seems important to underline the fact that counterbalancing the language of delayering, devolved management, empowerment and stress on the problem solving, creativity and innovation of individual workers, are the persistence of work regimes based on command and control systems, scripted interactions with customers, routinization of work tasks and often high levels of surveillance (on the latter point see, for example, Collinson and Collinson, 1997). The battle between these two opposite visions, a battle often being fought out within individual organizations, is of fundamental importance within UK management in the twenty-first century. Although management gurus, futurologists and many proponents of the LO model imply that the triumph of empowerment and creativity over command and control (theory

Y as opposed to theory X) is inevitable, the evidence adduced below and elsewhere suggests that this may not be so in all cases.

In any event, it is clear that many of the organizations who have been attracted to the idea of the LO have, in fact, been aiming more for enhanced organizational learning than for the full-blown model. This is hardly surprising given the requirements, in terms of value and culture change, that the textbook LO model demands. It is also apparent that the kinds of structural, procedural and cultural characteristics specified in the Marquardt and Reynolds model represent hurdles of varying heights for different organizations. Across a whole range of areas of managerial decision making, such as competitive and product market strategy, leadership style, organizational culture, job design, work organization, team design and operation, reward systems, control and reporting structures, management style and functions, appraisal and development systems, and information and participation procedures, any attempt to move towards higher levels of organizational learning will be encouraged or constrained by the prevailing norms, which will vary considerably between organizations.

A final point to make about this body of literature is that, as with many other areas of management writings, the bulk of what is available concentrates on definitional argument, model building, and is prescriptive. Broadly based, in-depth, longitudinal research of how the concepts and models play out in real-life organizations is in very short supply, and even detailed case studies are few in number (see Marquardt, 1996 for examples of what is available). In the UK, many of the examples seem to come from within the NHS, and the leading private-sector company associated with the concept has been the Rover Group. This organization's problems suggest that the timescale for any project to become a learning company and witness concrete effects on the bottom line, may be lengthy.

Moreover, while the LO literature displays a detailed interest in theoretical models of workplace learning (such as that advanced by Kolb, 1984; and Swieringa and Wierdsma, 1992), their practical utility may be limited. As Ashton (1998: 68) observes, 'learning theories derived from experimental observations and studies of the cognitive process abstracted from the realities of the organizational context are of little relevance to the practitioner . . . struggling to understand the process of learning as embedded in organizational structures'. Unfortunately, the LO literature on the whole offers limited recognition, and in some cases none, to wider research that has been undertaken into what actually takes place in terms of learning in the workplace (for examples of which, see Maguire, 1997; Tavistock Institute, 1998a; Darmon et al., 1998; Eraut et al., 1998; Ashton, 1998). As will be suggested below, there is much that can be learned from this detailed, fieldwork-based research.

The nature and extent of training and development

If large numbers of employers had succeeded in achieving the objective of becoming learning organizations, we would expect to find this reflected in a number of ways. First, we would find evidence that individuals were able to access formal training and informal learning opportunities in the workplace. Second, it would be possible to identify the adoption of training and development practices that could be considered as indicative of a commitment to the ideals of the learning organization. In this section, sources of evidence on individuals' experiences of training and development are examined, alongside survey evidence of company practices, updating our previous analyses of vocational education and training provision for the young (Keep, 1994) and the continuing training of adult workers (Rainbird, 1994).

Individual experiences

There are two distinctive features of British provision of vocational education and training for young people. The first has been the tradition of early school leaving. Until very recently, the majority of young people left education at the age of 16 and entered the labour market. This contrasted with most other developed industrial economies, where a far higher proportion of the 16- to 18-year age cohort remained in education, accompanied by an earlier development of mass, as opposed to elite, higher education systems. The education system in England and Wales has been characterized by early selection and low participation (Finegold et al., 1990) although the Scottish education system with its broader curriculum has achieved significantly higher participation rates (Raffe, 1991). Despite these observations, a combination of changes in employers' demand for young workers and a shift towards service-sector employment have contributed to decline in the proportion of 16-year-olds entering work from 62 per cent in 1975 to only 9 per cent in 1992. This has been accompanied by a sharp rise in the numbers remaining in full-time education post-16: by 1994–5 72 per cent of 16-year-olds and 59 per cent of 17-year-olds were in full-time education (Evans et al., 1997: 50). One of the knock-on effects of this growth has been its effect on the student population in higher education. In 1979 just one in ten young people entered higher education. By 1997 this had risen to almost one in three (DfEE, 1998a), and between 1980–1 and 1990–1 overall student numbers grew by 42 per cent, the growth of participation by women, mature and part-time students being particularly strong (National Commission on Education, 1993: 293).

It might be assumed that employers would compensate for the relatively low levels of educational attainment that, historically, have characterized new recruits into employment by having effective systems of vocational training. On the contrary, weaknesses in education participation and quali-fication have been reinforced by the second major failure of vocational education and training (VET) provision: the failure of employers to offer structured training to young recruits. Provision in the form of the institu-tion of apprenticeship existed primarily in manufacturing industry, but between 1970 and 1990 apprentice numbers plummeted from 218,000 to 53,600 (Keep, 1994: 310). Although partly reflecting the decline in manu-facturing employment, the proportion of apprentices in the workforce also declined during this period, with government training schemes, such as the Youth Training Scheme and Youth Training contributing to this outcome (Marsden and Ryan, 1989). Outside manufacturing industry, and especially in the services sector, there has been little formal training for early school-leavers, the one exception being hairdressing.

Perceived weaknesses in the VET system, in the quantity and the quality of training, evident in young people's acquisition of vocational qualifications gave rise to a series of reforms to youth training, which are documented in Keep (1994). Yet the persistence of weaknesses in foundation training deliv-ered by a voluntary system are all too apparent, leading Harrison (1997: vii) of the IPD to argue at that point that:

> For many observers, the present system of education and training for young people is not delivering the quality foundation learning that all interested parties are committed to. Few of the National Targets for Education and Training for the year 2000 look likely to be reached. The funding systems that support and drive education and training provision are out of alignment with the objectives they seek to achieve. Sir Ron Dearing's recommendations for qualifications for 16–19 year-olds are not in themselves sufficient to solve the deep-seated problems afflicting the education and training system.

Two positive developments need mention. The first of these was the re-instatement of apprenticeship as a model for work-based learning through modern apprenticeships (MAs), introduced by the Conservative Govern-ment in 1993. This has allowed public funding to support apprenticeship arrangements in the sectors where they have continued to exist and for their extension into new sectors of the economy, representing the creation of a relatively high-quality work-based education and training route. For a full review of the development and extent of modern apprenticeships see Maguire (1999). The second has been the provision under the Teaching and Higher Education Bill (1997) of a statutory entitlement for 16- and 17-year-olds to have time off during working hours to undertake study or training leading to a relevant qualification.

The initial education and training of young people undoubtedly shape their attitudes towards learning throughout their working lives. The evidence suggests that, to date, this has been inadequate compared to the experiences of their counterparts in other developed economies. There are therefore weaknesses in the foundations on which employers build their human resource development strategies. This has consequences, for managers' ability to adapt work organization to external competitive pressures, on the one hand, and for employees' own ability to learn and adapt, on the other.

So far, we have dealt with only the weaknesses in educational qualifications and initial vocational training in the UK workforce. If the objective is to achieve what Senge (1990: 1) defines as an organization 'where people continually expand their capacity to create the results they truly desire', then the evidence on individuals' experience of continuing training in employment requires examination. In an assessment of the nature and extent of continuing training (Rainbird, 1994), the weaknesses of the British data on individuals' experiences was highlighted. The major source is the annual Labour Force Survey, which records training received by the individual in the four weeks prior to the survey. Nevertheless, there may be differing perceptions of what constitutes training: the employees may only consider formal off-the-job training in these terms and discount on-the-job instruction and forms of learning that are more closely related to the transmission of organizational culture. Indeed, it is important to distinguish learning from training. For example, Eraut *et al.* (1998) have demonstrated that, certainly as far as highly qualified workers are concerned, the work environment itself is significant in providing learning opportunities through problem-solving activities and learning from colleagues and mentors that are unrelated to formal instruction.

The Department for Education and Employment reports that a further education college or a university is the most common location for off-the-job training received by employees (DfEE, 1996). An analysis of the sources of access to training reported in the Labour Force Survey demonstrates that training on employers' premises accounts for approximately one-third of continuing training, with 40 per cent of men's and nearly 50 per cent of women's continuing training being provided by education institutions (Payne, 1992).

Age, gender, ethnicity, educational background, hours of work and employment status exert considerable influence on individuals' access to learning, reinforcing patterns of inequality. Those lacking in initial educational qualifications are least likely to participate in continuing training at work and in adult education outside the workplace. As far as adults' experiences of workplace-related training is concerned Clarke's (1991: 41–42) analysis of the 1989 Labour Force Survey data concluded:

> The pattern of training provision for adult employees is a complex one with different groups of women and men having very different access to continuing training. Women part-timers in all occupations have substantially less access to training than full-time employees, both

women and men. Since a high proportion of women spend at least part of their working life in part-time employment, and over two fifths of all women employees currently work part-time, this is a major source of disadvantage for women in the labour market. Other groups of adult workers who are disadvantaged in terms of training are manual workers (the majority of whom are men), employees in small workplaces (who are disproportionately women) and employees in the private manufacturing sector (the majority of whom will be men).

This complex pattern continues to exist (McGivney, 1997; Blundell *et al.*, 1996). The relatively disadvantaged groups when it comes to access to adult education and training provision appear to be women, those with literacy and numeracy difficulties, people with few or no qualifications, ethnic and linguistic minorities, older adults, people with special needs and disabilities and ex-offenders (McGivney, 1997: 131). 'In other words, those who ostensibly have the greatest need participate the least' (ibid.). In 1997, the report of the National Advisory Committee on Continuing Education and Lifelong Learning was still able to observe that although there were many 'successful and imaginative elements of lifelong learning already occurring in the country' they did not add up to 'a learning culture for all'. One in three adults had taken no part in education or training since leaving school and a similar proportion reported that their employer had never offered them any kind of training (Fryer, 1997: 1–2).

Survey evidence of company training practices

Unlike other countries, which collect systematic data on training expenditure under the terms of their training legislation, there is little survey evidence in Britain on expenditure on training. Since the abolition of the Industrial Training Board's requirement on companies to complete levy returns, longitudinal industry-level data have not been collected. (For a history of the Industrial Training Boards see Perry, 1976 and Senker, 1992.) The major national company training surveys are the *Training in Britain* survey (Deloitte *et al.* 1989) and the Employers' Manpower and Skills Practices Survey (EMSPS) conducted by the (then) Department of Employment (see the series of working papers published by the Employment Department's Social Science Research Branch, for example Dench, 1993a and 1993b). In reviewing the findings of EMSPS, surveys of members conducted by the Institute of Personnel and Development and the Industrial Society, and research conducted by Felstead and Green (1994, 1996), Raper *et al.* (1997: 11) identify five major trends in company training practices:

1   the devolution of responsibility for training and development to line managers;
2   the declining use of external, off-the-shelf courses;
3   the increased use of in-company training;
4   the increased use of on-the-job training, planned work experience and coaching;
5   the influence of quality standards (such as BS5750 or ISO 9000) and health and safety regulations as motivators for training.

For a more detailed discussion of these changes and their implications for both line managers and training specialists, see Eraut *et al.*, 1998; Tavistock Institute 1998a; and Institute of Personnel and Development, 1999.

Raper *et al.* (1997) report that the EMSPS survey found that managers perceived market competition and customer demand as the main influence on quality improvements, which might support the view that adaptability to changes in the market environment, a feature of the learning organization literature, was significant. Nevertheless, in specific areas legislation clearly plays a role and the more recent surveys show that training budgets have been cut. Managers have become more directly involved in training, not because of their commitment to the concept of the learning organization but because the shift from off-the-job to less expensive on-the-job training in the workplace has required it (ibid.: 12).

Although at present there is little survey evidence that places training practices in the context of broader human resource policies, one yardstick is *Investors in People*, the national training standard introduced in the wake of the *Training in Britain* survey of 1989 and reflecting its concerns about the nature and the extent of the training taking place. The very ambitious target was set of achieving 70 per cent or more of organizations with 200 or more employees and 35 per cent of those with 50 or more by the year 2000. Initially, take-up was very slow: by the middle of 1996, scarcely 10 per cent of organizations had achieved the target (Employee Development Bulletin, 1996). By August 1998, however, 31 per cent of organizations with more than 200 employees and 16.8 per cent of organizations with more than 50 staff had gained IIP status, and many more (46.5 per cent of organizations with 200 plus employees and 26.2 per cent of those employing more than 50 people) had committed themselves to gaining IIP status (National Advisory Council for Education and Training Targets, 1998: 74). Moreover, there is evidence to suggest that some organizations, although not signing up for the formal process, have nonetheless adopted the good practice laid down in IIP.

Further survey evidence from the 1998 Workplace Employee Relations Survey shows that only 12 per cent of employers questioned reported that their employees received five days a year training and 27 per cent that most supervisors received training in employee relations skills (Cully *et al.*, 1998: 10). This gives scant support to the view that the LO model has been adopted in the larger organizations (those with more than 25 employees) that are included in the survey. Given that these are the organizations that are most likely to have sophisticated HR and training practices, it can be assumed that these percentages would be even lower for smaller employers. In the words of the Tavistock Institute (1998a: 26), there was 'a significant gap between the language or discourse of companies who viewed themselves as learning organisations and regarded people as their most important asset, and the actual practices of these companies'.

Organizational barriers to learning

Our attention now turns to the considerable barriers to learning that exist within UK organizations and wider society. To begin with organizational barriers, key aspects of the people management systems and structures of work organization and job design stand in the way of making learning the central pillar of organizational life and competitive advantage. Unless and until some of these are changed, more learning will often either be under-utilized or wasted.

Work organization, people management systems and competitive strategies

As Pevoto (1997: 212–213), reviewing another 'quick fix . . . cook book' on the learning organization, remarked:

> I keep asking myself why was this book written? What the world doesn't need is one more 'quick fix' book, or one more 'cook book' for how to make the organisation and its people work better. We have hundreds of those littering the shelves of authors, professors and libraries. I was reminded of the story of the farmer and the agricultural agent wherein the agricultural agent suggested the farmer attended a seminar on new farming methods, and the farmer replied, 'Why, I'm not farming now as well as I know how to'. The same could be said of organisations. Most are not managed or led now as well as people know how to.

This observation raises the important, and in much of the LO literature oft-ducked, issue of existing evidence on underemployment and the poor usage of existing levels of skills. The scale of the problem may be much larger than is generally held to be the case by employers and policy makers. In the UK, the evidence supplied by the Skills Survey (Green et al., 1997) suggests that underemployment and underutilization of existing qualifications held by employees may also be a reality for a substantial proportion of workers. The survey suggested that 32 per cent of degree holders believed themselves to be in jobs that did not require this qualification, 30.6 per cent of holders of sub-degree qualifications felt they were overqualified for their current jobs, and 22.4 per cent of workers with qualifications were in jobs where no qualification whatsoever was required. These figures suggest that, in many organizations, before any more learning is attempted there need to be greater efforts to harness existing pools of expertise and knowledge.

In order to do this, issues concerning work organization and job design may need to be tackled. As research by Dench *et al.* (1998) has illustrated, despite the textbook models of worker empowerment and the demands by some employers for workers with better skills in communication, problem solving and creativity, in reality in many organizations 'the generally low level of autonomy allowed to employees especially in non-managerial roles and in less skilled jobs was a theme emerging from many of our in-depth interviews' (ibid.: 58). Far from wanting self-monitoring, problem-solving innovators, Dench *et al.* conclude that, 'in reality most employers simply want people to get on with their job, and not to challenge things' (ibid.: 61). In these organizations it continues to be the case that managers undertake the planning, thinking, design and decision-making elements of work, while the non-managerial workforce get on with following tightly defined procedures and taking orders from above. The scope for real organizational learning (and for the learning to be utilized productively) at all levels in the workforce is hence limited.

Another issue concerns power. Learning is, in essence, a political process in that it leads to change and the disorganization of existing patterns of influence and control. The problem is that, in some cases at least, it seems likely that the necessary change will disrupt the continuity of power relationships and hierarchies. A better-educated workforce made up of autonomous, polyvalent knowledge workers needs far fewer managers, and managers whose role is one of facilitator, not hander-out of orders. Much of the writing on learning organizations appears to assume that a huge change in the role of managers (for example, Senge (1990) suggests that managers become servants of the workforce) is both possible and desirable. It is apparent that this is not likely always to be the case. Traditional models of management have cast managers as policemen and women, spies, controllers, dispensers of reward and punishment, sources of wisdom and expertise, order givers and arbitrators between competing claims. The new model of management tries to paint them as teacher, coach, mentor, facilitator, resource controller and 'servant' of the team.

It is not obvious that the majority of existing managers, recruited to perform the very different tasks of old model, possess the skills, behaviours and attitudes required to perform these new functions. Nor are the benefits for managers from such a dramatic change in roles clear. For example, if managers do become facilitators, with their ex-subordinates (now empowered) as the major source of competitive advantage, how do managers maintain their status and pay *vis-à-vis* the rest of the workforce?

This brings us to the wider problem of the LO's tendency to adopt, often implicitly rather than explicitly, a unitarist perspective. The emphasis on employers' and workers' mutual interest in learning in the learning organization model ignores the fundamental conflict embodied in the employment relationship between the employer and the employee. This is nowhere more evident than in management's desire to tap into the tacit skills of the workforce, which are embodied in collective knowledge of the production process, through mechanisms such as quality circles and suggestion schemes. Long ago, Marx recognized that tacit skills constituted a source of worker resistance to the degradation of manual work, commenting:

> The worker's continual repetition of the same narrowly defined act and the concentration of his attention on it teach him by experience how to attain the desired effect with the minimum of exertion. But since there are always several generations of workers living at one time, and working together in the manufacture of a given article, the technical skill, the tricks of the trade thus acquired, become established, and are accumulated and handed down.
>
> (1976: 458)

If workers are to allow management to learn from this source of expertise it raises serious questions about the guarantees that will be given to employees in exchange. Although management literature points to the need for employee commitment to the organization, there is little evidence of an understanding that this requires a reciprocal commitment to the employee. Scarborough *et al.* (1998) point out that the incentives needed to underpin employee commitment are rarely addressed. They cite a KPMG survey of 100 leading businesses, which found that 39 per cent of respondents said that their organization did not reward knowledge sharing and that this was considered one of the most important barriers to storing and sharing knowledge (ibid.: 51–52)

The structures of work organization and job design prevalent in many UK organizations are not the only barrier to the LO concept. Given the choice between trying to get employees to work harder/longer or to get them to do more by working in smarter ways, the evidence suggests that many (perhaps most) British organizations appear to prefer the tried and tested route of increasing working hours.

British workers currently work the longest hours in the EU, with a third doing more than 48 hours per week, and the UK is the only EU member state in which the average length of the working week has increased over the last decade (Milne and Elliott, 1999). In many UK organizations, a long-hours culture has become entrenched, with the standard response to increased market or customer pressures being simply to add further to the workload and working time of existing employees (Kodz et al., 1998). Evidently, long working hours render it more difficult for staff to find the time and energy to learn (the more so in organizations where the current norm is for more and more learning to be undertaken in the employee's own time rather than during working hours).

Perhaps the fundamental point is implicit in this example. The notion that a set of universalistic trends and competitive pressures is impelling organizations towards competition based on organizational learning is seriously flawed. Alternative avenues to competitive advantage remain viable, at least in the UK, and price-based competition continues to thrive above all in the service sector (see Keep and Mayhew, 1998). The figures on under-employment and working time reflect the fact that many organizations, far from opting for the high-skills route to competitive success (Keep and Mayhew, 1996a, 1998; Regini, 1995; Ackroyd and Procter, 1998; Foundation for Manufacturing Industry/Department of Trade and Industry/IBM, 1996), remain wedded to standardized, low-specification goods and services where the main factor of competitive advantage is consistent delivery of relatively simple goods and services at a low price. This Fordist or Neo-Fordist strategy is in turn reflected in Tayloristic forms of work organization that minimize the opportunities for creativity and discretion.

Not only that. If there is one thing the LO literature makes clear, it is that the whole project of becoming an LO is a long-term venture. It is not going to be accomplished in six months or a year. This means the organization has to maintain commitment, invest over a long time-period and stick with a strategy over several years. The evidence suggests that very few UK organizations are capable of this. Merger and acquisition, rather than internal growth through R&D activity, are the favoured route to 'success'. The evidence from the DTI's 1997 R&D scorecard international benchmarking exercise showed that in the previous five years UK companies' reinvestment of sales in R&D was the lowest in the G7 group of leading industrialized countries (Guardian, 1997) (see also DTI, 1997; Buxton, 1998).

The pathology of failing to master the basics

A major problem in much of the prescriptive literature on the LO is its near-automatic assumption that those running relatively large, sophisticated organizations, well equipped with specialist managers, will be capable of mastering the basic technologies and processes upon which their firms' operations were based and of moving from simple single-loop learning (Kolb, 1984) towards more complex and reflexive models of learning. The evidence of recent history suggests that such assumptions are not always correct, that even the most rudimentary single-loop learning is sometimes too demanding, and that in some cases managers are actually either incapable of or uninterested in mastering the basics of their trade, often with spectacularly disastrous results.

A few examples will suffice. British and Commonwealth started out life as a shipping company, but during from the late 1960s moved away from this into finance and brokerage activities. In the late 1980s the company decided to buy a US computer leasing company (an area of activity about which B&C knew little). A huge sum was expended purchasing a major US player, only to discover subsequently that the US company's figures were fraudulent and much of its business fictitious. B&C collapsed with losses of £500 million.

In the case of Barings Bank, the official inquiry (Board of Banking Supervision, 1995) into its collapse makes it clear that the senior managers had at best limited, and at worst no, understanding of the operation of the futures markets in which Nick Leeson was trading and upon which they were ultimately willing to stake a sum in excess of the net worth of the company. The report not does make it clear whether the underlying cause of this fatal lapse was an unwillingness to learn or a lack of the intellectual capacity to master the topic. In any event, the consequences were spectacular.

To offer a final example of these problems from the field of personnel management, we need look no further than the privatized train-operating company, South West Trains. Apparently unaware of the experience in the docks and elsewhere in similar circumstances, the management decided to offer an enhanced redundancy package to their drivers in order to reduce headcount and save long-term costs. The terms of the package were attractive and many drivers decided to avail themselves of the offer. Having let the drivers leave, management discovered that there were now insufficient staff to cover all the timetabled train services. As a result, there were numerous train cancellations and the company was fined £1 million by the Office of the Rail Regulator for service levels in breach of the company's franchise agreement. The next year SWT had to offer £6,000 bonuses to drivers to give up their holiday entitlement in order to avoid further cancellations and fines.

The scale and consequences of these disasters suggest that in certain circumstances, which may be bound up with company culture, complacency and overconfidence, or the intellectual resources of senior management cadres, the barriers to learning can be profound. Moreover, while it could be argued that such examples of disastrous failure to master the basic building-blocks of a firm's activities/technologies/process/productive techniques are aberrations, there are much more widely applicable examples of senior managers failing to learn. One example would be UK management's heavy reliance on mergers and acquisitions as a source of competitive advantage. The balance of research evidence suggests quite clearly that, in the majority of cases, mergers fail to produce the expected benefits (Dickerson et al., 1995). Despite this evidence, the UK economy continues to witness a higher level of merger activity than any other developed country because of the significance of financial engineering in the UK's business system.

The UK – a learning society?

The ability of learning organizations to emerge would, in part, seem related to there being a supportive institutional environment within the wider society in which the organizations operate. It has been argued that some nation states (for example, Japan), by virtue of elements of their societal organization, labour-market structures and cultural and historical inheritances constitute a learning society within which it is easier for individual organizations to improve and sustain organizational learning (Trivellato, 1997).

The argument that societal influences are important seems a powerful one. Organizations exist within a wider societal environment, which may or may not be amenable to the improvement of organizational learning. While the external environment does not necessarily determine what happens, it does influence the likelihood of a given outcome, not least because managers and others employees have lives outside the organization and bring into employment perspectives, attitudes and expectations that are, at least in part, moulded by the culture and traditions of the wider society in which they live (Chisholm, 1997).

In the UK, the notion of the learning society, region and city has become a popular one, and the creation of a learning society is now an element of official UK vocational education and training policy. Despite enthusiasm for the concept by policy makers, research undertaken for the Economic and Social Research Council's (ESRC) 'Learning Society' programme suggests that, in some respects at least, the UK has a long way to go before it becomes a learning society (Green, 1998; Coffield, 1997a, 1997b; McGivney, 1997; Keep and Mayhew, 1996b). A number of structural and cultural characteristics, such as the enduring legacy of our class structure; short-termism; a relatively deregulated labour market that encourages high levels of labour turnover and the perception of labour as a commodity; a tradition of low-trust employee relations; a shareholder rather than stakeholder model of capitalism; and conceptions of management as doing/action rather than reflection and analysis, all suggest that the UK offers an environment that may be relatively hostile to the swift and easy development of high levels of organizational learning.

One example of these environmental factors is the generalized 'common sense' assumption within British society that intelligence and ability are distributed across the population so that a fixed proportion of any given age group will be capable of achieving high levels of learning and academic excellence (however defined). To some extent at least this belief is coupled with a normally unspoken belief that ability is in large part a reflection of social class, or as the following leaked Conservative Party election proposals by former minister John Maples put it, while ABC 1s can conceptualise, C2s and Ds often cannot. They can relate only to things they can see and feel. They absorb their information and often views from television and tabloids. We have to talk to them in a way they understand.

(*Financial Times*, 21 November 1994: 10)

Attitudes such as these go some way towards explaining the tendency for workers in manual occupations to receive little training. Besides the limited nature of the jobs they occupy, in many cases their managers may believe that training would be wasted on them. Obviously the vision that only a certain section (usually rather limited) of the population, and by implication the workforce, is capable of benefiting from training and development sits uneasily with the concept of an LO.

There are also two specific issues that have to be resolved if there is to be a more general move towards a learning society. On the face of it, these would seem to be more immediately amenable to the influence of policy makers. Yet there continues to be a reluctance to confront them, raising doubts about the seriousness of the commitment to 'joined-up policy', if not the concept of the learning society itself.

A question of partnership?

In the same way that the power relationship between the employer and the employee is rarely considered within the unitarist framework of the learning organization literature, the dynamics of workplace industrial relations are equally absent. Since the late 1980s there has been a surge in interest among British trade unions in training as an item on the 'new bargaining agenda' (Storey *et al.*, 1993; Rainbird and Vincent, 1996). Emerging in response to the recognition of the significance of skills to competitive strategy and, in the British context, the unions' progressive exclusion from authoritative decision making in training policy, this has been manifested in the development of demands for a worker's right to training and union involvement in workplace training committees. Since the election of the Labour Government in 1997, a discourse on social partnership on training and learning in the workplace has emerged in official documents such as the Green Paper *The Learning Age* (DfEE, 1998b). This draws on experiences such as the Ford Motor Company's Employee Development and Assistance Programme and the UNISON/employer partnerships on employee development in the public sector (on the latter, see Munro *et al.*, 1997), which have used joint approaches in initiating and managing learning programmes).

Despite the official discourse on social partnership on training, British management vehemently opposed the suggestion, in the new Labour Government's *Fairness at Work* White Paper published in 1998, that training should be a matter of collective bargaining. In the event, rather than emphasizing the significance of the joint regulation of training to large numbers of working people, government ministers compromised. The Employee Relations Bill published in 1999 did not concede that the right to bargain on training should be included automatically where trade unions are recognized for the purpose of collective bargaining. Instead, it proposed rights to information and consultation on training that can be agreed on a voluntary basis, indicating that the government's consultations with employers and the CBI suggested that they were unready to accept a more extensive role for the trade unions in training.

Evidently, few British employers are disposed to European-style approaches to training and thus towards the forms of participation that would encourage joint approaches to learning. Some senior trade unionists, such as John Edmonds of the General, Municipal and Boilermakers' Union, have seen the incorporation of training into the bargaining agenda as a mechanism for moving the adversarial tradition of British industrial relations into the more co-operative forms of the 'European mainstream' (Storey et al., 1993). In contrast, Streeck (1992b: 252) argues that it is essential for unions to maintain, alongside areas of co-operation on skill formation, a strong independent power base that can be mobilized when necessary. The ideal of co-operation on learning embodied in the learning organization therefore requires a level of power sharing with employees and their representatives that is unanticipated in unitarist accounts. Indeed, the Tavistock Institute's (1998a) review *Workplace Learning, Learning Culture and Performance Improvement* argues that despite the promise of stakeholder empowerment in much of this literature, the reality is of 'an agenda of powerholders interested in a more vibrant capitalism' (ibid.: 9).

Paying for training

Government policy makers also seem to be reluctant to be precise in identifying responsibility for paying for training. In overall terms, they currently divide training/learning for adults into three categories: task-specific; general or transferable skills; and broader learning for intellectual development/ leisure/wider adult life. The evidence suggests that, with few exceptions such as Rover and Ford, companies are willing to pay only for the first, are often wary of paying for the second (for fear that such skills will either be poached or will enable staff to leave), and usually have little or no interest in paying for 'blue-skies' learning under the third category (Metcalf et al., 1994).

The official position appears in the Green Paper, *The Learning Age*. This argues that

> [i]ndividuals, employers and the state should all contribute, directly or through earnings foregone, to the cost of learning over a lifetime because all gain from this investment. Individuals enhance their employability

and skills, businesses improve their productivity, and society enjoys wider social and economic benefits.

(DfEE, 1998b: 25).

Yet the only aspect of workplace learning that is clearly identified for support on a shared basis between the state and employers is that of young people in work, modern apprenticeships being given as an example. For adults in work, it envisages the setting up of individual learning accounts whereby the state, the individual and (hopefully) the employer, will make contributions to a fund enabling individuals to undertake a course of study and training of their choice. In other words, major initiative is aimed at employee development, with pump-priming support from the state for the first million individual learning accounts, rather than training that is directly related to current and future job needs. Moreover, the emphasis on individual responsibility evades the question of the institutional structures required to develop mechanisms for socializing the costs of investment, so that individual employers who do invest in training are not penalized by the poaching of trained workers by those that do not. A continued reliance on the market model seems unlikely to promote an 'ecology of skills' (Streeck, 1992a) with incentives to organizations and individuals alike to invest in training and development, capable of allowing learning organizations to develop and thrive.

Conclusion

Perhaps the LO literature's greatest contribution to debates about learning, skills and knowledge is its implicit message that current obsessions with the individualization of learning are seriously misplaced and that the social and systemic dimensions of learning are the key determinants of how an organization successfully acquires, productively deploys, and develops its stock of skills. While interesting as a theoretical construct, however, the idea of the LO may be of limited value in serving as a blueprint for skills policies in the majority of UK organizations. In particular, its lack of contract with the often harsh realities of cost and time pressures and external environmental constraints raises serious problems. Given the evidence presented above, it seems reasonable to argue that there is little chance of achieving any very high level of organizational learning in the following circumstances, all of which are too prominent in the UK: cost-based competition; standardized products and services; a heavy reliance on economy-of-scale advantages; low-trust relationships; hierarchical management structures; people management systems that emphasize command, control and surveillance; an underlying belief that (whatever the overt rhetoric) people are a cost or a disposable factor of production; little slack or space for creativity; and a culture of blame where mistakes (particularly those of lower-status workers) are punished.

Whether the majority of organizations will be able to surmount the cultural and environmental barriers that currently often prevent an effective collective approach to organizational learning remains to be seen.

Recognizing what is possible seems a crucial requirement if many organizations are to reap competitive advantage from a more concerted attempt to systematize and collectivize learning (Ashton, 1998). Many organizations in the early to mid-1990s jumped on the LO bandwagon, at least in some cases without perhaps fully confronting what a wholehearted commitment to becoming an LO would imply for their competitive strategies, management structures and organizational culture. A first step might be to try to reorganize work systems and restructure job design in order to make better use of the existing stock of skills in the workforce. In many organizations, a large stock of latent talent, skill and knowledge is being underutilized. A second and allied approach is to look for hidden pockets of undertraining and to identify those sections of the workforce who are currently being offered few if any opportunities to engage in learning. As Mabey and Salaman (1995) underline, it is crucial to try to make learning apply across the whole organization rather than simply in isolated pockets of (usually high-status) staff. There is copious research evidence (McGivney, 1997) that tells us that structured learning opportunities tend to be concentrated on young entrants, managers and other workers with high levels of initial qualifications. Older workers, the outer layers of the flexible workforce, shop-floor and front-line staff and those with poor initial qualifications tend to lose out.

There is also a range of techniques that can not only boost the breadth of reach and effectiveness of structured learning opportunities within organizations, but which can also be deployed in support of cultural change within the organization that will assist in boosting the value of learning within the work routines of line managers and hence (in the longer term) within organizational strategy. These include better use of structured on-the-job training (Cannell, 1997), mentoring and coaching, job rotation, visits, work shadowing, the development of high-quality teamworking practices, project work, and the better use of professional networks (for further details, see Eraut et al., 1998). Interestingly, in their review of the use of a wide range of informal and semi-structured devices whereby individuals learned in the workplace, Eraut et al. (1998: 41) note that 'very few of our positive examples resulted from organisation-wide strategies or initiatives. Most were relatively informal and initiated by middle managers, colleagues or the learners themselves.'

A final, crucial point concerns conceptions of the managerial task. For as long as managers in the UK see themselves primarily as doers, firefighters or as Action Man/Woman rather than as reflective practitioners, the scope for wide-reaching and permanent organizational change will remain limited. If learning at a fundamental and deep level is not at the heart of what it means to be a successful manager, it seems highly unlikely that organizational learning will easily take root within the organizations that these individuals manage and lead.

References

Ackroyd, S. and Procter, S. 1998: British manufacturing organisation and workplace industrial relations: some attributes of the new flexible firm. *British Journal of Industrial Relations*, Vol. 36 No. 2, 163–183.

Ashton, D. 1998: Skill formation: redirecting the research agenda. In Coffield, F. (ed.), *Learning at Work*, Bristol: Policy Press, 61–69.

Blundell, R., Dearden, L. and Meghir, C. 1996: *Determinants of Effects of Work Related Training in Britain*. London: Institute of Fiscal Studies.

Board of Banking Supervision 1995: *The Report on the Collapse of Barings Bank*. London: HMSO.

Buxton, T. 1998: Overview: the foundations of competitiveness – investment and innovation. In Buxton, T., Chapman, P. and Temple, P. (eds), *Britain's Economic Performance*, 2nd edn, London: Routledge, 165–186.

Cannell, M. 1997: Practice makes perfect. *People Management*, Vol. 3 No. 5, 6 March, 26–33.

Chisholm, L. 1997: Lifelong learning and learning organisations: twin pillars of a learning society. In Coffield, F. (ed.), *A National Strategy for Lifelong Learning*, Newcastle: University of Newcastle, 37–52.

Clarke, K. 1991: Women and learning. A Review, *Research Discussion Series*, No. 1, Manchester: Equal Opportunities Commission.

Coffield, F. 1997a: Nine learning fallacies and their replacement by a national strategy for lifelong learning. In Coffield, F. (ed.), *A National Strategy for Lifelong Learning*, Newcastle: University of Newcastle, 1–35.

Coffield, F. 1997b: A tale of three little pigs: building the learning society with straw. In Coffield, F. (ed.), *A National Strategy for Lifelong Learning*, Newcastle: University of Newcastle, 77–93.

Collinson, D.L. and Collinson, M. 1997: 'Delayering managers': time–space surveillance and its gendered effects. *Organisation*, Vol. 4 No. 3, 375–407.

Cully, M., O'Reilly, A., Millward, N., Forth, J., Woodland, S. and Bryson, A. 1998: *The 1998 Workplace Employee Relations Survey. First Findings*. London: HMSO.

Darmon, I., Hadjivassiliou, K., Sommerlad, E., Stern, E., Turbin, E. and Danau, D. 1998: Continuing vocational training: key issues. In Coffield, F. (ed.), *Learning at Work*, Bristol: Policy Press, 23–36.

Deloitte, Haskins and Sells, 1989: *Training in Britain. A Study of Funding, Activities and Attitudes*. London: HMSO.

Dench, S. 1993a: What types of employer train? *Employment Department Social Science Research Branch, Working Paper No. 3*, November.

Dench, S. 1993b: Why do employers train? *Employment Department Social Science Research Branch, Working Paper No. 5*, December.

Dench, S., Perryman, S. and Giles, L. 1998: Employers' perceptions of key skills. *IES Report 349*, Sussex: Institute of Employment Studies.

DfEE (Department for Education and Employment) 1996: *Training Statistics, 1996*. London, HMSO.

DfEE 1998a: *Labour Market and Skill Trends 1998/99*. Sudbury: DfEE.

DfEE 1998b: *The Learning Age. A Renaissance for a New Britain*. London: HMSO.

Dickerson, A.P., Gibson, H.D. and Tsakolotos, E. 1995: The impact of acquisitions on company performance: evidence from a large panel of UK firms. *Studies in Economics*, No. 95/11, Canterbury: University of Kent (Department of Economics).

DTI (Department of Trade and Industry) 1997: *Competitiveness – Our Partnership with Business – a Benchmark for Success*. London: HMSO.

Employee Development Bulletin 1996: Making capital out of Investors in People, EDB No. 84, December, 11–16.

Eraut, M. 1994: *Developing Professional Knowledge and Competence*. Brighton: Falmer Press.

Eraut, M., Alderton, J., Cole, G. and Senker, P. 1998: Learning from other people at work. In Coffield, F. (ed.), *Learning at Work*, Bristol: Policy Press, 37–48.

Evans, K., Hodkinson, P., Keep, E., Maguire, M., Raffe, D., Rainbird, H., Senker, P. and Unwin, L. 1997: Working to learn, a work-based route to learning for young people. *Issues in People Management*, No. 18, London: Institute of Personnel and Development.

Felstead, A. and Green, F. 1994: Training during the recession. *Work, Employment and Society*, Vol. 8, No. 2, 199–219.

Felstead, A. and Green, F. 1996: Cycles of training? Evidence from the British recession of the early 1990s. In Booth, A. and Snower, D. (eds), *The Skills Gap and Economic Activity*, Cambridge: Cambridge University Press.

Financial Times (1994): 21 November, 10.

Finegold, D. and Soskice, D. 1988: The failure of training in Britain: analysis and prescription. *Oxford Review of Economic Policy*, Vol. 4 No. 3, 21–53.

Finegold, D., Keep, E., Miliband, D., Ratte, D., Spours, K. and Young, M. 1990: A British baccalaureat. Ending the division between education and training. *Education and Training Paper No. 1*, London: Institute of Public Policy Research.

Foundation for Manufacturing Industry/Department for Trade and Industry/IBM 1996: *Tomorrow's Best Practice: A Vision of the Future for Top Manufacturing Companies in the UK*. London: FMI.

Fryer, R.H. 1997: *Learning for the Twenty-First Century. First report of the National Advisory group for Continuing Education and Lifelong Learning*. November, Barnsley: Northern College.

Green, A. 1998: Core skills, key skills and general culture: in search of the common foundation in vocational education. *Evaluation and Research in Education*, Vol. 12 No. 1, 23–43.

Green, F., Ashton, D., Burchell, B., Davies, B. and Felstead, A. 1997: An analysis of changing work skills in Britain. Paper presented to the Low Wage Employment Conference of the European Low Wage Employment Research Network, CEP, LSE, December.

Guardian (1997): 26 June.

Harrison, R. 1997: Foreword. In Evans, K. *et al.*, Working to learn. A work-based route for young people. *Issues in People Management*, No. 18, London: Institute of Personnel and Development.

Institute of Personnel and Development 1999: *The Changing Role of Trainers*, London: IPD.

Jones, C. and Hendry, C. 1992: *The Learning Organisation: A Review of Literature and Practice*. London: HRD Partnership.

Jones, C. and Hendry, C. 1994: The learning organisation: adult learning and organisational transformation. *British Journal of Management*, Vol. 5, 153–162.

Keep, E. 1989: A training scandal? In Sisson, K. (ed.), *Personnel Management in Britain*, 1st edn, Oxford: Basil Blackwell, 177–202.

Keep, E. 1994: Vocational education and training for the young. In Sisson, K. (ed.), *Personnel Management. A Comprehensive Guide to Theory and Practice in Britain*, 2nd edn, Oxford: Basil Blackwell.

Keep, E. 1997: 'There's no such thing as society . . .': some problems with an individual approach to creating a learning society. *Journal of Education Policy*, Vol. 12 No. 6, 457–471.

Keep, E. and Mayhew, K. 1996a: Evaluating assumptions that underline training policy. In Booth, A.L. and Snower, D.J. (eds), *Acquiring Skills*, Cambridge: Cambridge University Press.

Keep, E. and Mayhew, K. 1996b: Towards a learning society – definition and measurement. *Policy Studies*, Vol. 17 No. 3, 215–231.

Keep, E. and Mayhew, K. 1998: Was Ratner right? – product market and competitive strategies and their links with skills and knowledge. *Employment Policy Institute Economic Report*, Vol. 12 No. 3.

Kodz, J., Kersley, B. and Strebler, M. 1998: Breaking the long hours culture. *IES Report 352*, Brighton: Institute of Employment Studies.

Koike, K. 1997: *Human Resource Management*. Tokyo: Japan Institute of Labour.

Kolb, D. 1984: *Experiential Learning*. Englewood Cliffs, NJ: Prentice-Hall.

Mabey, C. and Salaman, G. 1995: *Strategic Human Resource Management*. Oxford: Blackwell.

Mabey, C., Salaman, G. and Storey, J. 1998: Learning organizations. In Mabey, C., Salaman, G. and Storey, J. *Human Resource Management: A Strategic Introduction*. Oxford: Blackwell Publishers.

Maguire, M. 1997: Employee development schemes: panacea or passing fancy? In Coffield, F. (ed.), *A National Strategy for Lifelong Learning*, Newcastle: University of Newcastle, 143–157.

Maguire, M. 1999: Modern apprenticeship: just-in-time or far too late? In Ainley, P. and Rainbird, H. (eds), *Apprenticeship. Towards a New Paradigm of Learning*, London: Kogan Page.

Marquardt, M. 1996: *Building the Learning Organisation*. London: McGraw-Hill.

Marquardt, M. and Reynolds, A. 1994: *The Global Learning Organisation*. Burr Ridge, IL: Irwin.

Marsden, D. and Ryan, P. 1989: Employment and training of young people: have the government misunderstood the labour market? In Harrison, A. and Gretton, J. (eds), *Education and Training UK. Policy Journals*, 47–53.

Marx, K. 1976: *Capital, Volume 1*. Harmondsworth: Penguin.

McGivney, V. 1997: Adult participation in learning: can we change the pattern? In Coffield, F. (ed.), *A National Strategy for Lifelong Learning*, Newcastle: University of Newcastle, 127–141.

Metcalf, H., Walling, A. and Fogarty, M. 1994: Individual commitment to learning: employers' attitudes. *Employment Department Research Series* 40, Sheffield: ED.

Milne, S. and Elliott, L. 1999: How rich and poor must both pay the price of a workplace revolution. *Guardian*, 4 January.

Munro, A., Holly, H. and Rainbird, R. 1997: *Partners in Workplace Learning. A Report on the UNISON/employer Learning and Development Programme.* London: UNISON.

National Advisory Council for Education and Training Targets 1998: *Fast Forward for Skills.* London: NACETT.

National Commission on Education 1993: *Learning to Succeed. A Radical Look at Education Today and a Strategy for the Future.* London: Heinemann.

Payne, J. 1992: Motivating training. Paper presented to the Centre for Economic Performance's project on Vocational Educational and Training, January.

Pedler, M., Burgoyne, J. and Boydell, T. 1991: *The Learning Company.* London: McGraw-Hill.

Perry, P.J.C. 1976: *The Evolution of British Manpower Policy. From the Statute of Artificers 1593 to the Industrial Training Act 1964.* London: Eyre and Spottiswoode.

Pevoto, A.E. 1997: Book review. *The International Journal of Training and Development*, Vol. 1 No. 3, 212–213.

Raffe, D. 1991: Scotland v England: the place of home internationals in comparative research. In Ryan, P. (ed.), *International Comparisons of Vocational Education and Training for Intermediate Skills*, London: Falmer.

Rainbird, H. 1994: Continuing training. In Sisson, K. (ed.), *Personnel Management. A Comprehensive Guide to Theory and Practice in Britain*, 2nd edn, Oxford: Blackwell.

Rainbird, H. and Vincent, C. 1996: Training: a new item on the bargaining agenda. In Leisinck, P., Van Leemput, J. and Wilrokx, J. (eds), *The Challenges to Trade Unions in Europe. Innovation or Adaptation*, Cheltenham: Edward Elgar.

Raper, P., Ashton, D., Felstead, D. and Storey, J. 1997: Toward the learning organisation? Explaining current trends in training practice in the UK. *International Journal of Training and Development*, Vol. 1 No. 1, March, 9–21.

Regini, M. 1995: Firms and institutions: the demand for skills and their social production in Europe. *European Journal of Industrial Relations*, Vol. 1 No. 2, 191–202.

Scarborough, H., Swan, J.A. and Preston, J. 1998: *Knowledge Management and the Learning Organization: The IPD Report.* London: Institute of Personnel and Development.

Senge, P. 1990: *The Fifth Discipline: The Art and Practice of the Learning Organisation.* New York: Doubleday.

Senker, P. 1992: *Industrial Training in a Cold Climate: An Assessment of Britain's Training Policies.* Aldershot: Avebury.

Storey, J., Bacon, N., Edmonds, J. and Wyatt, P. 1993: The 'new agenda' and Human Resource Management: a roundtable discussion with John Edmonds. *Human Resource Management Journal*, Vol. 4 No. 1, 63–70.

Streeck, W. 1992a: *Social Institutions and Economic Performance: Studies in Industrial Relations in Advanced Capitalist Economies.* London: Sage.

Streeck, W. 1992b: Training and the new industrial relations. A strategic role for the unions? In Regini, M. (ed.), *The Future of Labour Movements.* London: Sage.

Swieringa, G. and Wierdsma, A. 1992: *Becoming a Learning Organisation.* Reading, MA: Addison-Wesley.

Tavistock Institute 1998a: *Workplace Learning, Learning Culture and Performance Improvement – A Report Prepared for the IPD*. London: Tavistock Institute.

Tavistock Institute 1998b: Intermediate Report to EU DGXIII on European Observatory on Innovations in Vocational Training. London: Tavistock Institute.

Trivellato, P. 1997: Japan as a learning society – an overall view by a European sociologist. In Coffield, F. (ed.), *A National Strategy for Lifelong Learning*. Newcastle: University of Newcastle, 185–206.

Chapter 6

The impact of the manager on learning in the workplace

Michael Eraut, Jane Alderton, Gerald Cole and Peter Senker

Introduction

Our research focused on the development of knowledge and skills in employment (Eraut *et al.*, 1998a). Briefly, our study involved double interviews, 6 to 12 months apart, with 120 people operating at a professional, management or technician level in 12 organisations. These organisations were in the engineering, financial services and healthcare sectors. The approach adopted was that of finding out what kinds of work activity our respondents were currently conducting, what kinds of knowledge and skill were entailed, how they had acquired the capability to do what they now did, and what factors had affected this learning process. Our findings showed that:

- Formal education and training provide only a small part of what is learned at work. Indeed, most of the learning described in our interviews was non-formal, neither clearly specified nor planned. It arose naturally out of the demands and challenges of work-solving problems, improving quality and/or productivity, or coping with change – and out of social interactions in the workplace with colleagues, customers or clients. Responding to such challenges entails both working and learning – one cannot be separated from the other. In retrospect it may be described as *learning from experience*. Although this leads to the development of knowledge, skills and understanding, such learning is often difficult to explain to others.
- Much learning at work derives its purpose and direction from the goals of the work. Achieving the goals often requires learning that is normally accomplished by a combination of thinking, trying things out and talking to other people. Sometimes, however, people recognise a need for some additional knowledge or skill that seems essential for improving the quality of their work, expanding its range or taking on new duties.

This is an edited version of an article previously published in F. Coffield (ed.) *Speaking Truth to Power*. 1999. Reproduced by permission of The Policy Press.

Learning goals are identified, which they pursue by a combination of self-directed learning and taking advantage of relevant learning opportunities as and when they appear. This sometimes involves undertaking some formal training, but almost always requires learning from experience and from other people at work.

- Learning from other people (Eraut et al., 1998b) is sometimes facilitated by organised learning support, which may be formally decided by central policy or informally arranged at local level. The former includes apprenticeships and trainee schemes; while mentoring, shadowing or coaching is more likely to be locally arranged, and generally more effective when it is. The most common form of learning from other people takes the form of consultation and collaboration within the immediate working group: this may include teamwork, ongoing mutual consultation and support or observation of others in action. Then beyond the immediate work environment, people seek information and advice, often on a reciprocal basis, from other wider professional networks. Only a minority of our respondents made frequent use of written or audio-visual materials like manuals, videos or computer-based training. The rest tried to circumvent materials by getting the information they needed from other people.

- Working for qualifications and short training courses are important for some people at particular stages in their career. Initial training was generally judged better when it was both broad in scope and involved periods in the workplace as well as in the classroom, laboratory or workshop. Mid-career management and professional qualifications were judged highly effective because they were able to use and build on prior experience at work; and management courses involving small groups and projects played an important role in helping people shift their thinking from an operational to a strategic level. What is less recognised, however, is the importance of less visible, work-based learning in developing the capability to use what has been learned off-the-job in work situations. This is especially true for short courses, which have very little impact unless they are appropriately timed and properly followed up at work.

- Increasing the amount of learning at work in order to realise the aspiration conveyed by the rhetoric of the learning organisation or The Learning Society depends on recognising how much learning occurs, or could occur on the job, and the factors that affect it. Our analysis at the individual level suggests that learning depends on confidence, motivation and capability – especially when capability is viewed as something to be acquired rather than something innate. This in turn depends on people's work having the appropriate degree of challenge, on how they are managed and on the microculture of the immediate work environment. The key person is the local manager whose management of people and role in establishing a climate favourable to learning, in which people seek advice and help each other learn quite naturally, is critical for those who are managed.

These findings have clear significance for the role of the manager, indicating that even the relatively novel concept of *the manager as staff developer* – novel, that is, to most managers – is too narrow. The Human Resource Management literature discusses managers as appraisers, mentors and even coaches. They assess the needs of those they manage, preferably is collaboration with them, and jointly prepare personal development plans. While the range of methods for supporting learning has widened, the underpinning concept is still based on learning goals being clearly specified and learning opportunities being planned. We found examples of this in our research. But we also found that much learning was neither clearly specified nor planned; indeed it was not easily separated out from the flux of daily living and working. For many people, learning arose out of the challenges posed by their work (McCauley *et al.*, 1994) and out of social interactions in the workplace. The most important factors, apart from the characteristics of the learners themselves, were the nature of the work, the way it was organised and managed, the climate of the immediate workplace and the culture of the organisation (Dubin, 1990). The local manager may influence learning more through their effect on the microclimate of the workplace and the organisation of work, and through personal example, than through formally recognised activities such as appraisal or sending people on courses.

Each of our respondents worked in unique situations, and the complex array of factors affecting learning could not possibly be subjected to any conclusive quantitative analysis. However, we did seek to collect evidence of how managers affected our respondents and how many of our respondents in their supervisory roles sought to facilitate the learning of those whom they supervised. This evidence is present here, so that it can be set alongside our earlier findings about respondents' formal and informal learning (Eraut *et al.*, 1998a), to assess how managers affect learning in the workplace. The evidence will be presented in three parts. The first will briefly described organisational policies that impact upon learning in the workplace. These include: short/long courses, external or in-house; apprenticeship/trainee schemes, induction and rotation; and appraisal systems, which range from a relatively informal annual interview to what is now being called performance management. The second will describe activities associated with the concept of the manager as staff developer: appraisal, mentoring and coaching, and other forms of planned learning support. The third will discuss the more informal influence of managers: the manager as role model, positive or negative; the manager as expert, leading professional or strategist; and the influence of managers' informal and incidental behaviour on the microclimate of the immediate workplace. Overlaps and links between these different types of evidence will be discussed in the conclusion.

Organisational policies

From a manager's perspective organisational policies can appear as dominant, enabling or disinterested. Taking courses as an example, centralised provision of in-house or bought-in courses is quite common. Such policies may be guided by perceptions of organisational weaknesses, strategies for building up particular future capabilities, the need for technical or legal updating, ongoing programmes of skill-formation and management development. Whether or not middle managers are consulted, there is an assumption of needs being similar across the organisation, which is sometimes true and sometimes false. More problematic is the difficulty inherent in a central system of timing courses appropriately. Our evidence suggests that timing is often a critical feature in learning from courses. In particular, courses need to relate to participants' current concerns, whether they are present or future orientated. The advantages of central provision, not always realised in practice, are economies of scale, relevance for the organisation and control over the quality of provision. But economies of scale may be counterbalanced by diversity of need; and relevance is difficult to achieve in fast-changing situations. Enabling strategies provide support in the form of funds and advice to managers seeking to meet the needs of their subordinates or directly to individual employees. In either case the initiative is more likely to come from the employee, and with it more motivation and commitment. The manager's role is to ensure relevance to needs that have been properly assessed and discussed; but with some managers this degenerates to laissez-faire. There is also a danger under either dominant or enabling regimes that too much emphasis is given to courses:

> The company thinks the only solution to learning is training courses rather than other types of experience or other methods.
>
> (Engineer)

Apprenticeship/trainee schemes are based on a variety of assumptions. There may be a set of planned learning outcomes, provided by off-the-job training (usually linked to qualifications), structured on-the-job training, or both. This planned learning will usually have a technical emphasis, and was regarded as providing a thorough technical grounding by *all* respondents who had experienced them. A second purpose, usually pursued by a system of rotations, was to acquire knowledge of the organisation. At its simplest, this provides some idea of what the organisation does, but it can also help employees to develop a network of contacts across the organisation who can be consulted later if it should prove necessary. This is more likely to happen where apprentices or trainees are welcomed and supported rather than just tolerated; and this in turn may be influenced by the length of rotations and the number of people being rotated. Apart from one management trainee in a bank and two actuarial trainees in insurance, all the examples encountered were in engineering. However, there are analogies in the placement arrangements for students taking initial and advanced/specialist qualifications in the health professions, particularly radiography. A third purpose, particularly relevant for graduates or qualified technicians, could be the development of a more holistic and strategic view of how the organisation works. One graduate engineering trainee was trying to achieve this, but finding it rather difficult in a relatively small company:

> I filled out the training form and I talked to the manager about it, and he sort of agrees that I would be able to have secondment/shadowing to other departments. I think I wrote four or five down, one I've already been to; and marketing would hopefully be about a four-week secondment; whereas the others would most likely be a week, a couple of days, just shadowing, just to give you a general picture ... But there is a difference between being supportive and actually doing it; 'cause obviously, the longer you're there the more valuable p'raps you become, and you get really involved in the project, and they can't afford [to be without you].

We did not encounter any other examples of this acquisition of a general view being planned, but there were sufficient examples of people gaining a range of experience across the organisation and clearly benefiting from their consequent increase in organisational understanding for it to be worthy of mention:

> You need to know about the company ... I've actually worked with an awful lot of departments within the company, and that's helped – ... so I actually know what goes on in customer services ... the central accounts office ... I know what happens in the retail industry, because I've actually worked there ... If you came straight in from outside, you couldn't do the job of corporate hospitality.
>
> (PR Manager, public utility)

Perhaps this should be conceived more in terms of job rotation during a person's early years in the organisation than as part of a post-entry training scheme.

All four financial organisations had performance management systems (Bevan *et al.*, 1992), but these differed according to:

- frequency of formal meetings
- approaches to performance criteria and target setting
- use of generic skills and competencies
- linkage to pay
- balance between performance evaluation and personal development.

These are illustrated by the following examples from our interviews.

Example 1: insurance manager

'They have a progress review three times a year and an annual review . . . So there's a lot of documentation on the person. You've got their file, you can see where they've developed, what their areas of strength and weakness are . . . You may already have some personal experience of their strengths and weaknesses . . . you can start to pick up on those issues, and by observing how their teams run, how they interact with their team, you can see what the morale and issues with the team are . . . We are very short-term. We may have one person who's very good at a particular job and we need them to do that job to keep us within target of our performance, so a manager focused on the short term would do that. When that person leaves, gets knocked over by a bus, has two weeks holiday, whatever they do, then suddenly the performance drops. Now what we should be doing and what we haven't done in the past is push those skills throughout the team, take aside three or four people who can do that, let's develop those people, let's develop that person as a trainer even and say, you push those skills through the organisation . . . The other thing we do that frustrates me is that that person will then become so expert, that when they want to move on, the manager says, "I can't lose them, I don't want them to go, it's six months before I can let them go". That individual is then stopped from all the potential benefits they could bring to the company and themselves by moving on and developing and imparting their knowledge elsewhere, simply because of a process need within one area. That is where I butted up against the culture very heavily . . . and that is not something I can compromise on.'

Example 2: senior sales manager in a bank

'I sign an annual contract at the beginning of the year and again that's based on numbers and performance, income and business objectives, so I get paid on the basis of an annual contract . . . Either you meet contract, you exceed contract or you fall short . . . As far as fall short is concerned I've given a "fall short contract" to a manager who works for me and it didn't sit very easily with me, I didn't like doing it but it had to be done, it was the right thing to do. That person is still with us and the way that I tried to deal with it was to turn it on its head and to look at those things that that person could change or influence to make sure that he certainly got a "met contract" next time round. But I think that if you then get a succession of fall short contracts, your career must be in question: that's not coming from the centre, that's my own personal view.'

Example 3: area manager for a bank

'We're working with a new system here, a performance management system . . . [It] starts off with business goals and takes it through to a personal development plan all in one document . . . It's a system we really like but we're still learning it . . . It's got a framework, a menu of attributes. So everybody picks out the ones they think are most relevant to their job and then assesses where they are on a level of one to four against definitions that we've got; and then the development plan should fall out of that. So it's much more personal than results focused, although that's in it as well.'

Example 4: finance manager, energy supply company

'These performance reviews tend not to be looking back, the emphasis is to look forward. They have some key skills, and you actually write down whether each skill is critical for the job, or important, or just nice to have. Then between yourself and your manager you decide where on each scale you ought to be, and then where on the scale you feel you are. If there's a gap, perhaps you need a little bit of training in that area; and then you decide between you and the personnel department what sort of training would be required . . . They're trying to make sure that performance reviews are not occasions where you say "Well, you haven't done very good in that this year", and start beating them around the head. It's meant to be a more positive approach. What can we do to help you become that much better in your job; and if you're quite satisfactory, what can we do to help you go still further? That's only just started, so let's see how it actually works, and whether the staff actually buy into it; 'cause apparently they've had fits and starts on appraisal systems and reviews, they've got a bit of a credibility problem.'

Example 5: accounts manager, energy supply company

'Our sector's very difficult, because we're split into areas. Some areas are harder to work in than others . . . so we have a team target . . . We all do equal amounts of work, we're all individually responsible for our own accounts regardless, but at the end of the day all of the figures are lumped together as a team target . . . and that forms part of our performance review.'

These examples indicate both the range of formal systems, and the ways in which individual managers try to interpret them in ways that match their own personal philosophies of management. They also demonstrate the tension between *performance management systems*, which focus on short-term results and key activities that directly affect 'the bottom line', and a *human resource development* approach focused on the development of staff capability over a longer timescale (Bevan and Hayday, 1994; Armstrong and Baron, 1998). Reconciling these two approaches depends on the skills of the manager. But even the most skilful manager will be constrained (a) when stakes are high because of possible promotions or contingent financial benefits; and (b) when their authority to make developmental responses to employees' learning needs is limited by finance and/or flexibility.

Performance management systems were not encountered in the engineering and healthcare sectors; but most organisations had a policy of annual appraisals. However, this did not always appear to be taken very seriously or to have been implemented in every department. One important limitation in engineering was the danger of those people who stood to benefit most from appraisal slipping through the net. Those who move departments frequently may leave one department just before they would have been appraised, and arrive at the next one just after appraisals have been completed. A proportion of such people may be having serious career/learning problems, which express themselves in frequent moves: it can happen that somebody in particular need of reviewing their career progress and learning misses appraisals for several years running. Nevertheless, many organisations had made recent improvements or were currently working on their implementation:

> There's a formal process in place by which you have to sit down and do this once a year informally and record it, it's a two-way thing between the employee and their immediate manager. I think some people should do it progressively during the course of the year but the mechanism is for making sure once a year you both sit down and actually record it. You can do it as many times as you want, it's really something that you should be working out together. So the company put quite a lot of effort into that, on the flip side because when they first introduced this it wasn't particularly successful. They had quite a long look at it, we had some consultants in; and it was identified that part of the reason for it not working was really the background of the managers. Like myself a lot of the managers were good at doing their previous job, so people assumed they'd be good at being managers; and they put engineers into managerial positions. And there wasn't a lot of support or help given to them in terms of development. So you had an organisation where there were an awful lot of technically competent people; but they were in managerial positions and they were not as confident in terms of doing the managerial bit. So there's been a lot of effort gone into really the managerial side over the last 18 months or so. Most of the managers have gone through the workshop where they sat down in small workshops and tried to work through their various strengths and weaknesses, areas where they need development . . .
>
> (Manager, engineering company)

I work with the coaches when we've been developing the performance management systems for each area . . . we haven't got many people with those skills to do the job because we have been brought up on good old command and control and tell [whereas] a coach is about enthusing you and encouraging you.

(Senior Manager, insurance company)

The manager as staff developer

The best indicator of whether a developmental approach is used by managers will probably be how they manage formal appraisal, informal feedback, and support for learning. These are the central features of 'the manager as staff developer' approach. In this section we summarise our respondents' experiences of appraisal, coaching and general support for learning.

Engineering in product development companies tended to be a little sceptical about appraisal. This may have been because managers, as suggested above, were not well trained in appraisal skills. But it also arises from the limited significance of the line management role when most work is done by project teams. Appraisal can play a useful part in reviewing an engineer's contribution in fairly general terms, both retrospectively and prospectively, but it may not have much impact on learning if the engineer's manager was not involved in any of their projects. Two relatively positive examples are given below, one at the level of general communication, the other giving useful feedback:

Appraisal is a lot better than it has been, it's something the company have taken more seriously over the last few years . . . It certainly lets me have a good feel for the major project that I'll be doing throughout the year . . . They look at what you're meant to have done last year, what you actually did last year, why they bear no resemblance, and whether that was your fault or their fault, and then you look at what you will be doing over the next year and how realistic that's likely to be. [Interviewer's probes about learning from appraisal yielded little response.]

(Manager, engineering company)

My current manager I think has been very fair. He's given a very good assessment synopsis of where I'm at and I think it will help, definitely, I mean, it focuses on strengths and weaknesses, which I think is important, because, you know, on the one hand you're told what you're good at, but on the other hand you're told what you can do better and what you can develop, improve on, and I think that's useful. You need to have feedback from both sides.

(Engineer)

Others commented that their appraisers did little more than discuss possible short courses.

The most interesting example came from a relatively senior manager in an insurance company who was trying to make the appraisal system work in the way it should, by changing managers' attitudes towards feedback from below:

> For my annual review I said to all my team: 'I've got my annual review in a month's time, can you pull together some feedback; and if my boss asks for it, give it to him.' I called him up on the E-mail and said 'Look, if you want some info for my appraisal, here it is.' He never asked for it, so they gave it to him anyway! They said: 'You haven't asked for it but here it is.' I was really pleased, 360° (collecting comments from seniors, juniors and colleagues at the same level) or whatever is not formally part of our appraisal process, but if you seek it and get it back, then you've got something in there that can be used. So we encourage it, and now, my team do it to their people. We are still a bit 'good news-ish', whereas my team go and bring informative stuff, their team didn't give them informative stuff so this honesty thing is probably not quite there yet. When I got the team back for their reviews I said 'Well you're good at everything and bad at nothing. You know what areas you need to develop here'; and they said 'We'll try to get them to be more open and honest.' But they're not there yet, not that confident with it yet, but they will get there.
>
> (Senior Manager, insurance company)

Radiographers missed out on formal appraisal but received a great deal of informal feedback from colleagues. Nurses, being more numerous, tended to be involved in hospital schemes from an early stage. They tended to focus more on the informal activities of their managers than formal appraisals, but there were some positive examples that significantly affected individual careers:

> The actual turning point was when my manager said to me, it was in an appraisal with him, he said 'Right, what are you going to do with the rest of your life? You've got a career. Like it or not you're a career nurse, you've been in it long enough.' I said 'Well I haven't really thought about it', and he said 'Well I think you really need to seriously think about doing your conversion course.' I actually said to him 'Oh I don't think I could do that, you know what do I want to do that for?'; and he said 'I think you've really got to realise that the enrolled nurses are going to be phased out. Your role will be eroded in one way or another.' It really made me think, and I just decided that I'd better go and do the O-levels then. I must admit I loved doing it at night school, I really enjoyed it. [This led to two years' night school, then a conver-

sion course to upgrade her professional status, which then led to further promotion and engagement in Continuing Professional Education.]

A similar example was provided by a healthcare assistant, whose fear of exams had prevented her from taking any further qualifications:

> I became interested in Complementary Medicines, and I was having, oh gosh what do they call them, a chat with the ward manager who assess what you've been doing over the last year, and she said 'Well, what are you going to do. Are you going to go through your whole life saying "No I can't?" . . . Go on, go for this.' And I said 'Yeah.' That was it.

Another nurse was preparing to discuss her need for some training in counselling at her next appraisal, in order to offer better support to patients at the oncology clinic where she worked. This was an example of a self-directed learner using the system, rather than an unconfident learner needing to be challenged and supported.

Given the project team approach, job descriptions were rarely significant in engineering. It was more a case of how best to use the assembled talent to get the job done. But in other sectors, the precise nature of the job was a frequent subject of discussion at appraisals, with modifications being used not only to reflect the changing demands but also for development purposes. Examples were cited of both job expansion and job redesign, the latter often occurring after an internal promotion rather than at an appraisal. In one case this involved expanding the work of a whole department by enlarging the roles of most of its members, with a consequent need for several staff to get further training for their new responsibilities:

> She's very good on helping people progress, she's very keen on post-grad studies. So quite a few of the radiographers here have been on the barium enema course because they're going to do barium enemas which takes some of the work load off the radiologists. Quite a few of us have been on the IV course so we can give (intravenous) injections ourselves, so we don't have to call the nurse or doctor to do it. Some of us have written up the instructions you know, as to what to give and how to give it and then we can get on and do it. So, she's very good from that point of view, but she can be a bit autocratic. She has a very forceful character.
>
> (Radiographer)

Not tea and sympathy but challenge, safety in numbers, and confidence that her staff were capable of doing what she asked of them.

A respondent from an engineering company described how he was being gradually eased into a team leadership role by his manager's phased withdrawal of support – an example of coaching, though not described as such.

He's given me an area to work in, but he's also kept me sheltered from the ravages of the customer . . . He's involved in the actual dates and timescales when we've got to deliver the project; and I'm involved in getting to that point, in the day-to-day running of the team . . .

Normally he's the guy whose chairing the meetings and I'm sitting in; but now he's there [only] 20 per cent of the time, looking in and I'm chairing the weekly meetings and inviting him along. Not on this project, because it's such a short timescale, but at some point down the line, I will be in charge of the whole project. I won't be the project manager, but I'll be the team leader in charge of delivering the software to the customer.

A nurse gave a somewhat similar but more opportunist example. She was involved as a witness in a disciplinary case, and rather nervous about it. Yet her manager realised that, if promoted, she would be expected to present such cases. So she involved her in discussions about the presentation, and debriefed her after the hearing, putting things into perspective.

Soon I'm going to be there doing exactly the same thing and also eventually you've got to be able to present. I've got to get used to that sort of formality.

The manager as role model and/or expert

We encountered many examples in our research of people learning from watching how their managers handled people and situations or from tuning into their manager's expertise. This learning did not depend on whether their managers saw themselves as staff developers and appraised, mentored, action planned or coached. It depended on how their managers performed when they were present:

I worked with a manager for a period of five years, who I believe to be one of the most capable people that I've ever met in the bank. I learnt an incredible amount from him just by watching him work. I don't think I would be doing the job I'm doing today unless I had that fabulous piece of experience of working with that one individual . . . One thing I especially learned was to put the right people in the right job.

(Senior Manager in a bank)

Negative models could be a source of learning as well as positive models, and often there were elements of both:

I have learned an awful lot from him . . . I still think some of the things he does are completely wrong . . . my manager feels that to get things done, the way to do it is to shout at people ... I disagree with that method ... so that's one major disagreement that I've learned *not to learn* from [him] ... the number one thing he's always taught me ... [is] that you can never presume something, and you'll be okay. Always know something for definite.

(PR Manager, public utility)

Many of the positive examples seemed to combine both personality and expertise:

My immediate manager was a very dynamic person, a driving force ... I learned a lot of design for cost from him ... Also, the management of the qualification of the machine. It's one thing to build the machine but when you're doing a new machine you have to qualify at the end of it to prove that it does what it's supposed to do, and he was very good at quantifying how to do that and I learned a lot.

(Development Engineer)

He seemed to have a clarity of objective. If you were given a task by him it was very clearly specified ... He would produce examples to show how to present a document ... One also saw J in operation, not only in the local setting but also in the European [context] ... There was modelling both of him as a person, and on examples of products [he showed you].

(Services Engineer)

Even from less sympathetic managers people learned about fairness, standards and loyalty to subordinates:

The manager I worked for during that period was a very demanding person. He was one of those people who expect a lot of you but he made it clear exactly what they expected. If you did something wrong he got you in and he told you off for doing it wrong. You did something right he praised you for doing right. And although he could be very critical of you inwardly, outwardly he would always give you total support. If he was dealing with someone else who was actually coming along and being critical about you he would support you to the Nth degree; but inwardly he might really be giving you a hard time.

(Product Development Engineer)

The manager as creator of a climate that supports learning

Many of the most positive comments about managers related mainly to the effect they appeared to have on the climate in the workplace (Kozlowski and Hults, 1987; Tracey *et al.*, 1995). Sometimes elements of the manager as staff developer or the manager as role model were also present, but this was just part of the story. What mattered most was that people felt it was a good working location where they were both stimulated and supported. It was especially interesting to note the wide range of personal styles that were described as being successful. The concepts underpinning people's praise for positive working environments, which were often contrasted with less positive examples, were achievement, support and participation.

The examples below demonstrate three contrasting styles of leadership, all praised for their high expectations, personal attention and development of individuals' confidence in their own capability.

> A wonderful manager, he was very good at making people feel they were important in their niche, and in encouraging them, giving that small amount of contact that is needed with a person to keep them going, which some managers do forget about. He actually comes round and says 'How are you, how are things going?' . . . and he kept tabs on all the projects which I always thought was wonderful.
>
> (Engineer)

> I've noticed with D she'll never say 'That's not what I want', or 'Why haven't you got this back to me within an X amount of time?' She's always so pleasant about it, not sort of excusing you or anything, but it's just the way she puts it, you know that she appreciates what's gone on, because she knows what's been happening or not, why you haven't the report or whatever it is. She never gives the impression she's on your back. She has this really nice way of getting you to do it, regardless of the whole place being on fire, without making you feel dreadful about it. Because you know you've got to do it, but you've had 50 million other things going on, or you might have completely forgotten about it.
>
> (Nurse)

> He's innovative, he wants to drive things forward, he's quite a mixture; he's very autocratic in many ways, but he also expects a high level of independence in his staff. He'll say 'Just go ahead and do it' . . . Yes I do feel incredibly supported and he does this, and if you go to him and say 'Look I don't quite understand why we're doing it this way, what about' he will listen and if he thinks it's reasonable he'll agree, so he's fairly open-minded.
>
> (Radiographer)

This last quotation provides an interesting mixture of challenge, participation and support. People need confidence in their manager as well as in their own capabilities.

If your manager is in a bit of a flap, then it will just trickle down and you'll see the stress not only in the staff but eventually in the patients as well, and the doctors, and the domestic, and absolutely everybody. But because she's calm and efficient and makes it look so easy just not hard at all, then it just sort of spreads, and people are generally more confident; and they know that she's such a confident manager that everything just seems to go like clockwork.

(Nurse)

This nurse also stressed the participative nature of management on her ward; as did a nursing assistant in another hospital:

Quite frequently we would get together all the E grades, and A and J, and discuss some of the other issues that were going in the ward at the time. So I think that A's the type of manager who likes staff to be involved with decisions, so I think that we're always aware of things that are going on even if we're not directly involved in having to make those decisions . . . Even though we're all part of a team, we each take on a certain amount of responsibility.

(Nurse)

If anything new is going to happen, then we get together. Sister will see as many of us as she can at one time, and talk to us about it and then a joint decision will be made. Or, if something is done above our heads then we all have to discuss it afterwards, you know, and we try and alter it if it's not right. But we do get consulted, sister is very good at consulting us over the various changes that are going to happen. I wish the upper management were as good.

(Nursing Assistant)

Another nurse appreciated a more low key, but still very supportive, approach:

Initially, I don't think I appreciate how good a boss he was; he's not a good boss if you don't know what you're doing because he does tend to let you feel your way. He's not breathing over your shoulder. If I need him I go to him and if he wants to ask me to do something he'll come to me, otherwise he has his, I have mine, we get on. He's not trying to influence me, he advises me; so he'll never say 'You're going to do it this way', he'll say 'Have you thought about doing it that way?' He's very good at supporting you and pushing you forward as well, so you find other members of staff will come to you and say, 'Oh M's said that perhaps you could help us with this.' And sometimes you think 'For God's sake', but he's very good at trying to raise your profile so that you're noticed. I always get amazed round that place that the bosses put their name on the other people's work, I think it's terrible. And M will never do that, to the point that he'll insist that you put your name on the front of it and insist that you're there to discuss it, even if you don't want to present it to be board, he insists that you're sat there so you're seen to be the one with the knowledge.

(Nurse)

Two engineers commented on environments that by most people's standards were good, but in their view could have been improved by giving greater attention to supporting new arrivals:

In the engineering environment . . . you could always go to people and they're always willing to help but you have to go and find the help, whereas when I moved into software everyone was coming up, offering advice, checking if I was OK . . . Not only the supervisor, the whole team were very very good . . . even now, you, you have to refer [to other people]. Because that guy really knows that particular area . . . he can . . . set you on a track to save you time.

We have the most wonderful people here. They really want to help you, want to make sure you understand. But I think you don't get involved enough as a team, like with new people coming in there's this mentor thing. It's very much this new person comes in, you meet them and slowly they might start getting socially involved with you, but on a work basis they're left on their own, to their own devices.

In neither case was this seen as weakness in management, rather as a limitation in the peer group culture. This might reflect the dominance of 'projects' in product development companies and a corresponding lack of attention to line managers.

A concept frequently cited or implied by our respondents when describing factors influencing learning in their workplace was that of a 'blame-free culture':

If you take a film somebody will look at that, and 'cause it's so relaxed here, you don't take it personally that it's not as good as it could have been. Or, if you do a good film, they'll say 'Oh that's good, well done.' Because they quite happily will say when something's good, you don't mind when it's not so good.

(Radiographer)

He's an exceptional boss, I feel very safe to say 'I really screwed up here and I could have done better.'

(Nurse)

People do not learn only from others' mistakes, as mentioned earlier, but also from their own. As one engineer commented:

> I don't really learn by being taught, I learn by cocking things up.

and another described how he learned forecasting:

> It was an acquired skill, basically I learned a lot and I made it up as I went along. You talk to people, you find out what they did, you copy it, you discuss with people what is working, what is not working; and what I basically did was to bring all the things I knew had gone wrong, and use that information to build a new system up in a different way, and make it work.

Conclusion

Our earlier paper 'Learning from other people at work (Eraut *et al.*, 1998b) demonstrated the major contribution to performance of learning from other people within and beyond the workplace. This learning was either facilitated or constrained by (a) the organisation and allocation of work and (b) the social climate of the work environment. While our methodological approach led to a greater emphasis on positive evidence of learning, our respondents not only volunteered negative evidence but implicitly provided it when they compared their personal experiences of different work contexts. The clear implication, sometimes explicitly stated, was that important learning opportunities were missed in certain kinds of activity or situation, with negative consequences for the quality and speed of work. These claims about missed opportunities were based either on self-evident misses ('it would have saved a lot of time', 'if only I had known . . .') or on comparisons with other, more learning-friendly work environments. Thus they were credible assessments of what was feasible in those contexts, not untested aspirations driven by hypothetical models of a 'learning organisation'. Some respondents may have been more cognitively aware of, and positively disposed towards, recognising and using learning opportunities at work; but they still had to know whom to ask and to feel that their requests would be positively received. An important corollary would be an orientation towards offering help rather than waiting to be asked. The positive effect on confidence and performance of being consulted by colleagues should also be noted.

This chapter argues that a major factor affecting a person's learning at work is the personality, interpersonal skills, knowledge and learning orientation of their manager. While approaches to management development normally emphasise motivation, productivity and appraisal, comparatively little attention is given to supporting the learning of subordinates, allocating and organising work, and creating a climate that promotes informal learning.

This imbalance may result from ignorance about how much learning does (and how much more learning might) take place on the job. There are also implications for the selection of people for management roles. In most organisations the practical implications of strengthening informal learning for developing the individual and collective capabilities of employees are not yet understood.

The main implications for policy at national level lie in two areas: management training, as already discussed; and the limitations of the dominant mode of policy discourse. Problems are treated as well defined and readily soluble, and therefore susceptible to formal, standardised types of training to clearly specified targets. Yet the concept of a knowledge-based economy and the metaphor of a learning organisation derive from recognition of the complexities and uncertainties of the modern world. Public discourse about training not only neglects informal learning but denies complexity by over-simplifying the processes and outcomes of learning and the factors that give rise to it.

References

Armstrong, M. and Baron, P. (1998) *Performance management: The new realities*, London: Institute for Personnel and Development.

Bevan, S., Thompson, M. and Hirsch, W. (1992) *Performance management in the UK: An analysis of the issues*, London: Institute for Personnel and Development.

Bevan, S. and Hayday, S. (1994) *Toeing the line: Helping managers to manage people*, Research Report No. 254, Brighton: Institute for Employment Studies.

Dubin, S.S. (1990) 'Maintaining competence through updating', in S.S. Dubin and S.L. Willis (eds) *Maintaining professional competence*, San Francisco, CA: Jossey-Bass, pp. 9–43.

Eraut, M., Alderton, J., Cole, G. and Senker, P. (1998a) *Development of knowledge and skills in employment*, Research Report No. 5, Brighton: Institute of Education, University of Sussex.

Eraut, M., Alderton, J., Cole, G. and Senker, P. (1998b) 'Learning from other people at work', in F. Coffield (ed.) *Learning at work*, Bristol: The Policy Press, pp. 37–48.

Kozlowski, S.W.J. and Hults, B.M. (1987) 'An exploration of climates for technical updating and performance', *Personnel Psychology*, vol. 40, pp. 539–563.

McCauley, C.D., Ruderman, M.N., Ohlott, P.J. and Morrow, J.E. (1994) 'Assessing the developmental components of managerial jobs', *Journal of Applied Psychology*, vol. 79, no. 4, pp. 544–560.

Tracey, J.B., Tannenbaum, S.I. and Kavanagh, M.J. (1995) 'Applying trained skills on the job: the importance of the work environment', *Journal of Applied Psychology*, vol. 80, no. 2, pp. 239–252.

Chapter 7

Knowledge creation in Japanese manufacturing companies in Italy

Reflections upon organizational learning

John B. Kidd

A study of all 47 Japanese–Italian production subsidiaries was undertaken during the early part of 1993. One analysis relating to the corporate governance in these firms was reported by Songini *et al.* (1993). They found the management styles of the companies were significantly related to company size and capital structure. They derived two styles, which may be called 'involvement' and 'hierarchy'; the arguments supporting these are based on the two principal components derived from factor analysis and regression analyses of the data.

This paper follows a different route in so far as it superimposes the work of Nonaka (1994) upon the data. He postulated that organisational knowledge is created through a continuous dialogue between tacit and explicit knowledge. Specifically we wished to see if this argument could be upheld when the organizations were not 'pure', given the enterprises in focus are managed by Japanese and Italian managers. We presumed the continuous dialogue between staff in a joint-venture firm may be expected to be less than seamless, given the gross differences in natural languages, the norms of business culture, and the different contexts in which business is conducted in Italy and in Japan.

The model of knowledge creation proposed by Nonaka seems to have many links – to other research on 'learning companies' and to the practical day-to-day operations of the Italian–Japanese production subsidiaries. We suggest that this model can be used to map how well firms handle knowledge creation and thus to imply how well they might achieve competitive advantage. While this point was not specifically researched it might be noted that some of the 'better' firms (in a Nonaka sense) in the response set are at the leading edge of their commercial sector.

The better firms are managed strongly by Italian CEOs. The Japanese partners work in conjunction, but in the background, offering technology, techniques and important financial support. In return the Japanese partners

This is an edited version of an article previously published in *Management Learning*, 29:2, 1998. Reproduced by permission of Sage Publications Ltd.

receive the benefits of strong product support in a 'happy' organizational environment. We suggest that in these firms the Italian managers themselves have absorbed some Japanese-ness and retranslated this to the Italian context for the benefit of their staff's learning.

Some firms are weaker performers, in the sense that they do not manage their knowledge creation process well. We feel this arises because both parties – the Italian and the Japanese managers – are each attempting to rule, and thus do not give clear communications to their workforce. They maintain a reliance on tradition, on hierarchy, on rules, and they hinder the implementation of knowledge generation schemes (for instance, by restricting workforce sociability they slow the development of tacit knowledge).

Finally we think that the model proposed by Nonaka deserves wider testing in different cultures and contexts since other research suggests that 'learning programmes' can take place in many diverse organizations. The Nonaka model draws these together in a simple, clear, dynamic framework.

A brief consideration of knowledge creation

Core competence

Many persons accept that a firm's advantage stems from its unique knowledge – one might talk of 'core competence' (Prahalad and Hamel, 1991). And few would disagree that the culture of the firm is often distinct and palpable – just walk through the entrance halls of major organizations, even those competing in the same economic or technology sector, and one 'feels' the differences; yet such culture is difficult to measure. It is the same with the creation of knowledge. In general the successful firm effectively transforms inputs to outputs employing unique competence, and, while so doing, it also generates new knowledge about novel combinations and processes – thus the organization is said to learn. It has also been suggested that organizational learning is under the managers' control and this has been the focus of many researchers (e.g. Hirschhorn, 1984; Kagono *et al.*, 1985; Nonaka, 1991, 1994; Nonaka and Takeuchi, 1995).

Knowledge, objective and tacit

Much is made of the notion of the rationality of science, which seeks to eliminate the sources of bias, yet it may be argued that knowledge is socially constructed (that we are the product of our initial nurturing at home, our learning and socialization at school, and our learning at work: Cook and Yanow, 1993). Further, there is no strictly private knowledge: knowledge gradually becomes evident through language and communication – thus we accept the definition of tacit knowledge as 'that which we know, but can't tell fully'.

Table 7.1 Firms in full survey, their sectors and market position (following Nonaka, 1994)

Sector	Up-stream	Down-stream
Electronic and electrical		A, J, M, H
Light vehicles		D, E, G, L
Heavy vehicles		F, I
Chemical processing	C, B, K	

Note: Coded to link with Table 7.2.

Polanyi (1962) drew a distinction between objective and tacit knowledge, the former being abstract and independent of the knower, while the latter is subjective and intimately tied to the knower's experience. It would seem that effortlessness is one characteristic of tacit knowledge. Polanyi notes this by referring to riding a bicycle: the knower can't exactly say what the body has learned, but the tacit knowledge is in fact displayed quite effortlessly. Tacit knowledge also has a collective component, which can be likened to the narratives of troubadours or to the constant repetition of folklore lest it be forgotten. In these cases one does not really know what one knows. It is argued that organizations retain their knowledge in 'organizational routines' that no single person fully understands (Nelson and Winter, 1982). And we find this collective experience occurs in the swapping of 'war stories' that may form the base for emergent good practice or the expression of clarity on some organizational issue that has previously defeated institutional rules (Brown and Duguid, 1991).

Formalization of contexts

One of the difficulties in sharing tacit knowledge is the need for formalization, the generation of a community of practice that may be seen in the workplace, in apprenticeships and even in the structuring of academic papers: if the context and layout become unusual, knowledge exchange does not occur. Wertsch (1985) and Scribner *et al.* (1991) have suggested that much of the expertise in the workplace lies in being able to formulate problems in ways that are embedded in understandable contexts – thus tacit knowledge may become formalized and articulated. This notion is in accord with the dynamic model of knowledge creation proposed by Nonaka, which forms the base by which we measure the interaction occurring in the Italian–Japanese firms in Italy. Importantly Nonaka and Takeuchi (1995) suggest that knowledge creation is an endless spiral, which may be promoted through a series of distinct stages and transformations.

Methodology

The aim of the original research was to explore the relationships and beliefs held by the CEOs in Italian–Japanese 'joint' ventures. The research programme was initiated by a long postal questionnaire sent to all Japanese manufacturing companies in Italy (47 at the time: spring 1993), with follow-up interviews with a sample of their top managers. In fact the questionnaire used was based on an earlier version (published later as Kidd and Teramoto, 1995a) with questions added by the Italian researchers to cover points relating to their primary interests. The questions elicited factual data on turnover, numbers of employees, and so on, or asked for subjective data. In the latter case we used a five-point Likert scale and occasionally allowed a free-form expression for the response. Even so, grounded in our own backgrounds and learned methodologies, we found we adopted a positivist approach to the questionnaire design – we inclined towards limiting the outcomes in any given question, even if we offered 'other' as a catch-all response on a multi-point scale.

In this paper we are not looking to produce data suitable for statistical interpretation, but to interpret the original data within the framework proposed by Nonaka. We thus hope to comment on the state of knowledge creation in the Japanese–Italian firms at that time, and to offer insight on the applicability of the Nonaka 'model'.

Due to time, distance and calendar restrictions our original interviews were restricted to 13 companies (see Table 7.1) although more firms returned the questionnaire. Generally the interviews were triggered by the early return of completed questionnaires – we took their return as a tacit acceptance of further involvement on the part of the management of the firms, thus we scheduled them into our calendar with their consent.

The questionnaire was offered in Italian and in English. The interviews were usually conducted in English, but occasionally in Italian or Japanese according to the respondent's need to explain a point in detail. They were relatively unstructured, although a reminder fax was sent to the CEOs highlighting points to be covered in the interview. Generally the researchers asked questions freely and followed leads as and when the CEO offered new data or avenues of exploration. We could, in this situation, be sensitive towards the contexts in which we and the CEOs found ourselves. Potentially, the verbal responses of the CEOs were interpreted differently by the researchers – since they were variously born and schooled in Italy, Japan, and the UK. Each person carried with them a set of overlapping cultural norms which, at the edge, remained a mystery to others, so naturally these may have affected their judgement – see Hall and Hall (1989).

The Nonaka model in a European context

Argyris and Schön (1978), and Huber (1991) to some extent, postulate learning to be at the level of the individual, and organizational learning may only be achieved if somehow individuals transcend their individuality and look for organization-wide data. Nonaka (1994) and Nonaka and Takeuchi (1995) however have defined a dynamic pattern of organizational learning wherein an individual's learning is merged with that of others, over time, in a dynamic spiral. They consider there are four stages in the knowledge conversion process linking one person to another, thus raising gradually the awareness of learning within the firm (see Figure 7.1). These four stages are reviewed briefly to offer a base for the discussions of our findings about the knowledge creation in Japanese–Italian firms.

Stage 1 – Socialization: from tacit to tacit (sympathized knowledge)
Here basic knowledge exchange is obtained by direct appreciation – being an apprentice is a good example. Knowledge is acquired from the master, not through abstract language but by observation, imitation and by practice. Nonaka notes the meetings held by Japanese firms, often outside the premises, to undertake 'brainstorming'. Herein there is a sharing of the realities of life: drinking, eating, generally chatting and experiencing communal bathing in a hot spring – it gives a 'throw-back' appreciation of the one-time good life in Japan, the situation relaxes everyone, and in so doing allows

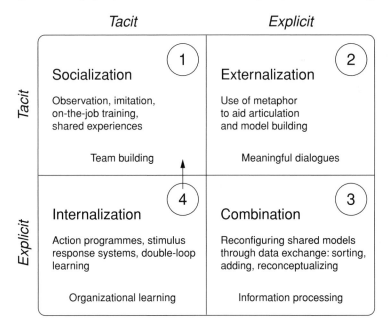

Figure 7.1 Stages of learning (following Nonaka, 1994).

deeper communion. Bartlett and Ghoshal (1989) have also stated firmly that a firm wishing to move into the global phase (to their Transnational type) must allow its staff to participate in a great deal of *socialization* (emphasis by Kidd).

Stage 2 – Externalization: from tacit to explicit (conceptual knowledge)
This mode relies upon analogies, metaphors, hypotheses and models being expressed through articulated language. Frequently there are gaps between the expressed knowledge and the 'W', or world-view of the perceiver. This may be emphasized when a model is inadequate and a metaphor has to be employed. This should lead an individual to reflect on the potential reasons for the gaps by searching for something in terms of something else. Donnellon *et al.* (1986) suggest that metaphor creates a novel interpretation of experience. The metaphor, based on an intuition, may be further refined by the use of analogy where logic, or analytic model, may be employed to give the ideas more substance.

It has been said the Japanese use a great deal of intuition, inferring much from what is said or not said; from the state of a room, or from a business layout. They view their world holistically, which can lead to better externalization of their internal knowledge base. On the other hand the European inherits a system of learning based on reductionist logic. They abhor intuition since it can't be justified – supposedly a French engineer was heard to say on studying a new machine while it was in operation, 'That's all very well – but logically it will not work!' The Italians are no exception to this 'rule'.

Stage 3 – Combination: from explicit to explicit (systemic knowledge)
This mode involves many channels of communication – face-to-face talking (socialization), using the written language (having aspects of externalization), as well as using the telephone, TV conferencing or electronic networking (e-mail). The receiving person will be able to reconfigure the data on a topic just as a computer reconfigures a database on command.

Middle management should exhibit a strong role model in this process. For instance, senior managers in Japan express their 'vision' statements in quite ambiguous terms, utilizing oblique language (Shenkar and Zeira, 1992; Kidd and Teramoto, 1995b). Interpretation rests with the middle managers. The decomposition–recombination process is well supported in Japanese firms by the single-year cadre who, even if dispersed round the world in their subsidiaries, will discuss intensely the meaning of the 'data' with respect to the organizations' intentions. This cadre have learned to respect each other and to support each other as they garner 'organizational learning' year by year. As they become more senior these managers may be dispersed to subsidiaries at home or abroad, or may even become managers in Keiretsu subcontractors. Nevertheless they will actively co-operate to promote their self-perceived managerial role of 'combination' and so be better able to guide their more junior staff.

Although the Italian cadres of managers are organized in 'family' units they receive quite direct visionary statements from the CEOs. The seniors have to be clear in their mission statements, since their middle managers, whilst leaders, are not the thinkers and combiners of concepts and data as in Japan. Furthermore, the process of 'combination' in Japanese firms is by preference a face-to-face process, while the more individualistic Occidental persons tend to use their technological support and look to electronic mail to pass messages quickly to their colleagues.

Stage 4 – Internalization: from explicit to tacit (operational knowledge)
Nonaka suggests this mode is close to 'learning by doing' and says it is only by absorbing and sharing the prior stages of socialization, externalization, and combination that an individual can develop his or her own internal assets, and thus bring them to bear upon the context and aims of the company. Furthermore, Nonaka suggests these internalizations are aided by the use of documentation, the creation of manuals and by oral traditions. Following this stage he suggests the knowledge spiral may commence again as an individual revises his/her world-view so leading to a new spiral of learning, commencing once more with new 'learning by doing', but at a more informed level.

We noted earlier the strength given to an organization by the oral tradition: something that is often overlooked – the 'war stories', the jokes, relating the little ways that individuals have found to make their organizational lives easier. Orr (1990) reviewed the stories that repair workers used to exchange. He found they operated a cohesive 'community of practice' that went far beyond the formal training given upon the design and operation of the machines they were repairing. This 'internalization' through such informal action programmes develops organizational learning, which combines at this fourth stage to uplift the organization along the spiral to the next phase of re-examining the tacit knowledge-base.

The knowledge spiral

Nonaka does not comment on the time to complete one cycle of the 'knowledge spiral', but clearly it is long. Naturally he has relied on the maintenance of the historic expectation of the 'job-for-life' that was the tradition in Japan, with staff 'promotion' and interfirm exchanges well organized so the juniors may perceive new parts of the organization. In many Japanese firms the organized personnel programme ensures that knowledge diffusion and acquisition take place in a planned fashion.

In many countries of Europe, prior to the demise of the iron, coal and shipbuilding firms there was a tradition of 'jobs-for-life' and even longer (!)

as sons succeeded fathers at the same enterprise. But there was no tradition and thus no support of the learning systems portrayed by Nonaka. This has led Japanese managers in the United Kingdom, for instance, to express surprise at the wealth of hidden skills at shop floor levels, yet also horror at the lack of networking or comradeliness that is normal in Japan when juniors and seniors stay after hours to work and to socialize. However, it has been shown in the United Kingdom that if innovation is directed towards cost cutting, and if benefits fall to the individual from teamwork, then a Kaizen-like atmosphere can be created; see Lewis (1995). But we see one difference – in Japan the staff (still) work generously for the firm, while Lewis finds continuous improvements in the UK only occur if individuals perceive a benefit. This is also likely to be the case in Italy (but for different reasons) as Italians first look to self-benefit, then to support their city, and a long way third to support their nation: Trompenaars (1993).

Classification of respondents

We found the sample of Japanese enterprises in Italy could be characterized by (i) the Italian situation, (ii) the relationships between themselves and their European regional HQ (if one existed), and (iii) their relationships with their headquarters in Japan. By this we mean the degree to which the firms may be seen to be more or less autonomously managed. However, localization of management is confounded with their capitalization, the origin of their equipment, and the development of their technology. These aspects are fully discussed by Songini *et al.* (1993).

We found, not surprisingly, that the dialogues between the Japanese managers and the Italian managers were fraught with difficulty as each party attempted to learn about the verbal and non-verbal exchanges that constitute their conversations. In entering a new market or country, a company has to be adaptive to deal with everyday problems that arise in a different context from the one it knows well. According to Hall and Hall (1990) there is a high chance in these circumstances that the culture-bound interactions of each party in a joint venture may cause a bewildering breakdown of good will as each person looks unfavourably on the 'demands' of the other. Yet interactions between individuals who are often very different in terms of culture, education and language can lead to new ideas or to new conceptualizations of what one of the parties already understands in their own-culture paradigm. Such transfers of knowledge take time. For instance, in one Japanese–Italian joint venture company – according to the Japanese management – 'the firm was not yet ready' to implement small-group activities within their factories, notwithstanding the fact that the company had operated in Italy since 1974. Similarly, while lean production and total quality concepts have long been promoted in Italy (typically in accord with

Table 7.2 Degree to which firms implemented the Nonaka stages

Nonaka stages	Degree of implementation		
	Strong	Average	Weak
1	F, H, K	A, C, D, E	B, G, I, J, L, M
2	F, H, K, D	B, C, J	A, E, G, I, L, M
3	F, H, K	B, D, G, M	A, C, E, I, J, L
4	F, H, K	G, I, M	A, B, C, D, E, J, L

Monden, 1994), the significant aspects of these innovations have taken time to be understood, absorbed, and thus implemented by Italian managers.

The data collected by the questionnaire and derived from the interviews prompted one to consider the exchange of knowledge between the donor (the Japanese firm offering machinery, capital and know-how) and the receiving firms (the Italians with their location in the European Union, their flair and their creativity). The model of organizational learning proposed by Nonaka seemed to hold promise in terms of allowing a subjective mapping to be made of the sampled firms with respect to the degree of fit to the model – and upon their management of their knowledge acquisition.

Table 7.2 shows the consolidated results of mapping the four stages of the Nonaka model against the degree to which the firms met each stage. Only three firms were thought to be 'strong' learners over all four stages. Otherwise no firms were consistently mapped wholly in the 'average' or the 'weak' categories of implementation (except for firm L).

Resulting contrasts between stages and firms

This research follows the model of learning postulated by Nonaka. However, we did not utilize any research instrument that would enable automatic categorization so naturally there is a degree of subjectivity in the interpretation of the data. We concentrate discussion on the 'strong' firms of the four stages and mention why other firms did not fare so well. The 'strong' firms were observed in three or four sectors – in chemical processing, electronic and electrical, and heavy vehicles sectors.

Stage 1 (socialization)   The 'strong' firms at this stage exhibited what has become commonplace in world-class firms – clear instructions are posted throughout the workplace. These are useful in many stages of the learning process, not just for the development of one's tacit knowledge, but for the successive stages where individuals can 'get together' and review their common findings or points that are of concern, not just to themselves but to others. In these firms there was ample evidence that training is taking place. The training might involve trips to Japan to learn how the parent firm sets up its machines and undertakes production and quality control, and to learn ahead of time how to use new machines prior to them being transplanted to the Italian firm. Moreover, this form of training develops the tacit knowledge of individuals, and it will join together the body of tacit knowledge in Japan as well as in Italy.

In the less-good firms we saw evidence of elitism. Attitudes were held by both the Japanese and by the Italians that prevented their minds being opened to better practices. Sometimes a heavy top-down management style prevented changes to working practices or precluded the peer group discussion that is the vital element at this stage of learning. As mentioned above, the focusing of the mind at the workplace through the use of diagrams, work hints or simple personal notes relating to 'work-arounds' leads to the development of tacit knowledge – stop the chit-chat, and gratuitous learning is reduced.

Also, if the work involved only 'screwdriver' assembly, there was no thought given to the amelioration of the boredom of the workforce. No opportunities were offered to empower these workers to discuss new methods of assembly – perhaps because the parent firm was stressing strongly all aspects of compliance with their original assembly specifications to achieve quality assurance. Naturally the latter is vital in any organization – but a little explanation given to the workforce would have inclined them to develop their tacit knowledge for their task, and potentially could have jump-started the firm along its knowledge learning track.

Stage 2 (externalization)   The firms that were 'strong' in Stage 1 were actively consolidating their tacit learning through displays at information points of plans and diagrams. These allow discussions to take place between peers and with persons from different parts of the firm, leading to the general betterment of the processes. During our interviews we were often offered quick tours of the site. In the 'strong' firms we observed there was an active involvement of the CEO in this display process: he (rarely she) often pointed out with some pride the utilization of this technique. It was clear the CEO *expected* the workforce to gather at these points and become more aware of the issues confronting individuals, groups, or the firm as a whole, and thus come to a resolution of a problem if it was within the power of the peer group.

In contrast, in our 'walkabouts' in weaker firms we heard the CEOs or senior managers making strong criticisms of the workforce, the factory layout, and other matters. While it was in their best interests to negotiate different systems that would facilitate the learning programme it was clear this was not taking place. Sometimes the strong notion of hierarchy (projected by both the Italians and the Japanese) prevented peer discussions on how to alleviate a process issue. All communications in these cases were being directed to the CEO, so tended to be lost in the mass of detail unless brought to a boiling point to generate a discussion. At this point the Japanese would feel they had lost face and the Italians might be thinking of strike action.

It might be clear by now that the Nonaka model may be used to map the performance of firms – if they can learn to work better, and smarter, they might raise their competitive advantage. If management actively prevents the workforce, or the middle administrators, learning better skills through the development of their tacit knowledge we may expect the general performance of the firm to decline.

Stage 3 (combination)   In the small number of better firms there were indications that their Italian 'inventions' were being transferred back to Japan through a process of dialogue: it may have been related to the generation of novel chemical processes, the use of materials created from machines originating in Japan, or the ergonomic layout of controls in vehicles organized to suit the European market. Italian flair, if you like, is treasured by the Japanese – they appreciated the creativity of the Italian persons. This form of praise rubbed off on the Italians, so they strove to do better through the better combination of their working practices and mental models. Once more the Nonaka model seems to 'fit' – tacit knowledge is appreciated, and 'war stories' and narrative are allowed to develop, so creating a new awareness of solutions that filter back to the head office in Japan.

In the average and weaker firms we perceived an overall pressure to conform to some ideal, be it the Japanese or Italian way of working or behaving. In some sense we may imagine powerful individuals sulking because of not getting their own way – and this might be transferred to the workforce to generate, in turn, a general sense of the firm sulking and being petulant. Whatever! The result is that an impasse is perceived by the staff, which prevents a good exchange of data and, more important, the development of cross-cultural models for the betterment of the persons: thus the firm is denied its rightful progress.

Stage 4 (internalization)   The strong firms in the fourth mode of Nonaka's model exhibit a liveliness that is in sharp contrast to the less-good firms. The workers in the good firms even look more alive – and seem to express a joy in being asked to carry responsibilities. Being empowered would be a description that would be well accepted by their staff. They have learned how to cope with their individual difficulties through their collective strength. They seem to be very Italian, and the Japanese offer little resistance to change.

The poorer firms continued with their difficulties inherited from their failure in Stages 2 and 3. No empowerment, no liveliness and so on – this led in some cases to an intense resistance to change, and to an intense wariness of 'the other side'. About one year after the survey one firm in the 'weak' segment of the matrix parted company with its partner – no doubt there were many reasons quoted officially for this action, but clearly they did not 'fit'; nor, in our terms, were they learning in their joint enterprise.

Discussion: following the 'Japanese way'?

Internationalization

In Italy in 1993 the Japanese companies seemed to be in the first phase of internationalization, in the sense that control was centralized in Japan, and that this control was exercised especially on capital and knowledge. For instance, a Japanese top manager in an office automation company told us 'that his parent company was sending a technical manager to their Italian joint-venture firm in order to complete the product development started in Japan, and to ensure that production *would follow* the designs made in Tokyo'. Conformity to quality specifications and to delivery performance are the most delicate criteria manufacturing companies must meet in order to be competitive. It is not surprising that several Japanese CEOs mentioned that quality control was an issue in the Italian subsidiaries. Yet to bring 'control from headquarters' in this way is to deny all forms of local organization learning – for both parties. Resentment would be the outcome – again for both parties due to their joint misunderstanding of the developing conflicts.

Strong control is also exercised by the Japanese parent firm with respect to managerial performance. When discussing human resource management, one manager said it was his opinion that local managers should head-up the European operations; but he said that senior Japanese managers in Tokyo did not agree, because of the high performance required. To some extent this refers to the expectation of long hours attending work (expected by the Japanese of the Japanese with their belief that other nationals do not put in such a long working week), and to some extent to the Japanese top managers' expectation that senior managers must be generalists. The former reason is not true anywhere in Europe – senior managers have to work long hours – but being a generalist is less often seen, as many senior managers rise from a functional specialization. Further problems arise if one adds the requirement of having worked in at least one other country prior to a senior appointment – and thus another issue relates to language skills. The European subsidiaries of a typical Japanese transnational firm use many European languages – German, English, French, Spanish and so on. For operational purposes within the Japanese–Italian firm at least three languages were needed, yet there were generally no senior Italian persons able to satisfy fully this requirement. Thus we are left with the unsatisfactory placement of a senior Japanese executive, able to speak English, and the senior Italian manager having to converse carefully in English on some detailed point that would be better addressed in Italian (or Japanese) but not via a common third language poorly understood by both parties.

There are differing perceptions on these points. Across Europe 92.9 per cent of surveyed personnel in Japanese manufacturing firms say there is 'enough autonomy to perform normal operations': JETRO (1994: 23). In the same survey there is said to be some difficulty in southern European countries (Spain, Italy and Portugal) in 'employing capable personnel' (quoted by 50 per cent of respondents), which is exacerbated by these same firms stating there is 'no need to employ a local-national CEO since their operations scale is small' (35.9 per cent of respondents) (ibid.: 25). In these countries only a few local staff are given senior responsibility, thus there are a high proportion of Japanese CEOs (in 57.6 per cent of firms). This aspect is out of tune with Japanese ventures in northern Europe, where there are a greater number of Japanese companies, most of which display a more egalitarian approach to the filling of senior positions by non-Japanese nationals.

Power base and decision making

Several Italian subsidiaries seemed to support firmly an 'Italian' form of management – very hierarchical, and very oriented towards the CEO as though he/she were a biological father. This structure is close to a traditional Japanese organization structure, except that the Japanese firm supports stronger peer group interactions and stronger superior/subordinate interactions in semi-informal situations (over drinks, after hours). Often the situation in Italy is rigidly hierarchical, and knowledge creation is limited by the power distribution, which creates a barrier against motivation – partly by not rewarding a positive attitude to knowledge creation. Of course this may be a consequence of factors quoted by Hall and Hall (1989, 1990) – the mismatch of contexts between parties. Some large joint ventures are hierarchical because one or both partners are themselves large organizations, and they have attempted to replicate their original structures. But this does not rule out the ability to support self-learning institutions in the joint alliances.

The Japanese have manufactured in Europe since 1966 (Pentel in France, and YKK in England) so they have gained many valuable managerial experiences, which now span several layers of the hierarchies in many major firms. Over this time indigenous Europeans have regarded employment by Japanese firms as a challenge, but not a sideline issue. In Italy it is only in recent years that first-class graduates and technicians have begun to enter Japanese firms since the (traditional) prestige and power the large Japanese firms enjoy in Japan is not so strongly evident in Europe at large, and least of all in Italy. In turn we see the Japanese managers also resisting a posting to a 'weak' country, which would not benefit their personal promotion: often they perceive their term of expatriation as a sideways promotion within their peer group. Thus at the commencement of an alliance the chiefs of both sides bring with them a hidden resentment, which is masked by the commercial need for the alliance, but which may surface later as hidden agendas become more open. This may be more evident in the Italian situation in contrast to Japanese ventures in northern Europe.

We found that specific organizational mechanisms such as a decision-making system, or personnel development schemes, differ according to the source of initial development – at the headquarters in Japan, or locally in Italy – although the implementation was independent of the nationality and gender of the CEO. However, a system such as the Japanese decision-making method, based on *nemawashi* and *ringi*, does little to motivate the Italian workforce – they are not able to see a goal however hard they try. This in turn contributes to the demotivation of individual skills and hence diminishes the search for knowledge acquisition. Although the *nemawashi* process is embedded in the first two stages of the Nonaka model, to disavow this process reflects the resistance to change by the Italians. If the *nemawashi* process is forced into the Italian firm, that decision reflects an insensitivity to the host partners by the Japanese. Due to the consequent unrest new organizational knowledge creation is also attenuated, although there may never be an explicit declaration to not search for it.

Information flows

There is a lack of horizontal communication between Italian companies in a given region. This contrasts starkly with the strong flow of verbal communication and the human networking of Japanese personnel between the Japanese head office(s), their European regional headquarters, and their local units. It is also unusual to find Italians moving from the local Japanese company to another European unit of the same firm. This effect is not unique to Italy – it has been observed elsewhere, in the UK, in France and Germany. With respect to data flows it is evident that the normal operational model in Italy is one of a centralized system, with the 'top' localized in Japan, but occasionally localized in a European regional headquarters administrative operation. There is a perception that little data flows 'down' to the Italian firm. These effects tend to slow down the acquisition of tacit knowledge by the Italians, and are a source of frustration for the 'tacitly' inclined Japanese managers.

It seldom happens that there is a flow of technology and know-how from local units towards their head offices. There are some exceptions. In the fashion and design sectors, Italy is among the world leaders, and the Japanese acknowledge this pre-eminence by requesting their subsidiaries in these sectors to deliver not only profits but know-how to the Japanese partner. We learned also that an Italian subsidiary in furniture and car industry products developed marketing strengths far greater than the Japanese parent would have imagined. Herein the Japanese managers declared that without the Italians it would have been difficult to reach satisfactory levels in product differentiation and marketing. On the other hand, companies in Japan who attempt to make use of Western technology, products and other managerial resources, as elsewhere in the world, are quite capable of invoking the NIH (not invented here) syndrome. That being so, the originators of the knowledge become depressed, sulk, and reduce their knowledge creation programme – 'Why bother?' is their cry.

Conclusions

The management of organization learning in Italy

We suggest that knowledge creation in Italy is influenced by three factors:

- the degree of local decision-making responsibility
- the presence of specific organizational mechanisms, both Japanese and Italian
- the clarity of the company objectives

The degree of local decision-making responsibility determines the capacity to generate and maintain autonomous knowledge-creating structures such as project teams, quality circles and organized small-group activity in keeping with the staff's perception of 'the Italian way'.

The importance of the alliance's objectives in Italy is fundamental in defining the presence and the possibility of supporting knowledge creation. If the company objective is simply to manufacture industrial products based on an imported process (at worse, the assembly of a kit of parts as a 'screw-driver operation'), it is difficult to see how new ideas and new knowledge may come out of these activities, be recognized as such, and be appreciated as a resource by the management team.

All companies declared their focus was on good productivity and the need to improve it through training and incentive systems. There should there-fore be a mechanism to motivate and involve people, especially local em-ployees. If the intent is to copy the Japanese processes the shortest cut is to send newly hired people to Japan, to a factory of the mother company, so on returning home they would be able to apply what they learned. They would be able to train their colleagues who stayed at home. Tacit and explicit knowledge exchanges are acknowledged by some Italian managers, but only one declared that 'we have learnt much from the Japanese, yet we are still independent in terms of technology and products'. At another site, the top Italian manager declared that 'as for creativity, the Italians are better, but for technical programs the Japanese are better, because they are precise, thanks to their different education'. But another Italian manager suggested 'there is too much individualism in Italy, and the "orchestra" requires too much attention to maintain harmony', which seems to say that the Italians will not spend the time needed to learn on a voluntary basis, only if pushed and guided by the CEO.

The applicability of Nonaka's model

The categorization of the 'Italian' production firms according to their responses to the questionnaire and according to the knowledge gained during the informal interviews suggests that it is possible to use Nonaka's model as a measuring tool. It allows insights to be made of the modus operandi of the firms. That being so, we may suggest his model has wider applicability than solely in Japanese firms having highly motivated workforces. It may be applicable to other Japanese alliances outside Italy, and even to non-Japanese firms.

However, there are some limitations to this conclusion. The review presented here is based on a small sample of firms, it is highly subjective, and there was no consistent test instrument applied to measure how well the firms met the criteria of each stage. And it is based upon Italian firms inclined to work with the Japanese in joint ventures. Nevertheless, earlier we noted research that indicated the broad nature of tacit knowledge generation, the way in which this may be shared, and thus how the firm benefits finally from a level of learning that was never explicitly put in place by the management. To the extent that this knowledge creation has been observed in different cultural settings we might accept that Nonaka's model may be generalizable and that it may offer a base by which firms can be compared.

Final remarks

Only three firms seemed to perform well over all four stages along the lines suggested by Nonaka. These are firms managed strongly by Italian CEOs. The Japanese partners herein work in conjunction, but in the background, offering technology, techniques and important financial support. In return the Japanese partners receive the benefits of strong product support in a 'happy' organizational environment. We may say the Italian managers themselves have initially absorbed some Japanese-ness and retranslated this to the Italian context for the benefit of their staff's learning. In these cases international contextual conflicts seem have been contained (at least to boardroom discussions). They are not apparent to the middle and lower management levels where Italian elitism, creativity and flair are controlled and guided by a respected Italian 'parent figure', who is clearly seen to be 'the boss'.

In the less good firms (in a Nonaka sense, though sometimes performing less well according to commercial economic indicators) we see there is more 'interference' by the Japanese managers – allowing conflicts to arise from divided loyalties. The Japanese perceive the Italians to be too 'theoretical' and not aligned to the practicalities of management. In turn, the Italians perceive the joint venture to be managed remotely from Japan; so the local Italian managers become strongly hierarchical, inward looking and apparently unhelpful, and the workforce follows suit.

We are not saying that the Japanese venture into Italy, date-lined in 1993, is a failure; far from it. Most of the firms were financially sound (notwithstanding the general difficulties with the lira, and the European recession). We are suggesting that there is a very strong culture and context clash that makes Japanese hands-on management quite problematical in Italy. But when there is a little freedom left for the Italian manager, better results have been achieved.

References

Argyris, C. and Schön, D.A. (1978) *Organizational Learning: a Theory of Action Perspective*. Reading, MA: Addison-Wesley.

Bartlett, C.A. and Ghoshal, S. (1989) *Managing Across Borders*. Cambridge, MA: Harvard University Press.

Brown, J.S. and Duguid, P. (1991) 'Organisational Learning and Communities-of-Practice: Towards a Unified View of Working, Learning, and Innovation', *Organisational Science* 2: 40–57.

Cook, S.D.N. and Yanow, D. (1993) 'Culture and Organisational Learning', *Journal of Management Enquiry* 2: 373–390.

Donnellon, A., Gray, B. and Bourgon, M.G. (1986) 'Communication, Meaning, and Organised Action', *Administrative Science Quarterly* 31: 43–55.

Hall, E.T. and Hall, M.R. (1989) *Understanding Cultural Differences: Germans, French and Americans*. Yarmouth, ME: Intercultural Press.

Hall, E.T. and Hall, M.R. (1990) *Understanding Cultural Differences*. Yarmouth, ME: Intercultural Press.

Hirschhorn, L. (1984) *Beyond Mechanisation: Work and Technology in a Postindustrial Age*. Cambridge, MA: MIT Press.

Huber, G.P. (1991) 'Organisational Learning: The Contributing Processes and the Literatures', *Organizational Science* 2(1): 88–115.

JETRO (1994) '10th Survey of European Operations of Japanese Companies in the Manufacturing Sector', *JETRO*, October.

Kogono, T., Nonaka, I., Sakakibara, K. and Omura, A. (1985) *Strategic vs Evolutionary Management: A US–Japan comparison of Strategy and Organisation*. Amsterdam: North-Holland.

Kidd, J.B. and Teramoto, Y. (1995a) 'Can the Japanese Localise? A Study of Japanese Production Subsidiaries in the UK', in S.-J. Park and M. Jovanovic (eds) *What is Behind the Japanese Miracle?*, pp. 136–152. London: Megatrends I.E.C.

Kidd, J.B. and Teramoto, Y. (1995b) 'The Learning Organisations: The Case of the Japanese RHQs in Europe', *Management International Review* 35(2): 39–56.

Lewis, K.C.E. (1995) *Kaizen: The Right Approach to Continuous Improvement*. Kempston: IFS International.

Monden, Y. (1994) *Toyota Production System: An Integrated Approach to Just-in-Time*, 2nd edn. London: Chapman & Hall.

Nelson, R.R. and Winter, S.G. (1982) *An Evolutionary Theory of Economic Change*. Cambridge, MA: Belknap Press.

Nonaka, I. (1991) 'The Knowledge-Creating Company', *Harvard Business Review* (Nov–Dec): 96–104.

Nonaka, I. (1994) 'A Dynamic Theory of Organizational Knowledge Creation', *Organizational Science* 5(1): 14–37.

Nonaka, I. and Takeuchi, H. (1995) *The Knowledge-creating Company*. Oxford: Oxford University Press.

Orr, J.E. (1990) 'Sharing Knowledge, Celebrating Identity', in D.S. Middleton and D. Edwards (eds) *Collective Remembering*. Newbury Park, CA: Sage, pp.169–189.

Polanyi, M. (1962) *The Tacit Dimension*. London: Routledge.

Prahalad, C.K. and Hamel, G. (1991) 'The Core Competence of the Corporation', *Harvard Business Review* 68(3): 79–91.

Scribner, S., Di Bello, L., Kindred, J. and Zazanis, E. (1991) *Co-ordinating Two Knowledge Systems: A Case Study*. New York: CUNY Laboratory for Cognitive Studies of Work.

Shenkar, O. and Zeira, Y. (1992) 'Role Conflict and Role Ambiguity of Chief Executive Officers in International Joint Ventures', *International Business Studies* 23(1): 55–75.

Songini, L., Gnan, L., Inumaru, K., Kidd, J.B., Teramoto, Y. and Piciozzi, F. (1993) 'Global Study on Management Issues in Italian–Japanese Subsidiaries', Presentation to Euro-Asia Management Studies Association 10th annual meeting, Nürnberg, November.

Trompenaars, F. (1993) *Riding the Waves of Culture: Understanding Cultural Diversity in Business*. London: The Economist Books.

Wertsch, J.V. (1985) *Vygotsky and the Social Formation of Mind*. Cambridge, MA: Harvard University Press.

Chapter 8

Managing institutional change and the pressures for new approaches to teaching and learning

Bruce King

John Bottomley (2000) has argued that education institutions in developed countries face a set of common challenges stemming from two decades of economic, political and sociocultural change. Indeed, the significance of these challenges is not limited to educational institutions; they are also creating a move towards flexible learning practices in the labour market and workplace. This chapter will consider the impact of such change specifically on the patterns of teaching and learning, and change management within higher education.

The general socio-political changes have created two main pressures for internal change within higher education institutions (HEIs). First, the context within which HEIs now have to operate influences the ways in which they approach change (and the rate at which these changes can occur). Second, there is more specific pressure for creating a new, more flexible teaching and learning climate, and for those administering HEIs to manage this change. These pressures have an impact on the organisational culture of HEIs, in that they dictate the way institutions deal with change and they require a fundamental shift in one particular part of their core activity – the delivery of teaching and learning programmes.

The issue for management is how to address the complexity of the required changes in circumstances. For instance, in areas where there is likely to be both internal resistance to changes in the core values embedded in current practices, and where conditions allow little scope for solutions, there is a requirement for significant additional expenditure.

Change and management in higher education institutions

There is some measure of agreement on the kinds of powerful forces affecting HEIs. Bradley (1997b: 1) identifies:

This is an edited version of an article previously published in V. Jukupec and J. Garrick (eds) *Flexible Learning: Human Resource Management*. 2000. Reproduced by permission of Taylor & Francis Ltd.

- globalisation of economic systems;
- rapid development of communications technologies, which are revolutionising both the way we do things and our contact with people across the globe;
- changing patterns of work and employment; and
- growing economic and social inequalities within and between nations.

Reid (1997: 1) mirrors some of these and adds:

- the political economy of higher education;
- the reconfiguration of knowledge within and between traditional fields of scholarship;
- the increasingly interventionist tendencies of government, the professions and employers;
- the funding and deregulation of higher education;
- competition for the potential client base for universities.

Both Bradley and Reid are vice chancellors of new Australian universities, moderately large institutions by the standards of that country, and each with a distinctive social agenda reflecting the needs of their local communities. As such, they are particularly aware of the difficulties confronting the institutions they are attempting to bring to maturity. But they are not alone. Reid (1997: 1) points to the remarkable similarity of 'multiple reforms and policy shifts of the last decade' across HEIs in OECD countries. Salter and Tapper (cited in Dopson and McNay, 1996) argue that these pressures are the attempts of governments to gain some degree of control over a university system that was educationally 'elitist' relating to 'pedagogical' merit and access policies. It was also costly and without much 'diversity'.

This is reflected in the English perspective of Ford et al. (1996: 8) who point to such pressures on all institutions arising from:

- the 'massification' of education;
- competition and control;
- changing student profiles;
- the demand for provision of learning resources.

These elements have all been present in the policies of reformist governments in Australia, but the election of a conservative coalition government in 1996 led to a changed political perspective. Simon Marginson (1998) has addressed what he describes as the 'deepening crisis' of Australian universities, comprising 'three mutually reinforcing but individually distinct' elements:

- the resource crisis caused by the decline in government funding, linked to a declining commitment to the nation-building role of the universities;

- the identity crisis caused by the corporatisation of internal university systems and cultures;
- and the crisis of global strategy: how do Australian universities make their way in a globalising university environment?

(Marginson, 1998: 3–4)

Marginson (1998: 5) holds that the proportion of government contribution to university funding in Australia dropped from 90 per cent to 60 per cent in the preceding decade. The implications of this have been dramatic. Large universities have abandoned courses long considered part of the stable provision of higher education. Ford *et al.* (1996: 9) comment on HEIs in the United Kingdom: 'Public sector funding per student has fallen by twenty-seven percent in the past five years and is likely to fall another ten percent, in real terms, over the next three years.' They say that 'it is increasingly difficult to maintain conventional patterns of working and traditional models of teaching and learning'.

The situation has become sufficiently serious that Sir John Daniel (1998: 2) has proposed cost reduction as one of the five aims to be pursued in the development of higher education programmes, the others being access, quality, flexibility and innovation. In an attempt to compensate for declining government revenue, institutions have been encouraged to adopt *user-pays* approaches, which bring additional pressures such as greater public surveillance and accountability for the provision of quality services. Politicians have been keen to exploit this new level of public accountability to ensure that universities are more efficient and attuned to the market place, and also to support government definitions of education and training. Such definitions at present are somewhat impoverished as they rest upon the interrelated rhetoric of industrial needs for a trained workforce, the 'user-pays' principle and instrumental views of education.

Funding cuts are accompanied by other pressures that compound their impact, for example the movement from elite to mass systems of higher education. Increased participation in higher education was a success of the Labor Governments in Australia between 1985 and 1995, with an increase in participation of 17- to 19-year-olds rising from 90 to 172 per thousand (Gallagher, 1997: 3). In Britain over 30 per cent of 18-year-olds entered higher education in 1996, and the projected increase was 40 per cent by the end of the century (Ford *et al.*, 1996: 9). This put pressure on HEIs both to do more with less government support and to increase their quality. As Yetton and Associates (1997: 2) observe, institutions differ in quality and 'they [students] can't all go to the "old" universities'. This commits institutions not just to increasing efficiency but also continuous improvement. Ford and his colleagues (1996: 12) argue that HEIs 'will increasingly have to adopt a typical service-based marketing approach' by asking such questions as:

- What are the investment factors that will determine how likely the institution is to acquire its funding?
- How will the balance be split between teaching and research?
- How important is teaching to a learning environment, how important is research?
- Is specialisation likely to lead to a satisfactory conclusion or will wider choice attract more students?
- Where are students likely to come from?
- What are students looking for?
- Are some students more financially attractive than others?
- Can we build a 'learning product' that will be attractive to them?
- Can we define and afford a learning infrastructure that will attract our target students?
- How do we publicise ourselves to our market?

(Ford *et al.*, 1996: 11)

I have no doubt that some of these questions would be anathemas to many academics; equally I am conscious that they are part of the day-to-day considerations of management in my own institution. What is at issue is the nature of the institution's organisational culture. Dopson and McNay (1996) consider this to be:

> a combination of rituals, routines, myths and symbols that give very clear messages about what is seen as acceptable and unacceptable behaviour. However, an organization's culture is also influenced by the way in which power is distributed in the organization, and how work is structured and controlled. Culture is therefore a combination of values, structure and power that has implications for every aspect of an organization's operations and external relationships.
>
> (Dopson and McNay, 1996: 20–21)

They continue:

> We also know from research in this area that there are other important influences on cultures, including the history, traditions and 'ownership' of the organization, its size, goals and objectives, the technology it operates with, the nature of the workforce and the environment in which it is situated.
>
> (Dopson and McNay, 1996: 20)

The questions from Ford and his colleagues are resisted by many academics because they are seen to bring such matters as the organisation's history, traditions and ownership into contest. Dopson and McNay (1996) cite Warren who suggested that when polytechnics became universities, they began to abandon the main features of collegiality, which were the corner-stones of their substantiality and vivacity. This led the new universities to display the signs of staff antipathy, contention and disharmony, together with bureaucratic-anomic life.

This is somewhat tendentious, but the point is important. For many academics, the demise of collegiality, i.e. the embodiment of institutional 'ownership', and the concomitant rise of managerialism in higher education strikes at the very nature of the 'enterprise'. Yet all universities are now more or less 'managed' institutions. In Australia, this is the product of quite explicit government policy (DEET, 1993), which saw intervention as appropriate to help bring about:

- strong managerial culture;
- consultation and accountability to government and other stakeholders;
- streamlined decision taking;
- institutional flexibility and efficiency of operations.

Four points need to be made about this. First, it is not simply the 'new' universities where problems exist. Government demands for efficiency, relevance and accountability are directed to higher education systems as much as individual institutions. Second, the recourse to private sector managerialism has occurred because HEIs have not themselves paid serious attention to the distinctive kinds of organisational management they might require at a time when the context within which they operate has forced significant change upon them (Tapper and Salter, cited in Dopson and McNay, 1996). Third, while there is academic resistance to new forms of HEI management, this is by no means consistent within institutions. Generally, university administrations are criticised by their own staff on two fronts. There are those who despise the kinds of changes being forced upon higher education and who regard 'management' as having capitulated to pressure that it should have resisted. Others, who have embraced entrepreneurialism in higher education, regard management as slowing them down by insisting on levels of internal accountability that frustrate their capacity to operate within the wider economy. Fourth, the conservative Coalition Government elected in Australia in 1996 removed some of the intervention of its predecessors but placed even greater reliance on market forces, competition and increasing privatisation of higher education institutions as mechanisms for improving overall quality in the sector (Meek and Wood, 1998: 4–6).

Like it or not, the relative insulation of universities from the wider community and the economy has disappeared. The need to deal in commercial terms with industry and the business end of the professions has posed substantial challenges to the culture of HEIs and in particular their decision-making structures, which are regarded by other elements of the community as incredibly slow and inefficient. The scale of change required involves a necessary shift in approach to management, administrative procedures, staffing arrangements and patterns of internal funding. The challenge for those who lead HEIs is how to bring such a complex range of changes about in circumstances where there is likely to be internal resistance to new practices and where there is little (or diminished) possibility for extra funding.

As a result, Ford *et al.* (1996: 33) argue that HEIs ought to consider:

- redefinition of their business scope;
- identification of core activities;
- assessment of the physical, human and intellectual resources available to them;
- assessment of the market at local, national and international levels;
- identification of strategies for exploitation that maximise quality and minimise costs.

These are critical dimensions of a comprehensive strategy for bringing change about in a large institution, but they are not sufficient to ensure success in higher education. I would also add a number of other elements, including:

- new organisational structures;
- consultative relationships with the stakeholders in the core enterprise;
- a planning and quality improvement cycle, including benchmarking;
- systematic development of a supportive administrative and technical infrastructure;
- introduction of an enterprise culture that incorporates both project management and business planning for new developments;
- a system of rewards for staff;
- appropriate processes for professional development.

I would now like to comment briefly on each of these additional elements.

New organisational structures

The organisational structures of higher education institutions tend to reflect some or all of the following:

- enterprise dimensions, e.g. management, administration and specialist support activities;
- areas of academic specialisation by field of study or cognate groupings of such fields;
- decision-making and approvals mechanisms, usually stressing collegial or representative group processes, with some acknowledgement of senior discipline expertise, e.g. the professoriate.

In very large part, the organisational structures are one embodiment of the culture of the institution. While it is not necessary for it to be so, they have frequently become barriers to change, constrained any customer orientation in the provision of services, reinforced exclusionary practices relating to diversification of the clientele or core business, and supported particular views of excellence based on selectivity, individualism, the quality of inputs rather than outcomes and increasing specialisation.

No distinctive organisational model for higher education has developed from within the sector and it may be that the best that can be achieved is 'competent leadership and managerial efficiency' drawing on private sector experience (Tapper and Salter cited in Dopson and McNay, 1996). What is critical is that institutions develop an organisational structure that can accommodate prompt decision taking within a framework that supports quality operations in areas of core business. Without wishing to recommend one particular approach over another, it is worth noting that several Australian universities are currently experimenting with larger rather than smaller aggregations of fields of study, in part to create a critical mass sufficient to afford the resource capacity to innovate and develop expertise in areas such as support for quality teaching and learning, application of new technologies to core business and revenue generation.

Consultative relationships with stakeholders

The need for consultation with stakeholders is in part simple recognition of the changing expectations of students, employers and the community at large about what universities do and who should judge the quality of how they discharge their function. Gallagher (1997: 8) cites one of Australia's most senior higher education civil servants as stating, 'the public will want to know more about provider capacity, performance, customer service and quality . . . Higher education providers will need to know their costs, their competitive advantages and their comparative performance.' This view has been reinforced by notions of user-pays in the provision of HEI services, increasing reliance on externally imposed performance indicators and published ratings of institutional performance, government-initiated audits of quality and the pressure of competition. There is increasing concern about self-assertion of quality in higher education, one manifestation of which is the expectation of certain generic attributes in the university graduates in addition to their subject expertise. This is reflected in the activity-based curriculum of such British institutions as Oxford Brookes University, Alverno college in the United States and the focus on developing graduate qualities in the Australian Technology Network Universities (see, for example, Otter, 1998).

Planning and quality improvement cycle

Planning and quality improvement cycles gained significant impetus in Australia from the establishment of a government-initiated quality audit process that rewarded and ranked institutions both on their achievements and the processes they implemented to ensure quality outcomes. Nonetheless, there can be a tendency for internal planning processes to be paper exercises, producing worthy documentation that bears varying degrees of relationship to what actually occurs within the component parts of the institution and destined for most of its life to gather dust. Competition and resource constraints will force HEIs to move to more sophisticated and helpful planning activity. To put it bluntly, if a discipline team cannot answer the question: 'Do staff know what courses will be introduced in three years time, why they will be, and what level of support they have from the relevant professional groupings?', then that part of the institution is just muddling along.

Supportive administrative and technical infrastructure

The administrative and support infrastructure of an HEI is an increasingly complex undertaking. The increase in the proportion of 17- to 19-year-olds moving to higher education has been accompanied by a greater diversification in the student body and consequently a greater range of student learning needs and expectations of support. Dopson and McNay (1996: 18) invoke the cybernetic law: 'a system must be as internally complex as is appropriate to reflect the degree of external complexity it has to face'. To which one would add, it must also be congruent (in the sense of the administrative system being sympathetic to the assumptions of the core business), appear as a seamless web of service to the clients and be sufficiently flexibly to cater for patterns of demand that fall outside conventional practice. The limitations of existing computer-based support and administrative systems are sometimes only recognised in their failure to accommodate an existing external demand. The presence of an outside agent can be a valuable stimulus. Open Learning Australia, which brokers subjects from several post-compulsory educational institutions on a fee-for-service basis, offers them to students in four teaching periods per year. The provider institutions typically found that their student information systems were incapable of dealing with such flexibility!

An enterprise culture

There are those in HEIs who do understand and operate with some success in contexts that derive their imperatives from the market place. Researchers who have an applied emphasis in their work and academics with personal experience in commerce and industry, often recruited precisely for that expertise, understand the pressures and time frames of business partners. Many, however, do not and often for quite good reasons. Factors mentioned previously, e.g. competition, customer service, revenue generation, account-ability and responsiveness to stakeholders have only taken on significant new force in recent years. Many academics have no training, indeed would have eschewed it, in business practice. Their professional context and the times supported them as discipline experts and, at best, talented amateurs in activities other than teaching and research. Projects undertaken with those outside HEIs were often characterised by:

- unrealistic time frames;
- ponderous and sometimes ineffective decision-taking processes;
- limited understanding of the actual costs associated with their activity;
- a failure to mount an adequate business case as part of the rationale for activity;
- quality asserted on the basis of inputs rather than demonstrated in outcomes;
- little sense of process management to bring collaborative activity to reso-lution.

In the current climate, these are the conditions of failure. HEIs have typi-cally sought to import such expertise as is necessary to cover these shortfalls, often in the form of business manager appointments or by establishing busi-ness development units to provide support for academics seeking to mount bids for funded project activity. This is only a partial solution. Until those who manage HEIs and a significant number of key academic staff within them develop some understanding and skill in such matters, then progress towards entrepreneurial and enterprise-based activity will be sluggish.

This has direct consequences for the development of teaching pro-grammes, too. Institutions can no longer sustain programmes offered on the basis of academic, rather than client, interest. The constraints on resources mean that responsible academics cannot justify demand for new courses on the basis of intuition; rather they require an adequately mounted business case, with defensible market research to establish levels of demand, likely competitors, and viability over time. This is particularly important in the case of distance education and flexibly delivered courses. Attention has to be given to the actual fixed and variable costs of production and delivery, the capacity to amortise expenditure over the years of offer, with some under-standing of the cost implications of methodological choices particularly where these involve new technologies. Without appropriate levels of busi-ness expertise, academics who conscientiously try to meet the changing mission of their institutions through their own endeavours can quite readily incur significant losses on activity.

Rewards for staff

If the changing context of higher education requires staff to operate in different ways, there is a legitimate question of whether institutional reward systems recognise their changed behaviour. Nunan (1996) has argued that the culture of HEIs is largely shaped by research and, in the case of teaching, focuses on the transmission of discipline knowledge. The consequence of the latter is 'a strong cultural devaluing of the concept of creating a learning environment as a part of intellectual work' (Nunan, 1996: 8). The enduring nature of cultural values suggests there will be resistance to different rewards systems. It will be argued later that a reorientation of teaching towards the creation of environments in which learning can occur is a critical part of the response of HEIs to the demands upon them. What is of consequence here is that despite the complexity of such an undertaking:

> the reward systems and measures of productivity are changed to account for skills and energies directed towards establishing teaching and learning environments where student learning interactions and outcomes are judged to be superior to other approaches.
>
> (Nunan, 1996: 8)

A similar argument could be made for other, non-traditional academic activity.

Appropriate processes for professional development

The new demands on HEIs changes the role of the professional developer. Bradley (1997a: 2) has argued that existing models of professional development in higher education not only fail to serve institutions but constrain action to bring about necessary change. She rejects prevailing collegial, professional service and counselling models (Webb, 1996) in favour of a model that recognises (1) whole-of-institution approaches to cultural change in pursuit of an agreed mission, (2) the contribution of all management positions to staff development and (3) a necessary commitment of staff developers to institutional strategic directions.

Bradley's prescription is to bring an analysis of strategic directions and planning about their achievement to the heart of professional development by having staff developers who:

- understand the strategic direction that the institution legitimates;
- are a part of the process of establishing the strategic direction;
- appraise the extent/strength of this legitimation;
- look for stakeholders and collaborators who will be affected by proposed changes;

- consider the processes that give effect to change – 'lighthouse examples, balance between top-down/bottom-up [strategies], working with collaborators';
- prepare the ground with 'starting points' to give effect to change through links with existing change processes and strategies for involving others;
- make judgements about strategic gains and the extent to which the change can take place, given particular contexts;
- do all the above in strategic dialogue with managers at all levels of the institution.

(Bradley, 1997a: 3)

Meeting the strategic commitments of the institution does not mean strictly educational ends are ignored. For example, at the University of South Australia, there have been attempts to conceive student support strategically, by seeing it in terms of the professional development of academic staff. Rather than accept the deficit model of student support, i.e. lecturers teach – students fail, trials have occurred to bring the expertise of study advisers into the shaping of the teaching and learning transactions in a proactive and collaborative manner. Having study advisers work with academics in addressing the scope and quality of teaching and learning opportunities allows all students taking the course to be exposed to activities directed to meeting concerns expressed by previous cohorts in the same classes (George and O'Regan, 1998).

The pressure for new teaching approaches

I wish to turn now to the question of how the pressures on HEIs explicitly impact on teaching and learning and what options institutions have by way of response.

In Australia, the costs of teaching provision comprise the largest component of recurrent expenditure in higher education, a situation presumably mirrored in other developed countries. Because the forces described above impact on expenditure, and resources are generally required to meet increasing needs, 'it is increasingly difficult to maintain conventional patterns of working and traditional models of teaching and learning' (Ford et al., 1996: 9).

Universities have to accommodate the simple fact that in relation to teaching provision they can no longer do what they used to do in the same way, but that there are increasing demands that they do different and additional things. Simple facts, of course, can give rise to complex and demanding challenges. Jan Reid comments:

At the locus of the curriculum, these and other factors come into play in ways that confront academic and support staff with new and complex challenges. Knowledge is not only exploding, but escaping the disciplinary territories in which it was once contained. Multidisciplinary studies are commonplace. Researchers are increasingly publishing across conventional disciplinary boundaries. The entry of new professional fields and diverse ideological, social and paradigmatic shifts create ongoing challenges to received knowledge. At the same time there are (though not always clear or consistent) demands from employers, professional bodies, students and the community for vocational relevance, generic skills, educational breadth and opportunities for lifelong learning.

(Reid, 1997: 1)

She adds:

Finally, the long-standing distinction between open learning or distance education and on-campus programs is being blurred by the realisation that flexible modalities are both appropriate for and expected by a range of students, and that resource based learning and creative timetabling are likely to become the norm, rather than special attempts to meet the access needs of certain groups.

(Reid, 1997: 1)

Reid's view involves an implicit assumption of some recognition of the breaking-down of distinctions between the teaching mode by academic staff and their preparedness to make appropriate educational responses. However, she recognises the potential for curriculum ideals to fall victim to budgetary pressures (Reid, 1997: 4). There is considerable correspondence between her position and that of Ford *et al.*:

HEIs are likely to move away from a pattern based on conventional teaching methods delivered in a fixed place at a fixed time, to a much more flexible system in which people learn how they want, when they want and where they want. Students will be independent, active learners, not passive recipients of teaching. They will make extensive use of technology in learning, and many of them will learn at a distance, from home or in the workplace, not on a campus at all. They will use an enormously wide range of learning resources: computer-based learning packages; printed open learning materials; networked information resources which they will seek out across the Internet; and books and other documents held in the library or resource centre. They will inhabit a much more diverse, richer information environment.

(Ford *et al.*, 1996: 15)

There is little doubt that such analyses of the near future of teaching and learning environments are correct. Roderick West (1998), Chair of the

Review of Higher Education Financing and Policy in Australia, has put this succinctly:

> Flexibility and responsiveness will be the watchwords for success over the next 20 years . . . Australians will demand flexibility over what, how, when and where they study, and it will be critical for our national well-being that those demands are met.
>
> (West, 1998: 69)

It is my view that flexible delivery of courses is both inevitable and already widely discernible across university systems in most industrialised countries. This is a product of recent higher education history and the responses of various governments and managerial hierarchies to rapid change. There is a sense in which any theoretical objections and consideration or alternatives may have been overtaken by events. To briefly summarise, I understand flexible delivery to mean:

> the provision of learning resources and the application of technologies to create, store and distribute course content, enrich communication, and provide support and services to enable more effective management of learning by the learner. In particular, the concept involves a view of learning in which a teacher does not predominantly mediate the student's experience.
>
> (King, 1998: 13)

By 'inevitable' I am bowing to the predictable impact of the pressures identified earlier in this chapter, although the particular response of flexible delivery is dependent on other things. These include the successful Australian history of distance delivery from conventional HEIs, the values that derive from theories of open learning and the transforming potential for education and developments in information and communications technologies. Technological developments provide the means for ends legitimated by the other two elements above: successful distance education practice and notions of the desirability of 'openness' in education.

Anecdotal evidence suggests those institutions that have made significant headway in relation to flexible delivery have done so either on the basis of redirecting distance education expertise and resources or by committing significant resources to the area. The University of Southern Queensland provides a strong example of the former; the University of Melbourne the latter. Fairly commonly, innovative developments in institutions of all kinds have been at the instigation of individual enthusiasts. This gives rise to three problems at institutional level.

First, individual innovation shares many of the characteristics of cottage industries, particularly the replication of development work, adoption of strategies that do not lead to mass application and unrealistic labour costings. Second, the capacity of the institution to support developments, both in terms of expertise and resources, is rapidly exceeded as individuals adopt incompatible technical platforms and proprietary software. Third, decisions to expand innovations to wider application are more influenced by the apparent success than systematic assessment of the merits of the technologies adopted. This is very evident in relation to cost considerations. To underline the latter point, researchers from the Fuijitsu Centre (at the University of New South Wales) surveyed 20 Australian HEIs and found 'almost universal agreement that information technology (IT) initiatives had both improved quality and reduced the costs of teaching and administration. But there was very little evidence . . . to support those claims' (Yetton and Associates, 1997: xi).

Several of the authorities cited here (e.g. Bradley, 1997b; Reid, 1997; Ford et al., 1996) suggest that the new learning environments that are the logical response to the pressures on institutions have to result from strategic decision taking. Ford, for example, suggests that in doing so, institutions should consider:

- new organisational structures;
- new learning methods;
- new delivery methods;
- new partnerships and collaboration.

(Ford et al., 1996: 9)

I wish to comment on each of these, using examples from my own institution, the University of South Australia. This is not to suggest any particular relative merit in the approaches we have taken but to indicate the kinds of considerations involved.

New organisational structures

The university has made four significant decisions about structure that impinge on its future learning environment: the establishment of a Flexible Learning Centre, consolidation of faculties into much larger aggregations (Divisions), creation of a Division of Access and Academic Support and management of the move to a universal on-line environment (UniSAnet) through a project team.

The rationale for the establishment of the Flexible Learning Centre is well documented in Yetton and Associates (1997) but at base involved bringing all those whose role is to add value to the activities of academic staff in support of teaching and learning into a single administrative entity. The Centre combines distance education operations, professional development activity, student counselling and advisory services, technical production facilities for the development of learning resources, on-line services and an academic group with policy making and advocacy skills. The critical dimension of the mission of the Flexible Learning Centre is that its priorities entirely derive from the academic groupings of the university, including the policy commitments of the institution as a whole. As a consequence, activities relating to support for professional development, production of learning resources, distance teaching services and support for students are negotiated in a service contract with teaching areas. The consequence of this development is that scarce professional development and support resources can be employed strategically across the institution, with some attempt to achieve economies of effort.

The creation of four divisions rather than nine faculties has served two particularly relevant functions. First, the capacity of the aggregated groups to generate funds to support innovation is significantly enhanced. Second, the divisional pro vice chancellors sit equally with their colleagues who have central co-ordinating responsibilities at senior management meetings. The capacity to secure decisions that are informed both by operational considerations and institutional imperatives is significant in a single group reporting directly to the vice chancellor. Equally, senior management accountability for supporting necessary steps to the future learning environment is much more tangible. The creation of a Division of Access and Academic Support that has no teaching functions but brings managers with responsibility for the Flexible Learning Centre, the Registry, the Library and Information Technology Systems into a single grouping both expedites and necessitates collaborative activity between key support staff within the university. The group considers, for example, plans for the development of new computerised student information and management systems with the capacity to inform developments that reflect a breadth of concerns previously missing. In particular, the insistence on an institutional focus in discussions has caused a breaking down of the 'silo' mentality that too often characterises operations in large institutions.

The introduction of a universal, common and user-friendly on-line environment within the university is managed through a project team, responsible to the Director of the Flexible Learning Centre and funded through resources channelled through the Information Technology Services Unit. This has allowed an institution-wide perspective, by combining staff with relevant expertise from different sections of the university. The approach impinges in no dramatic way on individual career development by moving too early to formal structures and the establishment of new positions and permits the involvement of necessary personnel on temporary attachment from their substantive positions. Similarly, the initiative has fostered the adoption of project management techniques focused on the imperatives of the central innovation rather than subsuming necessary functions within the activities of existing support centres.

New learning methods

Bringing relevant support expertise together in a single Flexible Learning Centre has enabled teaching and learning issues to be strategically targeted for action. The use of study advisers, previously concerned only to provide remedial support to students individually or in groups, in collaborative reshaping of teaching methods to incorporate necessary forms of study support, has been mentioned above. Similarly, institutional policy commitments to the development within graduates of an agreed set of generic attributes in addition to content mastery have fostered a programme of support activities such that teaching academics can obtain support with course documentation, planning of teaching and learning activities, the assessment of students and the evaluation of programmes that address those attributes. Staff are being encouraged to adopt teaching strategies that afford students opportunities to reflect on their personal development of the agreed set of graduate characteristics.

This support is critical. Perhaps the single most important professional development activity is that which enables an academic to reflect on the assumptions they hold about their own professional practice.

New delivery methods

The deflection of threats to academic competence through institutional commitment to new learning experiences that sit partially beyond the concerns of the discipline assumes grater significance with the application of new technologies to teaching and learning. These powerful resources confront transmission notions of education, alter the role of the academic as content expert to that of facilitator of learning, extend the range of available resources well beyond the capacity of an individual to prescribe, and offer students opportunities for interaction with each other and their teachers on an unprecedented level. They also make new demands on individual staff expertise with the technology itself. For this reason, the University of South Australia, through UniSAnet, has opted for initial movement on-line that can be managed without skills beyond those required for basic word-processing. Use of wizards, web forms and templates enables all academics a degree of success teaching on-line before additional skills are required.

New partnerships and collaboration

The university has opted for an essentially low-cost, low-technology approach to its initial on-line environment. The critical issue is how to incorporate the success of innovative and enthusiastic individuals who have gone their own way ahead of institutional commitments as well as incorporating new 'flagship' developments into our on-line presence, both for promotional and developmental reasons.

At base, our strategy has been to concentrate internal resources on the common, universal range of on-line services and to outsource expertise for those academics seeking specialist support, or who have the capacity through entrepreneurial activity to purchase additional complexity and sophistication in the on-line components of their programmes. The model adopted is to enter into commercial relationships with local IT companies who share the university's philosophy. Products, e.g. sophisticated on-line research tools, are developed using academic intellectual property and external technical expertise. The return to the university is a use-friendly but sophisticated addition to on-line resources; the external company gains a product eminently marketable to other HEIs.

Conclusion

The changes faced by HEIs internationally share several common characteristics, not least of which is the enduring imperative they create to bring about new environments for teaching and learning. This chapter has sought to elaborate on some of the sources of change and reflect on their implications for institutions. The source of most of the difficulty in finding appropriate responses to the challenges faced is the culture of the HEIs involved. The position taken here is that the culture can only be confronted and such difficulties overcome by systematic planning at management level. There is no single set of decisions that best enable this, but sharing examples of what has been tried already is a good beginning.

References

Bottomley, J. (2000) 'Reconfiguring institutional strategies for flexible learning and delivery', in V. Jakupec and J. Garrick (eds) *Flexible Learning, Human Resource and Organisational Development*, London: Routledge.

Bradley, D. (1997a) 'Staff developer as strategist', paper for The AHED Forum, *New Millennium, Four Winds, AHED of Change*, Glenelg, South Australia, 7 July.

Bradley, D. (1997b) 'Inventing the future: Australian higher education responses', keynote paper to the Third Indonesian Distance Learning Network Symposium, *Distance Education and Open Learning: Future Visions*, Bali, Indonesia, 17–20 November.

Daniel, J. (1998) 'Open learning and/or distance education: which one for what purpose?', in Commonwealth of Learning (ed.) *Open Learning for the New Society: The Role of Higher Education*, Vancouver: Commonwealth of Learning.

DEET (Department of Employment, Education and Training) (1993) *National Report on Australia's Higher Education Sector*, Canberra: Australian Government Publishing Service.

Dopson, S. and McNay, I. (1996) 'Organizational culture', in D. Warner and D. Palfreyman (eds) *Higher Education Management, The Key Elements*, Buckingham: The Society for Research into Higher Education and Open University Press.

Ford, P. *et al.* (1996) *Managing Change in Higher Education, A Learning Environment Architecture*, London: The Society for Research into Higher Education and Open University Press.

Gallagher, M. (1997) 'Current approaches and challenges in higher education', conference paper, on-line at: http:.//www.deetya.gov.au/divisions/hed/highered/pubs/mgspch1.htm

George, R. and O'Regan, K. (1998) 'A professional development mode of student support', paper prepared for *Transformation in Higher Education*, Annual Conference of the Higher Education Research and Development Society of Australasia, Auckland, NZ, 7–10 July.

King, B. (1998) 'Distance education in Australia', in H. Perraton (ed.) *Open Learning for the New Society: The Role of Higher Education*, Vancouver: Commonwealth of Learning.

Marginson, S. (1998) 'National-building universities in a global environment, the choices before us', presented in Public Lecture Series, *The Role of Universities in Australia in 2010*, Adelaide: University of South Australia, South Australia, 10 September.

Meek, V.L. and Wood, F.Q. (1998) *Managing Higher Education Diversity in a Climate of Public Sector Reform*, Canberra: Evaluations and Investigations Program, Higher Education Division, Department of Employment, Education, Training and Youth Affairs.

Nunan, T. (1996) 'Flexible delivery – what is it and why is it part of current educational debate?', paper presented at *Different Approaches: Theory and Practice in Higher Education*, Perth, Western Australia: Annual Conference of the Higher Education Research and Development Society of Australasia, 8–12 July.

Otter, S. (1998) 'Outcomes – a ten year perspective', paper given at the *Improving Student Learning Symposium*, Brighton, UK, September and on-line at: http://cs3.brookes.ac.uk/services/ocsd/abchome

Reid, J. (1997) 'Summary of discussions', paper prepared for Higher Education Council and the National Academies Forum: Joint Seminar on the Undergraduate Curriculum, University House, Australian National University, Canberra, 6–7 July, on-line at: http://www.deetya.gov.au/nbeet/hec/publicat/curricsem/reid.htm

Webb, G. (1996) *Understanding Staff Development*, Buckingham: Open University Press.

West, R. (1998) *Learning for Life: Final Report, Review of Higher Education Financing and Policy*, Canberra: Australian Government Publishing Service.

Yetton, P. and Associates (1997) *Managing the Introduction of Technology in the Delivery and Administration of Higher Education*, Sydney, Fujitsu Centre, Graduate School of Management, University of New South Wales, Evaluations and Investigations Programme, Higher Education Division, Department of Employment, Education, Training and Youth Affairs, Commonwealth of Australia.

Chapter 9

Professional education as a structural barrier to lifelong learning in the NHS

Becky Francis and John Humphreys

Introduction

This paper seeks to evaluate and comment upon the extent to which ideals of lifelong learning have been reflected in the training provision for health care workers in the United Kingdom (UK). We begin by providing a brief discussion of the notion of lifelong learning. The extent of demarcation between the education and roles of particular groups of health care workers are then explored, in order to ascertain whether a notion of lifelong learning appears to have been applied to training and career development across different occupational groups in the National Health Service (NHS). It is argued in this paper that professional demarcation perpetuated by various occupational groups is impeding lifelong learning in the health care sector. Finally, we discuss various options for educational routes, which might support lifelong learning in the health care sector and suggest some options for the future.

The notion of lifelong learning

The importance of education for economic development and growth in a global economy is argued in human capital theory, and indeed in many other economic, sociological and educational theories (Ashton and Green, 1996). These various theories maintain that a country can remain competitive in a global market only by providing the workforce with adequate skills, and with the knowledge to enable them to flexibly adapt to new technological innovations and directions (see NCIHE, 1997; Fryer, 1997; DfEE, 1998). This view has not been wholeheartedly embraced by all commentators: some urge a cautious interpretation (see, for example, Ashton and Green, 1996), while others are highly critical of the position. Ainley (1998), for example, argues that there is now a consensus amongst European leaders and policy

This is an edited version of an article previously published in *Journal of Educational Policy*, 15:3, 2000. Reproduced by permission of Taylor & Francis Ltd.

makers that a certain section of the workforce must remain unemployed in order to restrain national inflation, and to provide a reserve army of labour. Thus some potential workers will inevitably be marginalized despite their skill level, and their extra or re-education provided in any 'learning society' can be summarized as 'Education Without Jobs' (Ainley, 1998). However, the former, positive, view has been embraced in Britain by a Labour government, and indeed broadly represents the consensus view of governments and policy makers throughout the European Union (European Union, 1995; Ball, 1999). Indeed, the expansion of education and training at post-compulsory level, including continuing education or retraining for mature individuals, is seen by government as having the potential not only to secure Britain's continuing competitiveness in a global market (DfEE, 1998; Watson and Taylor, 1998) but also to contribute to solving problems of social exclusion.

The prolific body of research and extensive government policy relating to concerns over social exclusion and global competition have contributed to the development of the concept of the 'learning society', and to related concepts such as 'lifelong learning'. This latter term is a vague one, tending to reflect a particular discourse, which, as Ball (1999) points out, collapses educational policy into economic policy. Hence, although 'lifelong learning' technically concerns all learning from cradle to grave, the term is usually used to refer to the formal education and training of young people and adults. So when individuals participate in continuing education, learning new work-related skills or developing areas of knowledge, they are engaging in lifelong learning (OECD, 1996). Such updating of skills and knowledge is considered vital in the increasingly technological workplace (Watson and Taylor, 1998; DfEE, 1998).

Besides maintaining and upgrading skills for the sake of economic competitiveness, lifelong learning is also portrayed as a source of access to career development and mental stimulation for those who have, for one reason or another, been less successful in initial education (see Fryer, 1997; Watson and Taylor, 1998). This section of society contains a high proportion of individuals from socially disadvantaged groups (see Fryer, 1997), including working-class white men, individuals from certain ethnic minority groups, and women (although currently women are rapidly catching up with men in all areas of education, and overtaking them is some areas; see Francis, 2000). Fryer (1997) observes that social and economic inequality in Britain has widened in recent years, and suggests that lifelong learning has a major role to play in increasing the opportunities of the marginalized sectors of society (who are also often the least educated, leading Fryerto refer to a 'learning divide' in Britain). Hence lifelong learning is perceived as contributing to equal opportunities and to the erosion of social exclusion.

However, within mainstream popular perceptions, education and work tend to remain divided as concepts. Education tends to be understood as something in which children and young people engage until they are 16, after which they enter the world of work, their education complete. Such traditional views are incompatible with the concept of lifelong learning (Fryer, 1997). According to the Green Paper *The Learning Age* (DfEE, 1998), Britain lags behind countries such as Germany and France in terms of the proportion of the workforce qualified to level 3, and indeed there are seven million workers without any qualifications at all in the UK workforce. In order to foster lifelong learning attitudes throughout society, therefore, a major cultural and structural shift is required in our approaches to education and work, where the two are seen as complementary rather than mutually exclusive (Fryer, 1997).

This paper does not seek to evaluate the notion and effects of lifelong learning as a solution to the pressures of a competitive global market place, but rather reflects on these notions of lifelong learning and the learning society in the context of occupational groups within the National Health Service (NHS). It builds upon a previous paper, which analysed the professionalization of nursing via changes in nurse education during the last decade (Humphreys, 1996). Elsewhere we have examined occupational boundaries in the National Health Service and in relation to nursing particularly (e.g. Humphreys, 1997; Francis and Humphreys, 1999a, 1999b). In this earlier work we analysed developments in nurse education and professionalization strategies in nursing in terms of the logic of a professional project. Here we begin instead from the perspective of a British Labour government policy on lifelong learning. Downswell *et al.* (1997) have already explored the issue of nurses' learning patterns in relation to a learning society. This paper focuses rather on the implications of occupational boundaries for the notion of lifelong learning.

The NHS is one of the largest employers in Britain, and represents extremely high political stakes (Humphreys, 1997). It therefore presents an interesting and important case for the examination of occupational groups and the extent of their lifelong learning opportunities.

Doctors, nurses and health care assistants

Of the various occupational groups represented in the NHS, nurses, doctors and Health Care Assistants (HCAs) have been selected as those on which to focus here. These groups represent diverse sections of the NHS in terms of status and financial reward, but also comprise three important front-line groups in the provision of health services. These three occupations tend to be positioned as fundamentally different kinds of job: HCAs are seen as having an assisting role, nurses a caring role, and doctors a curing role (see Davies, 1995; Humphreys, 1997).

Medicine has traditionally been constructed as a scientific discipline, based on reason, objectivity and scientific experiment. A number of studies have analysed the development of the medical profession, revealing the ways in which this scientific discourse has been propagated and perpetuated by the profession in order to enhance its power (see, for example, Foucault, 1973; Dingwall *et al.*, 1988; Witz, 1992). The construction of the medical profession, and its demarcation from practices deemed to constitute nursing, has been gender-bound. Feminist writers have shown how reason and objectivity are constructed as male traits (Harding, 1991), and from the beginnings of its development, the medical profession deliberately excluded women from 'medical' practice, constructing the nursing and remedies provided by women as 'not medicine'. In recent years the numerical male dominance of the profession has been reduced, as women have entered the profession in ever-increasing numbers (DoH, 1992). However, the dominant construction of medicine as concerned with reason rather than emotion, and curing disease rather than caring for people, remains.

It was in the shadow of this dominant construction of the medical profession that nursing sought to build an identity during the development of the health care professions. *Caring* is portrayed as the fundamental and defining feature of nursing by the nursing profession (Briggs, 1972; McFarlane, 1976; Morrison and Burnard, 1991; Davies, 1995). However, caring is constructed as a feminine trait in society at large, as are the notions of selfless altruism with which 'caring' is often associated. For example, McFarlane (1976) referred to nursing as the process of 'helping, assisting, serving, caring'. This supports the argument that 'caring' is linked to feminine constructions of selfless altruism, utterly distinct from constructions of the medical role. The helping, nurturing role is often perceived as women's 'natural' role.

In recent years the construction of nurses as assistants to doctors has changed radically in the perceptions of the nursing profession: in the next section the growing confidence and autonomy of the nursing profession are discussed. However, the fundamental notion of nursing as the caring profession persists and is propagated within the nursing profession (see, for example, Morrison and Burnard, 1991; Davies, 1995).

Where the roles of doctors and nurses appear to be constructed in gendered opposition to one another, the care assistant role is constructed as similar to, but clearly distinct from, that of the nurse. They too are involved in assisting and caring. However, they are assistants to nurses. The United Kingdom Central Council's proposals for change in nurse education (the 'Project 2000' proposals, 1986) acknowledged that if nurses were to be qualified with higher education diplomas it was unrealistic to expect that health care employers would be able to afford to employ these nurses to perform 100 per cent of patient care work. They therefore included in their proposals a new type of aide to perform the most basic care tasks. That this new role was separate from nursing was emphasized in the *Project 2000* report, which endeavoured to find a title for the position that sufficiently delineated the divide between assisting and nursing. Having rejected the title 'assistant nurse' because it has 'nurse' in the title, which is misleading, the report settles for 'aide', which it argues conveys 'the notion of being a helper and not a practitioner' (UKCC, 1986: 43). The new 'helper' role was subsequently created, but was in the end titled 'health care assistant'.

Hence the three occupations on which this paper focuses are perceived to perform distinct roles. However, these distinctions are questioned here, and it will be argued that such boundaries are maintained by the professions in a manner that is deeply inconsistent with notions of a learning society.

The roles of nurses and doctors

In recent years the boundaries between the work performed by doctors and nurses has arguably become less distant (Mackay et al., 1995; Read, 1998). Nurse prescribing, and nurses' performance of tasks traditionally under-taken by junior doctors, are two well-publicized examples of an increasing overlap in areas of work. Read (1998) explains that following the govern-ment's commitment to improving the working conditions of junior doctors in 1991, it was felt that other professionals might perform some of the tasks then conducted by junior doctors. This led to the creation of new nurs-ing posts including Nurse Practitioners and Clinical Nurse Specialists. Nurse practitioners, particularly, have been found to 'blend' medicine and nursing, bringing a holistic approach to patient care as well as diagnosing diseases (Fenton and Brykczynski, 1993). Christine Hancock (general secretary of the Royal College of Nursing) maintained that nurse practi-tioners could provide between 60 and 80 per cent of the basic health care currently provided by doctors, and at a lower cost (reported in Nursing Times, 1997). Dowling (1997) has investigated this blurring of boundaries between the nursing and medical professions as nurses move into areas of practice traditionally carried out by doctors in hospitals. She observed that patients and staff often mistook senior nurses for doctors, especially when the nurses were required to wear white coats and were therefore physically indis-tinguishable.

However, a number of events also reflect the recent shift in the balance of power between doctors and nurses. For example, some of the primary-care pilots where local health services and surgeries are grouped together to pilot new ways of delivering primary care are nurse-led and actually involve nurses employing GPs. According to Porter (1997: 5), this illustrates a 'massive power shift between nurses and doctors'. The location of the basic Registered Nursing diploma course ('Project 2000' courses) in universities has improved the status of nurse training, and many key players in the nursing profession are now arguing for a graduate-led profession (see, for instance, Nursing Standard, 1997). It is claimed that a degree would reflect the high level of knowledge and practice now expected of nurses working in the NHS, and that the improved status of a degree would attract new applicants to nursing. But significantly, Moore (1998) has also pointed out that an all-graduate profession could finally extinguish the notion of the nurse as a doctors' hand-maid. The nursing profession is increasingly confident concerning the worth and ability of nurses, and is challenging the traditional hierarchy where nursing is subjugated to medicine.

And while the media focus tends to rest on nurses' progress into territory traditionally occupied by medicine, the movement has not only been one-way. According to May and Fleming (1997) doctors are increasingly appropriating the discourses of holism and care that have traditionally supported nursing. As patients become better informed and more assertive, some members of the medical profession have responded by taking up these holistic approaches that have proved so popular with the public (May and Fleming, 1997).

Hence the dualistic stereotype whereby male doctors cure the sick and women nurses care for them is being deconstructed as nurses take on doctors' tasks and doctors explore notions of holistic care. It is argued here that the benefits of this cross-fertilization also highlight the redundancy of the caring/curing dichotomy: nurses can use their skills and knowledge to help cure patients, and doctors care for (as well as about) their patients.

The role of RNs, ENs and HCAs

Similar blurrings of role also apply amongst lower grade nurses. Indeed, a lack of clarity or separation of roles in nursing has dogged the profession for more than a century (see Dingwall *et al.*, 1988). In the UK the nursing register is split between Registered Nurses (qualified on three-year courses) and Enrolled Nurses (qualified on two-year courses). Enrolled nurse (EN) training has now been phased out, following proposals from the United Kingdom Central Council for Nursing, Midwifery and Health Visiting (UKCC) and other nursing bodies (see UKCC, 1986; Humphreys, 1996; Francis and Humphreys, 1999b, for elaboration). One of the UKCC's main arguments for ending enrolled nurse training was the 'misuse and abuse' of enrolled nurses by employers who often expected enrolled nurses to perform the tasks of registered nurses, but with less status or remuneration (UKCC, 1986). Despite the cessation of enrolled nurse training, confusion over 'Rule 18' remains. (Rule 18 is the item in the UKCC's *Scope of Professional Practice*, 1992, which sets out the boundaries of enrolled nursing, but it is notoriously vague and tends to be interpreted differently by different employers, see Francis and Humphreys, 1999b.)

The potential of enrolled nurses as a group has been demonstrated by the large number who have succeeded in elevating themselves to the level of registered nurse via 'conversion courses'. These courses were mainly initiated following the decision to end enrolled nurse training, in order to alleviate fears that existing enrolled nurses were being abandoned and marginalized as a group (Hemsley-Brown and Humphreys, 1998). At the time the English National Board (ENB) had expected that, 'only 10–15% of existing ENs are likely to have the capacity successfully to complete the necessary [conversion] course' (ENB, 1986), but in fact the figure is closer to 50 per cent (Humphreys, 1997).

Yet the 'misuse and abuse' scenario now appears to be transferring to the case of HCAs, who represent a rapidly growing segment of the health care workforce. Alderman (1997) reports that two-thirds of enrolled nurses believe that they will be replaced by HCAs, supporting Humphreys' (1997) view that HCAs will become the new, but non-nurse, enrolled nurse equivalent. Certainly they are performing tasks that have previously been the remit of nurses (Snell, 1998; Francis and Humphreys, 1999b). While HCAs theoretically only 'assist' in care-giving, as with the case of enrolled nurses the confines of the role are not in practice clearly delineated (Francis and Humphreys, 1999b).

Opposition on the part of individual professions

Thus the boundaries between these health care options are somewhat blurred both in terms of the various tasks performed by each, and perceptions of their roles. The encroachment tends to be 'upward' in terms of the career hierarchy, as it is encouraged by two different forces: on the one hand, employers attempting to reduce costs by employing lesser-qualified workers to perform jobs previously performed by more highly qualified, and thus highly paid, workers; and on the other hand by the occupational movements attempting to improve the status of the occupational group. However, this encroachment by certain occupational groups into the traditional domains of others has been criticized and opposed by the professions into whose territory they are moving. As demonstrated by a report on discrimination against nurses by GPs (Kenny, 1997), some doctors are threatened by assertive nurses and rather prefer to see nurses as their assistants. The view of pseudonymed medical consultant Hippocrates Spratt (*Sunday Telegraph*, 1997) that nurses have grown 'stroppy' as a result of their new Project 2000 qualifications illustrates how confident and highly qualified nurses can be seen as a threat by doctors. Similarly, Sims (1997) reports that some doctors were initially concerned by the notion of nurse prescribing, as it represented an erosion of the doctor's role.

However, often there is also disquiet regarding the ability of individuals to carry out the new tasks. Nowhere is this anxiety greater than in relation to the role and functions of HCAs. Many in the nursing profession are concerned that because HCAs are relatively cheap, employers may be tempted to substitute HCAs for qualified nurses in order to cut costs, and indeed HCAs have been shown to be replacing enrolled nurses in the health care workforce (Francis and Humphreys, 1998a, 1999b). Recent reports have supported concerns that HCAs are indeed carrying out complex nursing tasks that 'ought' to be performed by nurses (e.g. Doult, 1998). Debate abounds within the British profession as to whether or not HCAs should be regulated by the nursing profession in order to prevent them from performing tasks outside their remit (see Francis and Humphreys, 1998a, 1999b). Indeed, from the logic of a professional project we have argued that there would be advantages in this for the nurses in that they could work to prevent the encroachment on their work and maintain the conceptual distinction between 'assisting' and 'caring'. However, as we have sought to show above, these jobs (doctor, nurse, HCA) in fact constitute a spectrum of roles, tasks and skills in which there are overlaps as well as differences, and a lack of fundament boundaries. It is argued here that rather than describing distinct roles and practices, such professional titles to a considerable extent reflect historical gender and class boundaries, and the endeavours and constructions of professional projects.

From occupational boundaries to social exclusion

Professions seek to increase their autonomy and status by self-regulation, and in particular, regulation of the professional entry gate (e.g. Moloney, 1992). Professional control over the level and content of education and qualification for membership of a profession maintains exclusivity (Ainley, 1994), and ensures that education is separate from employment issues (such as the cost concerns of employers, see Humphreys, 1997; Francis and Humphreys, 1998b), allowing the profession to decide the direction and nature of the profession. The programme by which these factors are increased has been termed 'professionalization' (Moloney, 1992).

The higher the entry gate to a profession, the more exclusive the knowledge provided in training. By maintaining exclusivity, the profession ensures that its skills and knowledge are scarce, and therefore highly valued (see Ainley, 1994). The medical profession has been extremely successful in defining and controlling the constitution of, and entry gate to, medical practice; and is one of the most powerful professions. It is no coincidence that nursing, an overwhelmingly female profession, is far less powerful: as was observed above, the nurse has traditionally been conceptualized and presented as the (male) doctor's helper. However, nursing has engaged in its own professionalization programmes (Witz, 1992). The move to Project 2000 diplomas, and the growing campaign for a graduate-led profession provide two examples where nurses have sought to raise the entry gate to their profession in order to enhance the status of nursing, and arguably to gain greater control over its regulation and autonomy (see Humphreys, 1997; Francis and Humphreys, 1999b). The Project 2000 proposals (UKCC, 1986) were keen to demarcate the HCA role from nursing. To HCAs who wished to train to become nurses, the report warned,

> The would-be entrant should be advised, however, that all the normal entry requirements will apply and that while work as a helper will serve to give an appropriate character reference, it cannot operate either as an entry gate or as credit towards professional preparation.
>
> (UKCC, 1986: 43)

Thus the nursing profession, like many other professions, has attempted to raise the entry gate to the profession and to draw clear divides between the nursing role and other less prestigious health care occupations.

If employers or government are empowered to influence professional education, they are likely to attempt to instigate changes in education, possibly with a view to producing more flexible, and possibly cheaper, future workers (see the case of health care consortia and nurse education, discussed in Humphreys, 1996 and Francis and Humphreys, 1998b, for a discussion of these processes). We have argued elsewhere (Francis and Humphreys, 1998b) that such employer control holds potentially negative connotations for the quality and direction of education provided. Conversely, however, our analysis here suggests that occupational control of educational institutions creates a barrier to lifelong learning. This is because occupational exclusivity mediated through education is fundamentally inconsistent with the amelioration of social exclusion. Yet, as the status of professions depends on the maintenance of demarcation and exclusion, it is predictable that the various health care professions would seek to maintain and perpetuate occupational boundaries.

So despite the reduction in distinction between the roles of health care professions and the increasing fuzziness of boundaries, practices of elitism and exclusion remain within the distinct occupational groups, and this is reflected in the limited or non-existent access to interprofessional training, or accreditation of prior learning schemes. In Britain it remains the case that, supposing that a nurse sought to become a doctor, or a doctor a nurse, each would have to start at the beginning of their respective new training, despite their existing knowledge (e.g. of human physiology, health care, clinical practice, etc.). This is not the case *within* professions. For example, nurses wishing to learn midwifery do not need to start again at the beginning, but can undertake an eighteen-month course rather than the normal three-year course, as their experience and qualification as nurses is deemed to contribute substantially to their knowledge and training for qualification as midwives. This inflexibility between occupational groups has been suggested to impact on levels of recruitment to nursing, at a time when the profession is suffering recruitment problems (Francis and Humphreys, 1998b): Foskett and Hemsley-Brown (1998) report that school pupils frequently mentioned inflexibility in education and occupational role between health care professions as a disincentive to enter nursing.

Such rigid delineation between occupational groupings is clearly in opposition to the concept of lifelong learning. Indeed, it is arguable that such occupational exclusivity maintains a form of social exclusion. Although notions of lifelong learning and structures for the accreditation of prior learning have been widespread, there is little evidence of coherent career development paths in the domain of health care and, particularly, in nursing. Indeed, there is much evidence that shows that while nurses spend a great deal of time and energy working for extra qualifications and gaining new skills, these endeavours go unappreciated by employers (Dowswell *et al.*, 1997). This tends to be due to a lack of career guidance (so that the new skills are not geared towards a particular career direction), and an absence of a clearly defined career structure in nursing. Butterworth (1998) argues that the clinical or academic career paths for nurses and midwives are ill-defined, in stark contrast with the medical profession. We would go further and suggest that any such defined career structure should explicitly include progression from one occupational group to another, and that curriculum development should be such that mechanisms like the accreditation of prior learning can be introduced to facilitate movement across occupational boundaries.

The achievements of enrolled nurses in progression via conversion courses provides an illustration of the potential here. It is recognized that the motives for enrolled nurses to take up conversion courses were mixed: some feared that their jobs might be phased out, and others were pressured to participate in the courses by their employers (Hemsley-Brown and Humphreys, 1998). Yet the majority declared excitement at the provision of the opportunity to upgrade, an enthusiasm for learning, as well as a commitment to successfully upgrading their position (Hemsley-Brown and Humphreys, 1998). That a large proportion of enrolled nurses were eager to take the opportunity to improve their qualifications and occupational position suggests the potential of individuals within the health care workforce to progress and achieve higher status and greater responsibility if provided with the opportunity. Moreover, as was observed above, the English National Board for nursing expected only a small fraction of enrolled nurses to achieve the conversion to registered nurse level. The English National Board had declared that, 'experience shows that only 10–15% of existing ENs are likely have the capacity successfully to complete the necessary course' (ENB, 1986). That their estimate was 'spectacularly incorrect' (Humphreys, 1997: 11), with numbers of enrolled nurses achieving conversion exceeding all expectation, arguably illustrates the embedded, erroneous prejudices of the professional bodies against lower-status groups. It appears that the English National Board's prediction was not based on an accurate assessment of the capabilities of those in lower occupational groups to progress, but rather reflected a preoccupation with professionalization, arguably at the expense of less powerful groups (Humphreys, 1997).

This analysis, then, suggests that the elitist and anachronistic approaches of health care occupations are currently impeding occupational and educational flexibility in the NHS, and are as such fundamentally inconsistent with any sophisticated and egalitarian concept of lifelong learning. This bears considerable significance for government agendas concerning lifelong learning, which will remain rhetoric rather than practice unless underpinned by more radical change to the occupational structures, occupational power and society generally.

Health care education: the future?

The above conclusion suggests the need for radical solutions in terms of health care education. In the current British health care environment where demand for care continues to exceed funding, and new innovations, technology, and a discourse of holistic care increasingly blur traditional occupational boundaries, it is unsurprising that a number of studies have discussed new interprofessional approaches to health care education. For example, Koppel (1998) and Freeth et al. (1998) have examined and evaluated 'interprofessional education'. This term refers to learning activities where members of different professions learn with and from each other (Koppel, 1998). Koppel identifies a number of benefits resulting from this interprofessional approach, such as improved qualify of care, a flexible workforce and greater cost-effectiveness in educational institutions. Freeth et al. (1998) maintain that such interprofessional learning might reduce the occurrence of communications breakdowns and ignorance of other team members' roles and expertise, in multidisciplinary health care teams, as well as avoid 'unhelpful protectionism' (see also Mackay et al., 1995). Like Koppel (1998), Freeth et al. suggest that interprofessional education can increase morale, efficiency, communication and the quality of care provision.

However, the interprofessional learning described in these studies in based on a notion of collaboration between bounded professions, rather than a deconstruction of professional boundaries in the workplace and educational facilitation for crossing them (lifelong learning). Moreover, both studies focus on small work-based schemes rather than on general pre-professional education. Koppel (1998) does allude to a different type of education, often confused with interprofessional learning: multiprofessional education. This he describes as a 'much wider enterprise', where learners share the same educational facilities. He argues that the vogue for such education reflects the scarcity of educational/health care resources, and a consequential attempt to reduce the expense of professional education. Koppel distinguishes this from interprofessional education where learners learn from each other with the intention of working together more efficiently.

Koppel's description of multiprofessional education echoes a widespread concern in health care circles. The fear that cost-cutting is driving the blurring of roles in health care has been discussed above, and has been demonstrated to be justified in some cases (Francis and Humphreys, 1999b). Notions such as that of the 'generic healthcare worker' (Health Services Management Unit, 1996), where a low-cost, flexible worker would be used to fill multiple roles, have generated consternation in nursing circles (see Francis and Humphreys, 1998b). However, it is argued here that multiprofessional education should not necessarily be perceived as a way to cut costs, or to produce a generic care worker. Rather, it is maintained that such education is required to ensure the opportunity for lifelong learning and development throughout the health care occupations.

Two interrelated educational strategies are suggested. The first concerns a more flexible basic education for health care workers. This would help to provide a suitable beginning point in order to facilitate diverse paths of future education and career development (enshrined in the discourse of lifelong learning) among health care workers. The second strategy concerns a clear structure of post-professional development, allowing individuals to maximize and develop their potential throughout their working lives, and hence helping to realize the principles of equality of opportunity and personal development maintained in the discourse of lifelong learning.

Responding to the shortage of recruits to nursing, the recently published report *Perceptions of Nursing as a Career* (Foskett and Hemsley-Brown, 1998: 3) argued that young people's perception of nursing as a future career would be 'enhanced by the establishment of a common basis for medical training in HE that was shared between medicine, nursing and Professions Allied to Medicine [PAMs]'. Foskett and Hemsley-Brown further maintain that transfers between the various health care careers should be facilitated. Our analysis supports that argument, and suggests the introduction of common basic higher education components for the health professions where roles, and therefore learning, overlap between them. Clear structures of accreditation should be introduced in order to allow capable HCAs and other lesser-status health care workers access to this Higher Education programme. For example, under the current system an NVQ in health care at Level 3 can be used to gain entrance to a nursing diploma course. However, able and experienced HCAs will already have learnt and practised many of the basic tasks taught in a nursing diploma course, and reteaching them such skills constitutes an inefficient use of time, money and energy. If a system of Accreditation of Prior Learning (APL) were introduced, the HCA would not be forced to 'relearn' those tasks, but could 'fast track' to other subjects. HCAs constitute a particularly appropriate group as potential beneficiaries from such strategies, representing as they do a relatively powerless and under-educated group in the health care workforce. As such, improving their personal and financial remuneration via structured training routes would particularly support the ethos of enfranchisement expressed in much discourse on lifelong learning (e.g. Fryer, 1997). However, this APL system would be equally applicable to a doctor or nurse wishing to change specialism.

This clearly defined structure of educational accreditation for all health care workers, then, would make the transfer from one level to another more accessible, and would widen participation and opportunity as a consequence. The success of the large proportion of ENs in completing conversion courses to RN level demonstrates that health care workers do indeed have the potential to develop new areas of knowledge beyond those anticipated by the dominant professional establishments or implied by their youthful performances in school. Workers already employed at lower levels in the health care workforce might provide an important source of recruitment in areas such as nursing, which are facing shortages (Buchan *et al.*, 1998; Francis and Humphreys, 1998b), or indeed medicine. It is vital, however, that quality and standards are maintained. The agenda would therefore be to ensure that the creation of any new educational approach in health care is driven by the values of opportunity, high standards and broad participation espoused in the rhetoric of lifelong learning, rather than by those simply of economic rationalization or occupational self-interest.

References

Ainley, P. (1994) *Degrees of Difference* (London: Lawrence and Wishart).

Ainley, P. (1998) Towards a learning or a certified society? Contradictions in the New Labour modernisation of lifelong learning. *Journal of Education Policy*, 13 (4), 559–573.

Alderman, C. (1997) On course for the future. *Nursing Standard*, 11 (45), 22–23.

Ashton, D. and Green, F. (1996) *Education, Training and the Global Economy* (Cheltenham: Edward Elgar).

Ball, S. (1999) Labour, learning and the economy: a 'policy sociology' perspective. *Cambridge Journal of Education*, 29 (2), 195–206.

Briggs, A. (1972) *Report of the Committee on Nursing* (London: HMSO).

Buchan, J., Secombe, I. and Smith, G. (1998) *Nurses Work: An Analysis of the UK Nursing Labour Market* (Hants: Ashgate).

Butterworth, T. (1998) This way up. *Nursing Standard*, 12 (29), 16.

Davies, C. (1995) *Gender and the Professional Predicament of Nursing* (Buckingham: Open University Press).

Department for Education and Employment (1998) *The Learning Age: Green Paper* (London: DfEE).

Department of Health (1992) *NHS Workforce in England* (London: HMSO).

Dingwall, R., Rafferty, A. and Webster, C. (1988) *An Introduction for the Social History of Nursing* (London: Routledge).

Doult, B. (1998) Concerns over HCAs' role in caring for children at home. *Nursing Standard*, 12 (24), 5.

Dowling, S. (1997) Life can be tough for the inbetweenies. *Nursing Times*, 93 (10), 27–28.

Dowsell, T., Hewison, J. and Millar, B. (1997) Joining the learning society and working in the NHS: some issues. *Journal of Education Policy*, 12 (6), 539–550.

English National Board (1986) Response to UKCC Project 2000 Proposals. (Held in UKCC Archive Index K3.2 (A5).)

European Union (1995) *White Paper on Education and Training, Teaching and Learning, Towards the Learning Society* (Brussels: EU).

Fenton, M. and Brykczynski, K. (1993) Qualitative distinctions and similarities in the practice of Clinical Nurse Specialists and Nurse Practitioners. *Journal of Professional Nursing*, 9, 313–326.

Foskett, N. and Hemsley-Brown, J. (1998) *Perceptions of Nursing as a Career* (London: DoH).

Foucault, M. (1973) *The Birth of the Clinic* (London: Tavistock Publications).

Francis, B. (2000) *Boys, Girls and Achievement: Addressing the Classroom Issues* (London: Routledge).

Francis, B. and Humphreys, J. (1998a) Regulating non-nursing health care workers. *Nursing Standard*, 12 (47), 35–47.

Francis, B. and Humphreys, J. (1998b) The commissioning of nurse education by consortia in England: a quasi-market analysis. *Journal of Advanced Nursing*, 28 (3), 517–523.

Francis, B. and Humphreys, J. (1999a) Rationalisation or professionalisation: a comparison of the transfer of registered nurse education to higher education in Australia and the UK. *Journal of Comparative Education*, 35 (1), 81–96.

Francis, B. and Humphreys, J. (1999b) Enrolled nurses and the professionalisation of nursing. *International Journal of Nursing Studies*, 36, 127–135.

Freeth, D., Meyer, J., Reeves, S. and Spilsbury, K. (1998) 'Of drops in the ocean and stalactites: interprofessional education within healthcare settings', presented at British Educational Research Association Conference, Queen's University Belfast, 27–30/8/98.

Fryer, R. (1997) *Learning for the Twenty-First Century* (London: NAGCELL).

Harding, S. (1991) *Whose Science? Whose Knowledge?* (Buckingham: Open University Press).

Health Services Management Unit (1996) *The Future Health Care Workforce* (Manchester: Manchester University).

Hemsley-Brown, J. and Humphreys, J. (1998) Opportunity or obligation? Participation in adult vocational training. *Journal of Vocational Education and Training*, 50 (3), 355–373.

Humphreys, J. (1996) English nurse education and the reform of the National Health Service. *Journal of Education Policy*, 11 (6), 655–679.

Humphreys, J. (1997) *Education and the Crisis of Nursing. Inaugural lecture* (London: University of Greenwich).

Kenny, C. (1997) GPs behaving badly. *Nursing Times*, 93 (11), 14–15.

Koppel, I. (1998) 'Evaluation of interprofessional education: State of art: The IPE JET study', presented at British Educational Research Association Conference, Queen's University Belfast, 27–30/8/98.

Mackay, L., Soothill, K. and Webb, C. (1995) Troubled times: the context for interprofessional collaboration?, in K. Soothill, L. Mackay and C. Webb (eds) *Interprofessional Relations in Health Care* (London: Edward Arnold) pp. 31–45.

May, C. and Fleming, C. (1997) The professional imagination: narrative and the symbolic boundaries between medicine and nursing. *Journal of Advanced Nursing*, 25, 1,094–1,100.

McFarlane, J. (1976) A charter for caring. *Journal of Advanced Nursing*, 1, 187–196.

Moloney, M. (1992) *Professionalization of Nursing* (Philadelphia: J.B Lippincott Company).

Moore, A. (1998) Degrees of separation. *Nursing Standard*, 12 (29), 14.

Morrison, P. and Burnard, P. (1991) *Caring and Communicating* (Basingstoke: Macmillan Press).

The National Committee of Inquiry into Higher Education (NCIHE) (1997) *Higher Education in the Learning Society* (London: NCIHE).

Nursing Standard (1997) News, 11 (31), p. 5.

Nursing Times (1997) News, 93 (52), p. 5.

OECD (1996) *Lifelong Learning For All* (Paris: OECD Publications).

Porter, R. (1997) Nurse practitioners beat doctors in value. *Nursing Times*, 93 (4), 5.

Read, S. (1998) Exploring new roles for nurses in the acute sector. *Professional Nurse*, 14 (2), 90–94.

Sims, R. (1997) Editorial: Satisfied in law. *Nursing Standard*, 11 (30), 17.

Snell, J. (1998) A force to reckon with. *Health Service Journal*, 9, 24–27.

Spratt, H. (1997) *Sunday Telegraph, RX Supplement*, 13/4/97.

UKCC (1986) *Project 2000: A New Preparation for Practice* (London: UKCC).

UKCC (1992) *The Scope of Professional Practice* (London: UKCC).

Watson, D. and Taylor, R. (1998) *Lifelong Learning and the University: A Post-Dearing Agenda* (London: Falmer Press).

Witz, A. (1992) *Professions and Patriarchy* (London: Routledge).

Chapter 10

Communities of practice and social learning systems

Etienne Wenger

You probably know that the earth is round and that it is in orbit around the sun. But how do you know this? What does it take? Obviously, it takes a brain in a living body, but it also takes a very complex social, cultural, and historical system, which has accumulated learning over time. People have been studying the skies for centuries to understand our place in the universe. More recently, scientific communities have developed a whole vocabulary, observation methods, concepts, and models, which have been adopted by other communities and have become part of popular thinking in various ways. You have your own relationships to all these communities, and these relationships are what enable you to 'know' about the earth's position in the universe. In this sense, knowing is an act of participation in complex 'social learning systems'.

This chapter assumes this view of knowing to consider how organizations depend on social learning systems. First, I outline two aspects of a conceptual framework for understanding social learning systems: a social definition of learning in terms of social *competence* and personal *experience*, and three distinct *modes of belonging* through which we participate in social learning systems: *engagement*, *imagination*, and *alignment*. Then I look at three structuring elements of social learning systems: *communities of practice*, *boundary* processes among these systems and *identities* as shaped by our participation in these systems. About each of these elements I use my conceptual framework to ask three questions. Why focus on it? Which way is up, that is, how to construe progress in this area? And, third, what is doable, that is, what are elements of design that one can hope to influence? Finally, I argue that organizations both are constituted by and participate in such social learning systems. Their success depends on their ability to design themselves as social learning systems and also to participate in broader learning systems such as an industry, a region, or a consortium.

The conceptual framework I introduce here is intended for organizational design as well as analysis. The questions I ask are meant to guide the inquiry of

This is an edited version of an article previously published in *Organisations*, 7:2, 2000. Reproduced by permission of Sage Publications Ltd.

the researcher as well as the actions of the practitioner: what to pay attention to, how to give direction to our initiatives, and where to focus our efforts. As Kurt Lewin used to say, there is nothing as practical as a good theory.

Aspects of a conceptual framework

A framework for understanding social learning systems must make it possible to understand learning as a social process. What is learning from a social perspective? And what are the processes by which our learning constitutes social systems and social identities?

A social definition of learning

In a social learning system, competence is historically and socially defined. How to be a physicist or how to understand the position of the earth in the universe is something that scientific communities have established over time. Knowing, therefore, is a matter of displaying competences defined in social communities. The picture is more complex and dynamic than that, however.

Consider two extreme cases. Sometimes, we are a newcomer. We join a new community. We are a child who cannot speak yet. Or we are a new employee. We feel like a bumbling idiot among the sages. We want to learn. We want to apprentice ourselves. We want to become one of them. We feel an urgent need to align our experience with the competence 'they' define. Their competence pulls our experience.

Sometimes, it is the other way round. We have been with a community for a long time. We know the ropes. We are thoroughly competent, in our own eyes and in the eyes of our peers. But something happens, we have an experience that opens our eyes to a new way of looking at the world. This experience does not fully fit in the current practice of our home communities. We now see limitations we were not aware of before. We come back to our peers, try to communicate our experience, attempt to explain what we have discovered, so they too can expand their horizon. In the process, we are trying to change how our community defines competence (and we are actually deepening our own experience). We are using our experience to pull our community's competence along.

Whether we are apprentices or pioneers, newcomers or old-timers, knowing always involves these two components: the *competence* that our communities have established over time (i.e. what it takes to act and be recognized as a competent member), and our ongoing *experience* of the world as a member (in the context of a given community and beyond). Competence and experience can be in various relations to each other – from very congruent to very divergent. As my two examples show, either can shape the other, although usually the process is not completely one-way. But, whenever the two are in close tension and either starts pulling the other, learning takes place. Learning so defined is an interplay between social competence and personal experience. It is a dynamic, two-way relationship between people and the social learning systems in which they participate. It combines personal transformation with the evolution of social structures.

Modes of belonging

Our belonging to social learning systems can take various forms at various levels between local interactions and global participation. To capture these different forms of participation, I will distinguish between three modes of belonging.

- *Engagement*: doing things together, talking, producing artefacts (e.g. helping a colleague with a problem or participating in a meeting). The ways in which we engage with each other and with the world profoundly shape our experience of who we are. We learn what we can do and how the world responds to our actions.
- *Imagination*: constructing an image of ourselves, of our communities, and of the world, in order to orient ourselves, to reflect on our situation, and to explore possibilities (e.g. drawing maps, telling a story, or building a set of possible scenarios to understand one's options). I use imagination here in the sense proposed by Benedict Anderson (1983) to describe nations as communities. Thinking of ourselves as a member of a community such as a nation requires an act of imagination because we cannot engage with all our fellow citizens. These images of the world are essential to our sense of self and to our interpretation of our participation in the social world.
- *Alignment*: making sure that our local activities are sufficiently aligned with other processes so that they can be effective beyond our own engagement (e.g. doing a scientific experiment by the book, convincing a colleague to join a cause, or negotiating a division of labour and a work plan for a project). The concept of alignment as used here does not connote a one-way process of submitting to external authority, but a mutual process of co-ordinating perspectives, interpretations, and actions so they realize higher goals.

Distinguishing between these modes of belonging is useful for two reasons. First, analytically, each mode contributes a different aspect to the formation of social learning systems and personal identities. Engagement, imagination, and alignment usually coexist and every social learning system involves each to some degree and in some combination. Still, one can dominate and thus give a different quality to a social structure. For instance, a community based mostly on imagination such as a nation has a very different quality from a community of practice at work, which is based primarily on engagement. I would in fact argue that these modes of belonging provide a foundation for a typology of communities.

Second, practically, each mode requires a different kind of work. The work of engagement, which requires opportunities for joint activities, is different from the work of imagination, which often requires opportunities for taking some distance from our situation. The demands and effects of these three modes of belonging can be conflicting. Spending time reflecting can detract from engagement, for example. The modes can also be complementary, however. For instance, using imagination to gain a good picture of the context of one's actions can help in fine-tuning alignment because one understands the reasons behind a procedure or an agreement. It is therefore useful to strive to develop these modes of belonging in combination, balancing the limitations of one with the work of another. For instance, reflective periods that activate imagination or boundary interactions that require alignment with other practices around a shared goal could be used to counteract the possible narrowness of engagement (Wenger, 1998).

Communities of practice

Since the beginning of history, human beings have formed communities that share cultural practices reflecting their collective learning: from a tribe around a cave fire, to a medieval guild, to a group of nurses in a ward, to a street gang, to a community of engineers interested in brake design. Participating in these 'communities of practice' is essential to our learning. It is at the very core of what makes us human beings capable of meaningful knowing.

Why focus on communities?

Communities of practice are the basic building blocks of a social learning system because they are the social 'containers' of the competences that make up such a system. By participating in these communities, we define with each other what constitutes competence in a given context: being a reliable doctor, a gifted photographer, a popular student, or an astute poker player. Your company may define your job as processing 33 medical claims a day according to certain standards, but the competence required to do this in practice is something you determine with your colleagues as you interact day after day.

Communities of practice define competence by combining three elements (Wenger, 1998). First, members are bound together by their collectively developed understanding of what their community is about and they hold each other accountable to this sense of *joint enterprise*. To be competent is to understand the enterprise well enough to be able to contribute to it.

Second, members build their community through mutual engagement. They interact with one another, establishing norms and relationships of *mutuality* that reflect these interactions. To be competent is to be able to engage with the community and be trusted as a partner in these interactions. Third, communities of practice have produced a *shared repertoire* of communal resources – language, routines, sensibilities, artefacts, tools, stories, styles, etc. To be competent is to have access to this repertoire and be able to use it appropriately.

Communities of practice grow out of a convergent interplay of competence and experience that involves mutual engagement. They offer an opportunity to negotiate competence through an experience of direct participation. As a consequence, they remain important social units of learning even in the context of much larger systems. These larger systems are constellations of interrelated communities of practice.

Which way is up?

Communities of practice cannot be romanticized. They are born of learning, but they can also learn not to learn. They are the cradles of the human spirit, but they can also be its cages. After all, witch-hunts were also community practices. It is useful, therefore, to articulate some dimensions of progress.

- *Enterprise: the level of learning energy.* How much initiative does the community take in keeping learning at the centre of its enterprise? A community must show leadership in pushing its development along and maintaining a spirit of inquiry. It must recognize and address gaps in its knowledge as well as remain open to emergent directions and opportunities.
- *Mutuality: the depth of social capital.* How deep is the sense of community generated by mutual engagement over time? People must know each other well enough to know how to interact productively and who to call for help or advice. They must trust each other, not just personally, but also in their ability to contribute to the enterprise of the community, so they feel comfortable addressing real problems together and speaking truthfully.
- *Repertoire: the degree of self-awareness.* How self-conscious is the community about the repertoire that it is developing and its effects on its practice? The concepts, language, and tools of a community of practice embody its history and its perspective on the world. Being reflective on its repertoire enables a community to understand its own state of development from multiple perspectives, reconsider assumptions and patterns, uncover hidden possibilities, and use this self-awareness to move forward.

Table 10.1 Community dimensions

	Enterprise: learning energy	Mutuality: social capital	Repertoire: self-awareness
Engagement	What are the opportunities to negotiate a joint inquiry and important questions? Do members identify gaps in their knowledge and work together to address them?	What events and interactions weave the community and develop trust? Does this result in an ability to raise troubling issues during discussions?	To what extent have shared experience, language, artefacts, histories, and methods accumulated over time, and with what potential for further interactions and new meanings?
Imagination	What visions of the potential of the community are guiding the thought leaders, inspiring participation, and defining a learning agenda? And what picture of the world serves as a context for such visions?	What do people know about each other and about the meanings that participation in the community takes in their lives more broadly?	Are there self-representations that would allow the community to see itself in new ways? Is there a language to talk about the community in a reflective mode?
Alignment	Have members articulated a shared purpose? How widely do they subscribe to it? How accountable do they feel to it? And how distributed is leadership?	What definitions of roles, norms, codes of behaviour, shared principles, and negotiated commitments and expectations hold the community together?	What traditions, methods, standards, routines, and frameworks define the practice? Who upholds them? To what extent are they codified? How are they transmitted to new generations?

The three dimensions work together. Without the learning energy of those who take initiative, the community becomes stagnant. Without strong relationships of belonging, it is torn apart. And without the ability to reflect, it becomes hostage to its own history. The work associated with each mode of belonging can contribute to these criteria. Table 10.1 illustrates how the modes of belonging interact with community elements.

What is doable?

When designing itself, a community should look at the following elements: events, leadership, connectivity, membership, projects, and artefacts.

Events

You can organize public events that bring the community together. Obviously, these may or may not be attended, but if they are well tuned to the community's sense of its purpose, they will help it develop an identity. A community will have to decide the *type* of activities it needs: formal or informal meetings, problem-solving sessions, or guest speakers. It will also have to consider the *rhythm* of these events given other responsibilities members have: too often and people just stop coming, too rare and the community does not gain momentum. This rhythm may also have to change over time or go through cycles.

Leadership

Communities of practice depend on internal leadership, and enabling the leaders to play their role is a way to help the community develop. The role of 'community co-ordinator' who takes care of the day-to-day work is crucial, but a community needs multiple forms of leadership: thought leaders, networkers, people who document the practice, pioneers, etc.

Connectivity

Building a community is not just a matter of organizing community events but also of enabling a rich fabric of connectivity among people. This could involve brokering relationships between people. It is also important to make it possible for people to communicate and interact in multiple media.

Membership

A community's members must have critical mass so that there is interest, but it should not become so wide that the focus of the community is diffuse and participation does not grab people's identities. Including those who are missing can be very helpful in consolidating the legitimacy of the community to itself and in the wider organization. Conversely, realizing that the membership is overextended allows the community to split up into subgroups. Finally, devising processes by which newcomers can become full members helps ensure access for newcomers without diluting the community's focus.

Learning projects

Communities of practice deepen their mutual commitment when they take responsibility for a learning agenda, which pushes their practice further. Activities toward this goal include exploring the knowledge domain, finding gaps in the community practice, and defining projects to close these gaps. Such learning projects could involve, for instance, assessing some tools, building a generic design, doing a literature search, creating a connection with a university doing research in the area, or simply interviewing some experts to create a beginner's guide.

Artefacts

All communities of practice produce their own set of artefacts: documents, tools, stories, symbols, websites, etc. A community has to consider what artefacts it needs and who has the energy to produce and maintain them so they will remain useful as the community evolves.

Boundaries

The term 'boundary' often has negative connotations because it conveys limitation and lack of access. But the very notion of community of practice implies the existence of boundary. Unlike the boundaries of organizational units, which are usually well defined because affiliation is officially sanctioned, the boundaries of communities of practice are usually rather fluid. They arise from different enterprises; different ways of engaging with one another; different histories, repertoires, ways of communicating and capabilities. That these boundaries are often unspoken does not make them less significant. Sit for lunch by a group of high-energy particle physicists and you know about boundary, not because they intend to exclude you, but because you cannot figure out what they are talking about. Shared practice by its very nature creates boundaries.

Yet, if you are like me, you will actually enjoy this experience of boundary. There is something disquieting, humbling at times, yet exciting and attractive about such close encounters with the unknown, with the mystery of 'otherness': a chance to explore the edge of your competence, learn something entirely new, revisit your little truths, and perhaps expand your horizon.

Why focus on boundaries?

Boundaries are important to learning systems for two reasons. They connect communities and they offer learning opportunities in their own right. These learning opportunities are of a different kind from the ones offered by communities. Inside a community, learning takes place because competence and experience need to converge for a community to exist. At the boundaries, competence and experience tend to diverge: a boundary interaction is usually an experience of being exposed to a foreign competence. Such reconfigurations of the relation between competence and experience are an important aspect of learning. If competence and experience are too close, if they always match, not much learning is likely to take place. There are no challenges; the community is losing its dynamism and the practice is in danger of becoming stale. Conversely, if experience and competence are too disconnected, if the distance is too great, not much learning is likely to take place either. Sitting by that group of high-energy particle physicists, you might not learn much because the distance between your own experience and the competence you are confronting is just too great. Mostly what you are learning is that you do not belong.

Learning at boundaries is likely to be maximized for individuals and for communities when experience and competence are in close tension. Achieving a generative tension between them requires:

- something to interact about, some intersection of interest, some activity;
- open engagement with real differences as well as common ground;
- commitment to suspend judgement in order to see the competence of a community in its terms;
- ways to translate between repertoires so that experience and competence actually interact.

Boundaries are sources of new opportunities as well as potential difficulties. In a learning system, communities and boundaries can be learning assets (and liabilities) in complementary ways.

- Communities of practice can steward a critical competence, but they can also become hostage to their history, insular, defensive, closed in, and oriented to their own focus.
- Boundaries can create divisions and be a source of separation, fragmentation, disconnection, and misunderstanding. Yet, they can also be areas of unusual learning, places where perspectives meet and new possibilities arise. Radically new insights often arise at the boundaries between communities.

The learning and innovation potential of a social learning system lies in its configuration of strong core practices and active boundary processes (Wenger, 1998).

Which way is up?

Not all boundary processes create bridges that actually connect practices in deep ways. The actual boundary effects of these processes can be assessed along the following dimensions:

- *Co-ordination.* Can boundary processes and objects be interpreted in different practices in a way that enables co-ordinated action? They must accommodate the practices involved without burdening others with the details of one practice and provide enough standardization for people to know how to deal with them locally.

- *Transparency*. Do boundary processes give access to the meanings they have in various practices? For instance, forms like US tax returns enable co-ordination across boundaries (you know how to fill them out by following instructions line by line), but often afford no windows into the logic they are meant to enforce.
- *Negotiability*. Do boundary processes provide a one-way or a two-way connection? For instance, a business process re-engineering plan may be very detailed about implementation (co-ordination) and explicit about its intentions (transparency), but reflect or allow little negotiation between the perspectives involved. Boundary processes can merely reflect relations of power among practices, in which case they are likely to reinforce the boundary rather than bridge it. They will bridge practices to the extent that they make room for multiple voices.

Table 10.2 explores how the three modes of belonging affect these qualities of boundary processes.

What is doable?

Boundary processes are crucial to the coherent functioning of social learning systems. A number of elements can be intentionally promoted in an effort to weave these systems more tightly together. Here, I will talk about three types of bridges across boundaries: *people* who act as 'brokers' between communities, *artefacts* (things, tools, terms, representations, etc.) that serve as what Star and Griesemer (1989) call 'boundary objets', and a variety of forms of *interactions* among people from different communities of practice.

Brokering

Some people act as brokers between communities. They can introduce elements of one practice into another. Although we all do some brokering, my experience is that certain individuals seem to thrive on being brokers: they love to create connections and engage in 'import–export', and so would rather stay at the boundaries of many practices than move to the core of any one practice. Brokering can take various forms, including:

- *boundary spanners*: taking care of one specific boundary over time;
- *roamers*: going from place to place, creating connections, moving knowledge;
- *outposts*: bringing back news from the forefront, exploring new territories;
- *pairs*: often brokering is done through a personal relationship.

Table 10.2 Boundary dimensions

	Co-ordination	Transparency	Negotiability
Engagement	What opportunities exist for joint activities, problem-solving, and discussions to both surface and resolve differences through action?	Do people provide explanations, coaching, and demonstrations in the context of joint activities to open windows on to each other's practices?	Are joint activities structured in such a way that multiple perspectives can meet and participants can come to appreciate each other's competences?
Imagination	Do people have enough understanding of their respective perspectives to present issues effectively and anticipate misunderstandings?	What stories, documents, and models are available to build a picture of another practice? What experience will allow people to walk in the other's shoes? Do they listen deeply enough?	Can both sides see themselves as members of an overarching community in which they have common interests and needs?
Alignment	Are instructions, goals, and methods interpretable into action across boundaries?	Are intentions, commitments, norms, and traditions made clear enough to reveal common ground and differences in perspectives and expectations?	Who has a say in negotiating contracts and devising compromises?

Brokering knowledge is delicate. It requires enough legitimacy to be listened to and enough distance to bring something really new. Because brokers often do not fully belong anywhere and may not contribute directly to any specific outcome, the value they bring can easily be overlooked. Uprootedness, homelessness, marginalization, and organizational invisibility are all occupational hazards of brokering. Developing the boundary infrastructure of a social learning system means paying attention to people who act as brokers. Are they falling through the cracks? Is the value they bring understood? Is there even a language to talk about it? Are there people who are potential brokers but who for some reason do not provide cross-boundary connections?

Boundary objects

Some objects find their value, not just as artefacts of one practice, but mostly to the extent that they support connections between different practices. Such boundary objects can take multiple forms.

- *Artefacts*, such as tools, documents, or models. For instance, medical records and architectural blueprints play a crucial role in connecting multiple practices (doctors/nurses/insurers, architects/contractors/ city planners).
- *Discourses*. A critical boundary object is the existence of a common language that allows people to communicate and negotiate meanings across boundaries. This was an important thrust behind the quality movement.
- *Processes*. Shared processes, including explicit routines and procedures, allow people to co-ordinate their actions across boundaries.

Boundary objects do not necessarily bridge across boundaries because they may be misinterpreted or interpreted blindly. Rethinking artefacts and designs in terms of their function as boundary objects often illuminates how they contribute to or hinder the functioning of learning systems. An organizational structure, for instance, is often considered as an overarching umbrella that incorporates multiple parts by specifying their relationships. But, in fact, it is more usefully designed as a boundary object intended to enable multiple practices to negotiate their relationships and connect their perspectives.

Boundary interactions

- *Boundary encounters*. These encounters – visits, discussions, sabbaticals – provide direct exposure to a practice. They can take different forms for different purposes. When one person visits, as in a sabbatical, it is easier to get fully immersed in the practice, but more difficult to bring the implications home because the very immersion into a 'foreign' practice tends to isolate you from your peers. When a delegation of two or more people visit, as in a benchmarking expedition, they may not get as fully immersed, but they can negotiate among themselves the meaning of the boundary interaction for their own practice, and therefore find it easier to bring their learning back home.
- *Boundary practices*. In some case, a boundary requires so much sustained work that it becomes the topic of a practice of its own. At Xerox, as in many companies, some people are charged with the task of maintaining connections between the R&D lab and the rest of the corporation. They are developing a practice of crossing these boundaries effectively.
- *Peripheries*. Communities often have to take steps to manage their boundaries to serve people who need some service, are curious, or intend to become members. Many communities have found it useful to create some facilities by which outsiders can connect with their practice in peripheral ways. Examples of such facilities include lists of 'frequently asked questions', visitors' rooms on websites, open houses and fairs.

Cross-disciplinary projects

In most organizations, members of communities of practice contribute their competence by participating in cross-functional projects and teams that combine the knowledge of multiple practices to get something done. Simultaneous participation in communities of practice and project teams creates learning loops that combine application with capability development. In these double-knit organizations, as Richard McDermott (1999) calls them, the learning and innovation that is inherent in projects is synthesized and disseminated through the home communities of practice of team members.

People confront problems that are outside the realm of their competence but that force them to negotiate their own competence with the competences of others. Such projects provide a great way to sustain a creative tension between experience and competence when our participation in a project leverages and nourishes our participation in a community of practice.

Identities

As I said, you probably know that the earth is round and in orbit around the sun. Of course, it is not a flat plate in the way it appears to be at first glance. You actually want to make sure you know this. It is part of your identity as the kind of well-educated adult you probably are if you are reading this article. You may even know that the orbit is not an exact circle, but a slight ellipse. Chances are, however, you do not know the exact distance between the earth and the sun or the precise difference between the apogee and the perigee. This kind of ignorance, your identity can accept without existential angst because your relationship to the communities where such knowledge matters is very peripheral at best. My point is that, if knowing is an act of belonging, then our identities are a key structuring element of how we know.

Why focus on identity?

Knowing, learning, and sharing knowledge are not abstract things we do for their own sake. They are part of belonging (Eckert, 1989). When I was working with claims processors in an insurance company, I noticed that their knowing was interwoven in profound ways with their identities as participants in their community of practice. Their job did not have a high status in the company (and in their own eyes, for that matter), so they were careful not to be interested in it more than was absolutely necessary. What they knew about their job, what they tried to understand and what they accepted not to understand about the forms they had to fill out, what they shared with each other, all that was not merely a matter of necessity to get the job done, but it was also a matter of identity. Knowing too much or failing to share a crucial piece of knowledge would be a betrayal of their sense of self and of their community (Wenger, 1998).

In the landscape of communities and boundaries in which we live, we identify with some communities strongly and not at all with others. We define who we are by what is familiar and what is foreign, by what we need to know and what we can safely ignore. We define ourselves by what we are not as well as by what we are, by the communities we do not belong to as well as by the ones we do. These relationships change. We move from community to community. In doing so, we carry a bit of each as we go around. Our identities are not something we can turn on and off. You don't cease to be a parent because you go to work. You don't cease to be a nurse because you step out of the hospital. Multimembership is an inherent aspect of our identities.

Identity is crucial to social learning systems for three reasons. First, our identities combine competence and experience into a way of knowing. They are the key to deciding what matters and what does not, with whom we identify and whom we trust, and with whom we must share what we understand. Second, our ability to deal productively with boundaries depends on our ability to engage and suspend our identities. Learning from our interactions with other practices is not just an intellectual matter of translation. It is also a matter of opening up our identities to other ways of being in the world. Third, our identities are the living vessels in which communities and boundaries become realized as an experience of the world. Whenever we belong to multiple communities, we experience the boundary in a personal way. In the process, we create bridges across communities because, in developing our own identities, we deal with these boundaries in ourselves.

Which way is up?

Our identities are not necessarily strong or healthy. Sometimes, they are even self-defeating. In fact, a whole self-help industry has flourished by offering advice for building healthy identities (Giddens, 1991). Navigating the social landscape defined by communities and their boundaries requires a strong identity. Progress can be described in terms of a few crucial qualities that must coexist to constitute a healthy social identity.

- *Connectedness.* Where are enduring social relationships through which an identity gains social depth? An identity is not an abstract idea or a label, such as a title, an ethnic category, or a personality trait. It is a lived experience of belonging (or not belonging). A strong identity involves deep connections with others through shared histories and experiences, reciprocity, affection, and mutual commitments.
- *Expansiveness.* What are the breadth and scope of an identity? A healthy identity will not be exclusively locally defined. It will involve multi-

Table 10.3 Identity dimensions

	Connectedness	Expansiveness	Effectiveness
Engagement	Is there a community to engage with? How far back do you go? What kinds of interactions do you have? What do you do together? Do you trust and are you trusted?	Is there enough variety of contexts and identity-forming experiences, such as logging on the Internet and chatting with strangers, going on a blind date, or visiting a foreign country?	Do you have opportunities to develop socially recognized competences by participating in well-established practices? Are your communities ready to embrace your experience into their practices?
Imagination	Do you have good conversations? Do you talk about your deepest aspirations? Do you listen well?	Can you see yourself as a member of large communities, for instance, a world citizen, the heir of long-lived traditions, the pioneer of a world to come?	Do you understand the big picture well enough to act effectively?
Alignment	Do you keep your commitments to your communities? Do you uphold their principles? Do you give and receive feedback?	Do you follow guidelines that align your actions with broader purposes, such as saving energy or recycling for the sake of the planet?	Do you know the regimes of accountability by which your ideas, actions, and requests will be judged? Can you convince others of the potential of a new idea?

membership and cross multiple boundaries. It will seek a wide range of experiences and be open to new possibilities. It will identify with broad communities that lie beyond direct participation.

- *Effectiveness*. Does an identity enable action and participation? Identity is a vehicle for participating in the social world, but it can also lead to non-participation. A healthy identity is socially empowering rather than marginalizing.

There are potential tensions and conflicts between these qualities. How 'big' can your identity be and still be engaged as well as effective (not merely an abstract kind of identification)? Can you really think globally and act locally, feel like a citizen of the earth without losing your ability to connect with specific communities? In other words, it is the combination of these qualities that matters. Table 10.3 explores how each mode of belonging contributes to these three qualities.

What is doable?

To help identities achieve simultaneously high degrees of local connectedness, global expansiveness and social effectiveness, below are some design elements to consider.

Home base

Identity needs a place where a person can experience knowing as a form of social competence. Think of a project-based organization, for instance, where people go from one project to the next, spending a few days inbetween on the 'available' list. The learning that they do in their projects does not have a social 'home', unless they can also belong to a community of practice. In such a community, they are not only recognized as competent for the sake of a project, their need to develop their competence is also part of their belonging.

Trajectories

Identity extends in time. It is a trajectory in progress that includes where you have been and where you are going, your history and your aspirations. It brings the past and the future into the experience of the present. Apprentices in traditional apprenticeship, for instance, are not just learning skills, they are exposed to possible futures. By observing and working with journeymen and masters, they develop a sense of trajectory that expands their identity in time (Lave and Wenger, 1991). Members of a community embody a set of paradigmatic trajectories that provide material for newcomers to construct their own trajectory through a community and beyond. Trajectories can be of various types. Inbound trajectories invite newcomers into full membership in a community. Peripheral trajectories allow a person to interact with the community without making a commitment to becoming a full member. Outbound trajectories, such as the ones offered by schools, point to forms of participation outside the current communities.

Multimembership

Identity extends in space, across boundaries. It is neither unitary nor fragmented. It is an experience of multimembership. It is not something we can turn on and off. When we go to work, we don't cease to be parents, and when we go to the theatre, we are still an engineer or a waitress. We bring these aspects of our identity to bear to some extent in everything we do. Even though certain aspects of our identities become more salient in different circumstances, it would be an oversimplification to assume that we merely have a multiplicity of separate identities. Such a view would overlook the extent to which our various forms of membership can and do conflict with, influence, complement, and enrich each other. The work that we do in attempts to combine, confront, or reconcile various aspects of our identities has a double effect. It is a source of personal growth. It is also a source of social cohesion because it builds bridges across practices. As a result, our identities shape the social structures we live in. The work of identity constantly reshapes boundaries and reweaves the social fabric of our learning systems.

Combining concurrent forms of membership in multiple communities into one's experience is a way to expand an identity. Of course, we can only combine core membership in a limited number of communities, but we can also have more peripheral forms of participation, or even transitory ones, such as visits, sabbaticals, immersion, or one-time projects. Communities that can include in their forms of participation a large portion of the multi-membership of their members are more likely to engage their whole identity. If I do not have to pretend that I am not a parent when I am at work, I am more likely to put my heart into what I do.

Fractals

Identity extends across levels. You may belong to a local church, but this belonging is usually an expression of your belonging to a religion that includes many other people in many other churches. Engaging at the local level of your church is a way to belong at the broader level of your religion by combining such engagement with imagination (you can picture many other churches) and with alignment (in your church you follow rituals that conform with liturgical formats adhered to by all other churches). Note how the three modes of belonging complement each other.

Combining modes of belonging this way creates 'fractal' layers of belonging. More generally, if a community is large, it is a good idea to structure it in layers, as a 'fractal' of embedded subcommunities. If a community is large and does not have a fractal structure with local subcommunities in which people can engage actively, then it can easily happen that beyond a small core group various segments of the community feel disconnected. Subcommunities could be defined regionally as local 'chapters' of a global community. Some representatives of these local communities then form a global community among them, whose purpose is to connect the local subcommunities into one large global one. This is how some global communites of well engineers have structured their forms of participation at Shell Oil. Subcommunities could also be defined by subspecialities as engineering communities are at DaimlerChrysler, where engineers can join communities specialized in specific components (e.g. wipers, seats, or dashboards) but clustered into broader communities defined according to systems (e.g. body or powertrain). With such a fractal structure, by belonging to your own subcommunity, you experience in a local and direct way your belonging to a much broader community.

Conclusion: participation in social learning systems

The perspective of a social learning system applies to many of our social institutions: our disciplines, our industries, our economic regions and our organizations. This view has implications at multiple levels.

- For individuals, this perspective highlights the importance of finding the dynamic set of communities they should belong to – centrally and peripherally – and to fashion a meaningful trajectory through these communities over time.
- For communities of practice, it requires a balance between core and boundary processes, so that the practice is both a strong node in the web of interconnections – an enabler of deep learning in a specific area – and, at the same time, highly linked with other parts of the system – a player in systemwide processes of knowledge production, exchange, and transformation.
- For organizations, this perspective implies a need to learn to foster and participate in social learning systems, but inside and outside organizational boundaries. Social learning systems are not defined by, congruent with, or cleanly encompassed in organizations. Organizations can take part in them; they can foster them; they can leverage them; but they cannot fully own or control them.

This paradox could be bad news because the organizational requirements of social learning systems often run counter to traditional management practices (Wenger and Snyder, 2000). The currency of these systems is collegiality, reciprocity, expertise, contributions to the practice, and negotiating a learning agenda; not affiliation to an institution, assigned authority, or commitment to a predefined deliverable. But there is also good news. The knowledge economy will give more primacy to informal systems. In a traditional industry setting, the formal design of a production system is the primary source of value creation. Think of an assembly line where value derives from the quality of the design of the formal process. Informal processes still exist, but they produce value to the extent that they conform to and serve the formal design. In the knowledge economy, this relationship is inverted. The primary source of value creation lies in informal processes, such as conversations, brainstorming, and pursuing ideas. Formal organizational designs and processes are still important, but they contribute to value creation to the extent that they are in the service of informal processes.

This framework suggests two directions for organizations. On the one hand, they must learn to manage themselves as social learning systems and develop such systems internally. This means:

- giving primacy to the kind of informal learning processes characteristic of communities of practice and designing organizational structures and processes that are in the service of the informal;
- placing a lot of emphasis on the meaningfulness of participation in the organization, on the possibility of building interesting identities, and on community membership as the primary relationship to the organization (Handy, 1989):
- organizing for complexity, working to link the various communities that constitute the learning systems in which the organization operates; offering channels, shared discourses, processes, and technology platforms by which local forms of knowledgeability can have global connections and effects; and providing co-ordination among practices to create complex knowledge beyond the purview of any practice.

On the other hand, organizations must learn to participate in broader learning systems in which they are only one of many players. Companies have learned to participate as one of many players in economic markets to sell products and services to customers taken as individual decision makers. In the knowledge economy, however, they must learn to participate in learning systems as well. Knowledge production is becoming more distributed, complex, and diversified, in disciplines and industries (Gibbons *et al.*, 1994); in regional economies such as Silicon Valley (Saxenian, 1996); and among consumers who have the potential of forming communities (Snyder, 1999).

In these learning systems, organizations find the talents they need, new ideas, technological developments, best practices, and learning partners. The rules of participation in social learning systems are different from those of product markets. You don't simply compete; in fact, your most threatening competitor may be your best partner when it comes to learning together. If you hoard your knowledge in a social learning system, you quickly appear as taking more than you give, and you will be progressively excluded from the most significant exchanges.

In a knowledge economy, sustained success for any organization will depend not only on effective participation in economic markets, but, just as importantly and with many of the same players, on knowing how to participate in broader social learning systems.

References

Anderson, B. (1983) *Imagined Communities*. London: Verso.

Brown, J.S. and Duguid, P. (1999) 'Organizing Knowledge', *Reflections* 1(2).

Eckert, P. (1989) *Jocks and Burnouts: Social Categories and Identity in the High School*. New York: Teachers College Press.

Gibbons, M. *et al.* (1994) *The New Production of Knowledge: The Dynamics of Science and Research in Contemporary Societies*. London: Sage.

Giddens, A. (1991) *Modernity and Self-identity: Self and Society in the Late Modern Age*. Stanford, CA: Stanford University Press.

Handy, C. (1989) *The Age of Unreason*. Cambridge, MA: Harvard Business School Press.

Lave, J. and Wenger, E. (1991) *Situated Learning: Legitimate Peripheral Participation*. New York: Cambridge University Press.

McDermott, R. (1999) 'Learning across Teams: How to Build Communities of Practice in Team-based Organizations', *Knowledge Management Review* 8 (May/June): 32–36.

Saxenian, A. (1996) *Regional Advantage: Culture and Competition in Silicon Valley and Route 128*. Cambridge, MA: Harvard University Press.

Snyder, W. (1999) 'Organization and World Design: The Gaia's Hypotheses'. Submitted to the Academy of Management, Division of Organizations and the Natural Environment, John M. Jermier, College of Business, University of South Florida, Tampa, FL.

Star, S.L. and Griesemer, J. (1989) 'Institutional Ecology, "Translation," and Boundary Objects: Amateurs and Professionals in Berkeley's Museum of Vertebrate Zoology, 1907–1939', *Social Studies of Science* 19: 387–420.

Wenger, E. (1998) *Communities of Practice: Learning, Meaning, and Identity*. New York: Cambridge University Press.

Wenger, E. and Snyder, W. (2000) 'Communities of Practice? The Organizational Frontier', *Harvard Business Review* January–February.

Chapter 11

The learning city in the learning society

Sue Cara, Charles Landry and Stewart Ranson

Moving learning centre stage

Introduction

Education and learning need to move centre stage to secure our future well-being – and especially so in periods of rapid, yet consistent social transformation (Ranson, 1998). Only if learning is placed at the centre of our daily experience can:

- individuals continue to develop their skills and capacities;
- organisations and institutions recognise how to harness the potential of their workforce and be able to respond flexibly and imaginatively to the opportunities and difficulties of this paradigmatic period of change we are living through;
- cities act responsively and adapt flexibly to emerging needs;
- societies understand that the diversity and differences between communities can become a source of enrichment, understanding and potential.

A learning society is much more than a society whose members are simply well educated; it goes well beyond merely learning in the classroom. It is a place or a society where the idea of learning infuses every tissue of its being: a place where individuals and organisations are encouraged to learn about the dynamics of where they live and how it is changing; a place that on that basis changes the way it learns whether through schools or any other institution that can help foster understanding and knowledge; a place in which all its members are encouraged to learn; finally and perhaps most importantly a place that can learn to change the conditions of its learning democratically.

This is an edited version of an article previously published in *The Richness of Cities: Urban Policy in a New Landscape*. 1998. Reproduced by permission of Comedia.

The lineages of the learning city

The idea of a 'learning society' became enormously influential during the 1990s. In the UK it has provided one of the guiding assumptions for the renewal of the economy and society for national politicians, the National Commission on Education, the European Commission White Paper on education and training, city policy makers, corporate strategists and industrial trainers. The vision that informs the idea of learning societies or communities has in particular become central to creative strategies for regenerating cities, towns and regions. The ideas and concepts have inspired the formation of the Learning Cities Network in the UK, which has grown rapidly and includes a number of cities, including Derby, Hull, Liverpool, Milton Keynes, Norwich, Nottingham, Sheffield and Stockton, as well as places with Learning City initiatives including Birmingham, Brighton, Co. Durham & Darlington, Gloucester, Greenwich, Tyneside and York. Cities and communities are increasingly understanding that the mutual learning processes unleashed, and the potential uncovered, by involving the various publics in cities is immense, as is the power of synergy through building partnerships of traditional and non-traditional organisations concerned with learning. This enhances the capacity for economic and social renewal in a period of global change. In Europe too there is a similar interest in taking forward this set of ideas.

The concept of the *learning city* was promoted initially by an OECD/CERI study in 1992 (Hirsch, 1993) and this became a major influence upon the development of the Learning Cities Network in the UK. Ideas in relation to how *individuals best learn*, and how *the learning organisation* learns as well as historical connections to the idea of the *village college* have also contributed to our understanding of the different aspects and levels of learning in the learning community.

Learning thus needs to be understood at different levels:

- how individuals can continue to develop their skills and capacities throughout their lives;
- how the 'learning institution', be that a school, a training agency or a company with nothing specifically to do with learning, is enabled to respond openly and imaginatively;
- how the 'learning city and town' can provide for itself the preconditions to develop a sense of direction for its future;
- how the 'learning region' can understand the resources and cultural traditions it has to tap into in order to enable it to support economic and social development.

The learning city or the educated city?

The terms 'learning' and 'learning city' are used rather than 'education', 'educating' or 'educated city'. Why do we wish to distinguish these terms? We do so because the concept of 'education' is restrictive, leading to a focus on a particular institutional system. Learning is a more overarching process that embodies education. Learning is both concerned with the way educational and learning processes proceed as well as with a whole raft of skills and core competencies well beyond the satisfaction of immediate vocational needs, or indeed those traditionally considered as educational. The capacity for learning, and thus enrichment and understanding of the place one lives in and how one relates to it, includes as preconditions a strong focus on human and social capital development.

It is easy to envisage the learning city merely as a place that both enables and encourages its citizens to educate themselves as they have greater 'leisure' time while simultaneously being increasingly responsible for their own education and development. Yet in that model of the learning city, the defining characteristics are the nature and extent of educational investment and its take-up by citizens. Thus the city with a high number of university and college places, extensive investment in apprenticeships and vocational training and an active adult education sector may be described as a learning city. It would have comprehensive ladders of educational opportunity at the formal and informal level.

But this is a very limited definition. It could be argued that it does no more than state the obvious fact that cities with a high proportion of students are better educated than those that, for reasons of poverty or short-sightedness, have failed to invest in higher education. Critically, as a concept, it fails to deal with issues of collective learning, of quality or to present a developmental challenge. There are towns that can demonstrate a high degree of success in some respects such as Kirklees, which do not have highly ranked universities. So a definition of a learning city that considers only the extent of its educational sector, even with some qualitative measures, may be inadequate.

The other danger is that it offers little guidance to cities beyond the suggestion that they should invest in educational infrastructure. The UK, for example, saw an explosion of further and higher education in the 1990s with cities like Derby and Portsmouth witnessing a huge expansion. In 1990, Derby College of Further Education had fewer than 1,500 students: by 1998 it had 14,000 and it is still expanding. It now has a very big 'learning factory' yet the impact of this on the city remains to be seen. A definition of the learning city that restricts itself to easily identifiable and measurable areas such as the formal and informal education sectors, vocational and in-service training and similar activity is entirely feasible. But, just as there is a difference between knowledge and understanding, we would argue that this is an unnecessarily limited concept of the learning city: indeed, a better term would be the educated city.

A learning city is a reflexive city

There is another way of envisaging the learning city. A true learning city is one that develops by learning from its experiences and those of others. It is constantly on the lookout, searching out examples of success and failure and always asking why is this so. It benchmarks itself to appropriate other cities to get a grip on how well it is developing. It is thus a place that understands itself and reflects upon that understanding – it is a 'reflexive city'. It is a place where individuals feel they can become empowered, where organisations – public, private and voluntary – are open-minded, and most importantly a place where this amalgam of various actors with differing cultures coalesce to work together towards an agreed set of objectives for its city. The key characteristic of the learning city is its ability to develop successfully in a rapidly changing socio-economic environment. In order to do this it nurtures the potential of all, because it understands that in the emerging knowledge based economy it is the capacity to learn and reflect in all its facets, in responding to urban challenges, that will largely determine success or failure. It knows that knowledge is more than information. Today cities have one crucial resource – their people. It is their cleverness, ingenuity, aspirations, motivations, imagination and creativity that are today of crucial economic significance, as the old locational factors – raw materials, market access – diminish to the point of insignificance. Thus the objective of far sighted urban leaders should be to 'embed a culture of learning into the genetic code of their city'.

Where the unreflective city flounders by trying to repeat past success for far too long, the learning city is creative in its understanding of its own situation and wider relationships, developing new solutions to new problems. The essential point here is that any city can be a learning city. It is not a factor of size, geography, resources, economic infrastructure or even educational investment (though this will play an increasingly important role if a city is to sustain itself as a learning organism in the emerging knowledge economy). To some extent, it might be argued that the fewer natural or historical advantages a city enjoys, the more important it is that it should rethink itself as a learning city.

The learning city is thus strategic, creative, imaginative and intelligent – it looks at its potential resources in a far more comprehensive way. It sees competitive edge in the seemingly insignificant; it can even turn weakness into strength. An example from Huddersfield might suffice. The town not particularly renowned for its creativity drew up a strategic programme called the Creative Town Initiative made up of 20 projects based on the idea of the cycle of urban creativity. Some projects actively encourage individuals and groups to have ideas and generate projects, such as their 'creativity forum'. Others are concerned with turning ideas into practice, such as the 'advisory service for inventors' or the 'creativity investment services'. Products and services need to be circulated and here the Northern Creative Alliance is an example. Then there are projects for people to work on ideas and showcase them and finally to disseminate them.

By this definition the learning city is both richer and more complex than the educated city, though it encompasses it. It requires investigation not only of a city's educational inputs, but many areas such as the open-mindedness and flexibility of city institutions, the quality of partnerships, the track record of innovation, vitality of democratic and political activity, questions of empowerment and so on. But this very richness does make both definition and evaluation of the learning city more complex. The learning city/society concept is thus a multifaceted idea. Just remember the range of learning environments as one instance (devised by R. Balsam, Kent County Council):

- *Obvious*: Pre-school groups, nurseries; schools; colleges; universities; adult learners' centres, homes; libraries; television.
- *Less obvious*: Businesses; community centres; arts centres; museums and attractions; health centres; post offices; citizens advice bureaux; cities; towns; villages; the Internet; nature reserves; the outdoors; newspapers; bookshops.
- *Surprising*: Old people's homes; homeless shelters; refuges; prisons; shopping malls; hospitals; churches; trains; stations; football stadia; service stations; restaurants; hotels; cafes; nightclubs; local parks.

The importance of the city unit

The CERI/OECD (Hirsch, 1993) report concentrates its attention specifically on cities pointing out that the majority of people in OECD countries live in cities or urban areas with populations greater than 100,000. While recognising that the city is not the only geographical area on which to base education and training – accepting for example that national and regional governments may be best placed to initiate broad policy changes – it argues that the city unit in particular is capable of making a significant difference in terms of advancing lifelong learning.

The city provides an area of a size that offers scope for collaboration and a sizeable learning infrastructure. However, Hirsch also identifies a sense of urban identity as being important and indicates the difficulty in some conurbations of using the concept of the learning city because a strong sense of self-identity may not exist. Within the range of British places that call themselves learning cities there are places that are either too small or too diverse to fit the pattern but that have nevertheless found value in either the concept or the way of working that underlies it. However in terms of the development of lifelong learning other sizes and kinds of community have felt that they could use similar strategies and need similar kinds of initiative.

What seems to have attracted a number of British towns and cities about the ideas in the CERI/OECD report were the 'ideas for action' and in the reports of what cities had been doing. These included Norwich, Nottingham, Hull and Derby. Thus by the end of 1996 about twenty British cities had either adopted a title reflecting the idea of a learning city or were considering doing so, and a network of learning cities was meeting on a regular basis.

Part of the attraction of the concept of a lifelong learning strategy that focuses on the local is that it allows for variation according to the needs and aspirations of the community concerned. This is apparent in the international examples given in the CERI/OECD report but, even given the shared national context of the British examples, there are differences of emphasis that reflect the priorities of those involved. However, there are common themes that run through the concept as developed both in the OECD work and also through the thinking of European and world lifelong learning initiatives.

The now many examples of practice show that what has actually been done has varied and continues to vary from community to community. Thus Sheffield has been seriously concerned to involve communities in decision-making on learning within the city, Hull has been concerned to build the education and training work of the City of Learning into the economic development plan for the city as a whole and Norwich has marketed and promoted learning through a guidance shop and a festival.

Learning in the community

In education, the interpretation given to learning cities typically focuses upon developing the opportunities for individuals to develop education and training throughout their lives. The learning city movement by contrast argues that the city, and the strategies it adopts, can make a difference to lifelong learning. This is for several reasons:

- People relate their participation in learning activities to their immediate environment, and a lifelong learning culture is hard to achieve through national initiatives alone.
- It is important to create coherence among a very large number of actors now involved in the planning and delivery of education and training. Beyond initial schooling, there is no single 'system' conveniently managed by a centralised public structure. Here, again the city can be a useful focus, as illustrated by the 'Further Education Council' developed in Edmonton, which acts as co-ordinator and policy forum for the many

providers of adult learning. In Norwich and in Sheffield 'Learning City' initiatives developed from post-16 provider partnerships.

- The nature of much adult learning is community-based. This makes it possible to build learning elements into city-led community activity – from health awareness campaigns to support for small enterprises. Conversely, learning in a city can be seen as a means of community action. In Kakegawa, Japan, lifelong learning has been a way of involving citizens in the revitalisation of their city (Hirsch, 1993).

The strategies of partnership – inside and outside local authorities and in and outside 'classic' educational institutions – and the more holistic, cross-departmental governance implied throughout the learning city discussion is promoted strongly by the European Learning Cities movement (Hirsch, 1993), which argues for:

- the development of city-wide coalitions co-ordinating all relevant actors in both public and private sectors of education;
- the co-ordination of work-oriented and general/leisure-oriented education and training, in a way that allows all citizens easily to relate their development as individuals to their development as workers, exemplified in the public sector union Unison's Return to Work scheme;
- the co-ordination of learning at different stages, for example by encouraging different generations to learn together and to learn from each other; whether this be in a library, the workplace or a school, or as shown by family literacy initiatives;
- the use of local media both as teaching tools in themselves and to raise awareness of learning opportunities, such as Eastern Counties Newspapers' supplement for the Norwich Learning Festival;
- the promotion of the concept of the 'learning city', in which communities attempt to learn collectively through public dialogue as a means of changing their own futures.

Regenerating the city through public dialogue

Michael Piore (1995) brings out the need for public dialogue in local regeneration brilliantly in a study of the significance of dialogue for local development: whereby a form of double-loop learning is instigated as the key to regeneration. This involves going beneath the surface of a problem to locate its source in underlying differences of interests and values and recognising that shared understanding and agreement can only grow out of a dialogue that addresses these difficult differences.

In traditional economic development, the nation state and the large corporation were the central change agents when it was being driven by the logic of mass production. Then growth was perceived to depend upon highly specialised resources, dedicated capital equipment and narrowly trained semi-skilled workers. Now, in the context of globalisation, roles are changing. Subnational communities become more dependent on their own initiative and this requires them to become clear about who they are and how their traditions and resources can be developed for world markets. Piore (1995: 80) suggests:

> In the new environment, development is about the community finding a place for itself in world markets and thinking about how to turn its particular cultural heritage into an asset in that endeavour. It is no longer a question simply of negotiating among local interests to obtain resources . . . it is more a question of purposeful reflection and debate within the local community.

This is where the learning city or community comes in as it needs to deliberate upon both the nature of its own community and how it can adapt to the changing outside world in which it must live. Many examples reinforce the notion of groups, businesses, communities 'learning to support each other' and develop the 'capacity for co-operation'. The role of government in this new world is 'to catalyse that learning process', enable the creation of a denser network of collaborative relationships.

Cities learning together

In one example, given by Michael Piore (1995), small teams of community leaders drawn from different economic and social groups in the city were sent overseas to visit cities that might serve as models for economic regeneration. Piore describes how these visits served a number of purposes including enlarging the vision of team members, and providing materials to catalyse the debate at home. However the most significant benefit is:

> the experience of travelling together in a foreign environment helps people from different, often antagonistic segments of the local community get to know each other: it breaks down the barriers among them and provides a common set of experiences and shared knowledge base upon which to build a more co-operative relationship.
>
> (1995: 81)

Similar evidence of the centrality of this type of learning comes from two other sources. In the first, a Comedia study of how the Swedish public library system was innovating itself assessed how different forms of communications assisted learning and innovation, whether this be through reading books, talking to friends, television, conferences, seminars, the Internet and so on. It found that the most profound learning experiences came from librarians

jointly visiting another place, preferably another country, to see a best practice example, but using this opportunity for discussing the new ideas or
innovations that they were trying out at home.

The other example comes from the work of the Washington-based
Partners for Liveable Communities described in 'The State of the American
Community: Empowerment for Local Action'. It notes:

> A representative group must find pleasure in the association and
> profit in learning together. One way is shared experience, retreats, study
> trips, seminars that build first name familiarity and personal bonds that
> foster collaboration. For example 60 people from all walks of life in
> Chattanooga visited Indianapolis. Those 60 people discussed Indianapolis
> proposals to improve how the city worked, how Indianapolis has been able
> to depoliticize issues too important for political division. But in the process
> of learning about Indianapolis they learnt about one another. They
> travelled by bus returned home then created Chattanooga Venturer, a
> vision for the city; now 10 years later they have completed Re-vision 2000,
> an encore of their original vision. Indeed the example was so successful
> that it won one of the Habitat best practice awards.

In Britain, urban regeneration projects increasingly provide illustrations of
Piore's theme of dialogue being central to learning for community development. Initiatives include the setting up of local forums, or citizens' panels,
Planning for Real sessions; developing joint Parish Maps; Community
Appraisals; Action Planning techniques to promote effective dialogue
between different interest groups as well as between members of the community or local economic developers about the key local issues of poverty,
unemployment and social exclusion. Planning partnerships are formed, or
coalitions built, between local developers, voluntary associations and local
communities to support credit unions, access courses, or new jobs, because
there is recognition that economic access of excluded groups (e.g. the young
black unemployed, or single mothers) to training and jobs develops the social
and economic wealth of the community. The social capacity (and thus
wealth) of disadvantaged communities has also been enhanced through
organised action of local 'user groups' seeking to identify gaps in services
that are vital to support women if they are to contribute to the labour market
or take up learning opportunities, as well as support young children.

Understanding the learning city

A learning city is much more than an educated city, it is a living urban
system where the idea of learning is put centre stage to the city's development. It is a place that:

- learns about itself and how it is changing;
- needs to change the way it learns;
- develops in a way in which all its members are learning;
- can learn to change the conditions of learning, democratically.

These ideas will be explored in turn.

A place that learns about itself and how it is changing

A learning society is a society that needs to learn about itself and the significant changes that it faces if it is to survive and flourish in the future. The great theorist of the learning society has been Donald Schön (1971), whose *Beyond the Stable State: Public and Private Learning in a Changing Society* was presented as the Reith Lectures in 1970. Its analysis sought to help a society confront transforming change by understanding that placing learning at the centre was the key to future viability. Societies and institutions are, he argued, routinely characterised by 'dynamic conservatism'. The belief in the virtue of a stable, unchanging order as the best protection against the threat of destabilising change is very deep. In an ordered world, we know who we are, what our roles are and thus how to act. Change threatens crisis because we will not know how to act, will lose the stabilising sense of who we are. We are plunged into uncertainty.

Yet societies face unprecedented and continuing change that erodes the possibility of ever recovering the traditions of stability. In the current period of transformation, stable views of occupations, religions, organisations and value systems have been lost. We must learn to live 'beyond the stable state'.

- The loss of the stable state means that our society and all its institutions, including the educational ones, are in *continuing* processes of transformation. We cannot expect new stable states that will endure even for our own lifetimes.
- We must learn to understand, guide, influence and manage these transformations. We must make the capacity for undertaking change integral to ourselves and to our institutions.
- We must, in other words, become adept at learning. We must be able not only to transform our institutions, in response to changing situations and requirements; we must invent and develop institutions or networks or partnership forms that are 'learning systems', that is to say, systems capable of bringing about their own continuing transformation.
- The task that the loss of the stable state makes imperative for the person, for our institutions, for our society as a whole, is to learn about learning.

What are the conditions for institutions and societies to become learning systems – 'social systems [that] learn to become capable of transforming themselves without intolerable disruption' (Schön, 1971: 60)? Schön finds models of learning societies in studies of social movements and the constellation business firm, which present 'paradigms of learning systems for the society as a whole' (ibid.: 61). Their characteristics include emphasis on flexibility, apparent lack of structure, no fixed centre, overlapping networks and feedback loops that enable learning and self-transformation. Societies, like organisations, need to learn about how they learn.

These characteristics are comparable to those discovered within the Comedia Creative City project (Landry et al., 1996) where urban decision makers felt the key attributes required from their cities to adapt to the future were: encouraging more open internal and external communications; enhanced networking capacity; a greater harnessing of skills right through the organisation; recreating governance structures to unleash potential of individuals and thus allowing individuals to learn through empowerment; the capacity to be able to break rules and for organisations to reassess success and failure; encouraging pilot projects, catalyst events and catalyst organisations and on occasion importing outsider talent to bring in new ideas and perspectives.

A place that needs to change the way it learns

If a society or city is changing, it needs to learn how it is changing and thus probably needs to change the way it learns. How we learn is shaped by our social structures and the influence of historical traditions. Torsten Husen's work on the learning society (1974, 1986, 1990) has been particularly influential in educational studies and practice because of its preoccupation with reflection upon and reform of traditional forms of learning. The task of reforming education to meet the needs of a changing society required, Husen argued, a critical review of the institutionalised nature of schools without moving to the excess of 'deschooling'. The reform of education would require a number of system level conditions to enable the creation of a learning society: first, a massive expansion in participation in education; second, the appropriate technology to support the knowledge explosion and the processing, storing and retrieval of information; and third, the need to individualise instruction so that each student develops a programme of learning that suits them best.

The learning society will need to provide a foundation of general education and vocational training. The purpose of education should be to prepare young people for 'general citizenship'. The inexorable trend to a society ruled by specialists and experts (a 'meritocracy') needs to be balanced by 'a common liberal schooling' that encourages communications skills so that citizens can speak to and understand each other. Education should also prepare young people for changing careers and the continuing need for re-education, and will accomplish these purposes more effectively in the future if it concentrates on inculcating certain fundamental learning processes, 'by providing a basic repertoire of skills as well as attitudes of flexibility and a taste for more, a motivation for going on with education' (Husen, 1974: 199).

A place in which all its members are learning

A learning society or city is a place that recognises that learning cannot be separated from society and is not just for the young but for all throughout their lives. Radical educators from the 1970s onwards already understood that only more far reaching reforms could facilitate the learning society and help it respond to the transformations of the late twentieth century. The deep learning required by the learning society is the need to learn two indispensable capacities:

- *the capacity for co-operative action*: the predicaments of our time, such as the environment, or human rights and justice, can only be resolved by human beings together and in common;
- *the capacity for agency*: that cities will flourish when their members cease being passive spectators and become active citizens participating in and sharing responsibility for the well-being of their communities.

Crucially adult educators have been most likely to build upon this heritage to develop analysis of a learning society for all.

If learning as doing is to be promoted more widely, then imaginative approaches are needed, for example developing 'learning exchanges' that enable people to get in touch with those who have knowledge or skill they wish to benefit from. Public libraries, moreover, have the potential to become centres for this kind of learning exchange, and to

> make available not just books and a few audio visual materials, but musical instruments, music practice rooms . . . and the equipment needed to do a wide range of arts and crafts . . . libraries might also keep and lend toys, games, elementary scientific equipment, chemistry and electronic kits, sports equipment, skates, rackets and so on.
>
> (Holt, 1977: 43).

Institutional flexibility is the central quality as institutions respond to diverse and changing needs by developing connections across traditional boundaries of school, college, work and community. Moreover, as Robert Aitken (1983: 46) argued, 'we need to break away from a rigid delivery system of fixed entry points, of hours in the day, terms, academic years and self-contained levels and entry qualifications. Diversity, accessibility, transferability, partnership and accountability become the defining characteristics of a comprehensive system of continuing education. As Flude and Parrott (1979) suggest, the role of the educator changes in such a system from formal provider of given, unchangeable learning experiences, to the 'educator as impresario, as course compiler, as guide, as counsellor and link man [sic] – these will be the new specialisms in a recurrent system'.

A place that learns to change the conditions of learning, democratically

A society that is to learn about how it is changing has to learn the conditions of learning and these fundamentally are social and political. A learning society must be a learning democracy. Different aspects of this idea have been grasped by educators in the past. The task of reforming education from an elite (selective) to a socially just (comprehensive) system can never be a purely educational or pedagogical problem, but has to be conceived as a social and political one.

> The problems facing educational planners are not just problems of pedagogy. They are problems of social justice, of national economy and of preparation for a rapidly changing society where lifelong learning becomes imperative. Educational problems in rapidly changing society are too important to be left entirely to educators.
>
> (Husen, 1974: xvi)

The need is for new institutional processes to be created and old structures to be discarded. Governments have typically been inept at the process of public learning, at learning about the mistakes of the past, and, for example, in creating overcentralised public bureaucracies. If governments are to become learning systems, they must recognise that the movement of learning is not from centre to periphery, as in traditional models, but from periphery to periphery, or from periphery to the centre. Much of the initiative for reforming education has come bottom up, viz. comprehensives, bilingualism, equal opportunities, etc. Continuing adaptation is best supported through fostering new ideas, enabling local networks of learning, creating task groups responsible for projects, and an intelligence function that monitors and evaluates them. As Schön (1971: 189) suggests, the need is for differentiated, responsive, continually changing but connected reaction': such constellations allow diversity at the periphery without giving up central control. The emphasis is upon networks, facilitation, co-ordination, knitting together. A central role is given to the roles of change agents, who might be entrepreneurs, consultants, researchers, reflective intellectuals in any organisation or institution.

New urban values

The above definitions of a learning city as a place of constant innovation, change, and of experimenting with new forms of partnership and democracy involve confronting the contemporary world with different and often conflicting conceptions about the values that should shape society. Learning to understand and reconcile those differences so that communities with ostensibly incommensurable values can share the same social and institutional space is the task of politics.

A society with the capacity to learn about itself depends upon the quality of political institutions to enable that learning. A learning society can only grow out of a learning democracy. The *polis*, as Aristotle understood, is the only arena in which contending claims and interests can be deliberated, transcended and aggregated in collective decision. A society can only remake itself when the different groups within decide they can act together, and such collective action depends upon reaching shared understanding about the purposes of change and the conditions that will enable all to develop and realise their capacities. This learning democracy is of course also a place that is likely to be more economically prosperous as it harnesses potential and reduces social exclusion.

The purposes of the learning community

The learning community has two principal and interconnected purposes (Cara and Ranson, 1998): to support the learning of individuals throughout their lives and to learn how to promote social and economic regeneration:

- *Lifelong learning: encouraging individuals and institutions to involve themselves in learning throughout their lives*
  The changing nature of work will require people to adapt and upgrade their skills and knowledge throughout their lives if they are to survive in the labour market. Employment will be attracted to high skill communities. Successful cities and towns are attractive places to live as well as providing employment opportunities. Learning needs to support and enrich the life of communities as a whole. The more people participate in learning activities of both a formal and informal nature the richer, more successful and attractive their community is likely to become.
- *Regeneration: learning about how the community is changing*
  The learning community is one that strives to understand how it is changing in order to be able to shape its future. It needs to learn about the context of change – in population movements, growth as well as decline in its industrial and commercial base, the impact of new technologies on communication systems – if it is to influence change to create the knowledge society. Thus communities that are in the process

of regeneration need to learn, not merely to develop the skills of their citizens but to understand how the different parts of city life – social, cultural and political as well as economic – can connect together more effectively to sustain the future well-being of the community.

The tasks of the learning community

If learning is to be made attractive then communities will have to learn to create new forms of partnership between sectors and ways of listening to and involving the public.

- *Partnership*
  A fragmented education and training sector – with inadequate connections between sectors and competition between providers particularly in the post-school phase – does not facilitate the participation needed for the learning age. An early phase of the learning community work is to build the partnerships between sectors and institutions that encourage participation and progression in learning of all members of the community. Such partnerships:
  - develop community-wide coalitions bringing together relevant partners from public and private sectors;
  - co-ordinate approaches to the various kinds of learning offered within the community whether formal, informal or work based;
  - make contacts across sectors and educational phases;
  - use the media to promote an appetite for learning.
- *Participation*
  These partnerships need to become part of a broader public dialogue, the purpose of which is to clarify the future of the city, town or region in an era of global change. Traditionally, public services have been delivered to the public with too little consultation and involvement. Democracy has been at a distance from the communities it was created to serve. Now, however, many cities and towns are looking to find new ways of strengthening the important traditions of local democratic practice and understanding the contribution of participation to regeneration. This understanding has been learned in a number of European communities.

Real learning communities will learn new kinds of engagements with their citizens to involve them in determining how their communities will be governed and change. This process demands citizens who have the skills to articulate their needs and aspirations, which are the same skills needed for work and leisure in a society that is in a state of change. The educational system has an important part to play in moving to such a culture of learning but other parts of the community – its democratic and cultural traditions – also have a key role to play in renewing the quality and vitality of public life.

If the learning community is to encourage its citizens to commit themselves to learning it will have to be imaginative in the way it provides learning opportunities:

- developing variety and flexibility in the kinds of involvement people can have in the learning process;
- recognising and valuing all kinds of learning within and for the advancement of the community.

Learning here is not only engagement in the formal educational processes but the connecting of the many kinds of learning, in the workplace, the voluntary organisation and the family with the purpose of making the community a better place to live.

How do learning city initiatives begin?

How have learning community initiatives been started? Looking at those places that term themselves learning communities in England, the way that things have begun has been almost as various as the places themselves. The most we can do is to pick out a number of key elements that seem to be necessary and then to look at the way things have grown.

- *Key individuals*: Individuals seem to be important in two ways, those who believe in the idea of the learning city/town and who start to persuade others to consider the idea and those powerful individuals who can give an initiative credibility within the community by their support and patronage.
- *Key institutions*: The adoption of the idea of the learning community by a particular institution and the leadership and support provided by that institution are crucial to building the initiative in the early stages. Although partnerships may develop, the groundwork has to be undertaken and resourced. Training and Enterprise Councils, universities and local authorities have all played this role.
- *A core group*: Once the idea has captured the enthusiasm of a number of influential people and been taken on by a specific institution, time has to be devoted to drafting papers, convening meetings, networking with potential contacts and sponsors. An embryonic organisation will need to be created. This will include an advisory or steering group composed of key organisations in the city or town. Membership of such an advisory or steering committee will involve willingness to commit at least time and possibly other resources to enable the fledgling initiative of the learning city to get off the ground.
- *Wider interests*: The germ of an idea, even if a small number of the influential are drawn to it, will only really take hold if the wider community

are persuaded of its validity and significance. The task of developing support from the wider community suggests the importance of seminars and conferences that can engender the necessary groundswell of enthusiasm. These events can be accompanied by strategies of consultation to test the degrees of support for the idea of the learning city. A conference can be followed up by a feedback questionnaire that tests opinions.

- *Launch events*: Sometimes overlapping with the conferences mentioned above, following a period of development work and consultation, the preparations may lead to a formal launch event with significant media coverage.

There is no simple system to be implemented: it has to be made to measure for each organisation. Problems can occur with:

- lack of commitment from key people
- inappropriate organisational culture
- too little time devoted
- inadequate staff expertise
- defining indicators and obtaining the appropriate information

A learning community that reflexively monitors and evaluates its development will ensure that the different sectors of the city, town or region are aware of, seek to learn from, and replicate where appropriate imaginative and effective practices of regeneration and lifelong learning.

Conclusion

In an age of global transition learning becomes central to the future of communities, local and national. The creative achievement of a growing number of cities and towns is to recognise that regeneration depends upon learning to reconstruct their communities through partnerships and public participation while reflecting back upon what has been achieved. They are learning that only a more active democracy that enables citizens to make and remake the communities in which they live and work can sustain their future.

References

Aitken, R. (1983) *Comprehensive Education For Life*, Coventry, Coventry City Council.

Cara, S. and Ranson, S. (1998) *Practice, Progress and Value: The Learning Community Assessing the Value They Add*, Sheffield, DfEE; Learning City Network.

Flude, R. and Parrott, A. (1979) *Education and the Challenge of Change: A Recurrent Education Strategy for Britain*, Milton Keynes, The Open University Press.

Hirsch, D. (1993) *City Strategies for Lifelong Learning*, Gothenburg, CERI/OECD.

Holt, J. (1977) *Instead of Education*, Harmondsworth, Penguin.

Husen, T. (1974) *The Learning Society*, London, Methuen.

Husen, T. (1986) *The Learning Society Revisited*, Oxford, Pergamon.

Husen, T. (1990) *Education and the Global Concern*, Oxford, Pergamon.

Landry, C. et al. (1996) *The Creative City in Britain & Germany*, London, Anglo-German Foundation.

Piore, M. (1995) Local development on the progressive political agenda, in C. Crouch and D. Marquand (eds) *Reinventing Collective Action: From the Global to the Local*, Oxford, Blackwell.

Ranson, S. (ed.) (1998) *Inside the Learning Society*, London, Cassell.

Schön, D. (1971) *Beyond the Stable State: Public and Private Learning in a Changing Society*, New York, W.W. Norton.

Chapter 12

Learning for active citizenship
Training for and learning from participation in area regeneration

Marjorie Mayo

Introduction

Lifelong learning has emerged in recent years as a key issue on the policy agenda, with an apparently widespread consensus that 'it is going to be central to the economic well-being of the UK for us to create a learning society' (Tuckett, 1997: 1). This emphasis upon lifelong learning as a means of enabling individuals to adapt to changes in the world of work has been characteristic of debates not only in Britain but in the European Union and beyond (Edwards, 1997). While there has been a predominant focus upon lifelong learning in relation to the goal of increasing economic competitiveness this has not been the only policy objective. As Jacques Delors, then president of the European Commission reflected, lifelong education must, in addition,

> constitute a continuous process of forming whole human beings – their knowledge and aptitudes, as well as the critical faculty and ability to act. It should enable people to develop awareness of themselves and their environment and encourage them to play their social role at work and in the community.
>
> (Delors, quoted in NAGCELL, 1997)

In addition to 'securing our economic future', the Secretary of State for Education and Employment in the UK reflected, in his introduction to the Green Paper *The Learning Age*, that learning has been valued for its wider contribution and the promotion of active citizenship. It 'enables people to play a full part in their community' (DfEE, 1998: 7).

There might seem to have been increasing interest in developing connections between lifelong learning and community capacity-building. Policies for the development of social capital have been linked with strategies to

This chapter was first published by NIACE in *Studies in The Education of Adults*, 32:1, April 2000.

combat social exclusion and facilitate wider processes of democratic renewal. In the UK these concerns can be traced in the NAGCELL Report (1997) as well as in policy papers on urban regeneration, on social exclusion and on the revitalisation of local democracy. The NAGCELL Report (1997) argued that support should be given to projects and initiatives that 'build capacity, strengthen voluntary organisation and contribute to social and economic regeneration ... [lifelong learning] with its opportunities for critical reflection and creative initiative can strengthen democracy and community development'. This recognises the vital role of voluntary organisations and community groups in the development of education for active citizenship.

Does this apparent convergence of interest demonstrate an underlying analytical consensus? Is there even consensus on the definitions of the key terms in question or are (catch) phrases such as 'lifelong learning', 'community capacity-building', 'active citizenship' and 'community empowerment' actually being used with varying and contested meanings? If, on closer inspection, this apparent convergence were seen to be more problematic, what might be the differing implications for policies and practice?

There is a range of evidence to support the case for co-ordinating policies – 'joined-up thinking' – for lifelong learning and active citizenship. Community participants need access to appropriate education and training *for* capacity-building, just as professionals need appropriate education and training, if they are to work with communities in empowering ways. What 'appropriateness' might mean in practice, however, depends upon how capacity-building and empowerment are defined, by whom and according to whose agendas.

Conversely, the process of participating can, itself, provide learning experiences, both for individuals and for community organisations, learning *from* active citizenship, which may be more – or indeed less – effectively facilitated by adult educators (Elsdon, 1991; Elsdon *et al.*, 1993). This chapter considers evidence from research on education and learning in area regeneration, as a means of exploring these different aspects. The two research projects, later referred to in more detail, were both based upon UK experience. However, the questions that these experiences raise may have potential implications for debates elsewhere, including theoretical debates on the transformation and development of adult knowledge through participation in social practice (Billett, 1998).

As Schuller has argued, in face of the 'suspiciously unchallengeable' consensus that seems to pervade so much of the debate on the 'learning society', it is important 'to sustain traditional social scientific concerns with relationships of power and be alert to claims of vested interests' (including the vested interests of adult educators) (Schuller, 1998: 11). The research that this chapter draws upon also raises questions about this apparent consensus. In practice there are questions, too, about who is doing this learning for active citizenship – who, conversely, is not – and who emerges as effectively excluded. How is this learning being facilitated most effectively – or not? What lessons are actually being learnt, in terms of whose definitions and agendas for active citizenship and empowerment, whether for transformatory aims – or not?

Having explored these questions, the chapter concludes by identifying a number of policy implications, if lifelong learning and active citizenship are to be supported as part of concerted strategies to promote social inclusion and democratic renewal, while safeguarding the space for varying approaches and continuing debate. Although the chapter focuses upon UK experience and research findings, in view of the wider interest in lifelong learning, social capital and democratic renewal, there may be resonances with debates and trends in Europe and elsewhere (Bron et al., 1998).

Contested concepts: varying agendas

Despite the 'suspiciously unchallengeable consensus' that appears to surround it, the concept of lifelong learning has in fact been used in differing ways, as part of varying agendas. As Edwards (1997: 13) has pointed out:

> Within the discussion of lifelong learning and a learning society we have, for instance, the discourses of learners, lecturers, managers, policy-makers, academics, professional bodies, employers, trade unions, awarding bodies, think tanks, journalists and commentators. Each has their own discourses through which the terrain is constructed, contested and challenged, for example, liberal humanist, human resource management, skills training, social action.

In addition 'not all discourses are equal and the power embedded within them also seeks to construct certain discourses as more valid, "truer" than others' (ibid.).

In the current context the 'modernisers'' version of lifelong learning has been predominant – a focus upon lifelong learning in terms of the needs of the economy and the requirements of the market. In this version of the learning society, institutions provide services for individuals as a condition for supporting the competitiveness of the market. Such an approach has characterised employers' bodies and a range of policy think-tanks, in response to the perceived need for economic restructuring since the 1970s.

UK government policy papers such as *The Learning Age* (DfEE, 1998) do also refer to other meanings – lifelong learning for active citizenship, equal opportunities and social inclusion. The citation from the Secretary of State's introduction has already illustrated this point. Active citizenship, in this context, focuses upon both the rights and duties of citizens (although these are not spelt out in a written constitution in the UK, which differs from many other states in this respect). However, the section on 'Learning at home and in the community' is addressed in five paragraphs in the main body of the text of *The Learning Age*. This would be consistent with the predominance of the 'learning market'. The learning society as 'an educated society, committed to active citizenship, liberal democracy and equal opportunities', the meaning that Edwards (1997: 184) associated with the social policy framework of post-World War II social democracies, would seem to be more peripheral. The question here is not simply one of differing definitions, then, but of the varying and indeed competing agendas that underpin them.

Definitions of social capital have been similarly problematic, with varying measures of how its accumulation may be assessed. Putnam, whose work on social capital has been key, has defined it as follows: '(B)y analogy with notions of physical capital and human capital – tools and training that enhance individual productivity, "social capital" refers to features of social organisation such as networks, norms and social trust that facilitate coordination, and cooperation for mutual benefit' (1995: 67). He argues that '(f)or a variety of reasons, life is easier in a community blessed with a substantial stock of social capital' (ibid.: 67). While emphasising the benefits of social capital, however, and the correlations with social trust and civic engagement, Putnam also recognised the potential disbenefits of closely knit social, economic and political organisations (including the potential for corruption and organised crime). As he pointed out in a subsequent article (Putnam, 1996), social capital could enable participants to act together more effectively to pursue shared objectives. Whether or not their shared goals are praiseworthy is, of course, entirely another matter. The varying implications of social capital emerge again, subsequently, in this chapter. Putnam himself also recognised the complexity of the concept and the need for further exploration of the different dimensions of social capital which, in his view (Putnam, 1995: 76) was 'clearly not a unidimensional concept'.

Both aspects, the complexity of the concept and the varying implications of social capital, have been explored in subsequent discussions. For example, Schuller (1997) has identified three different versions of the notion of social capital, drawing upon the works of Putnam, Fukuyama and Coleman. There are differences of emphasis, here, despite considerable common ground between the three, and there are particular complexities when it comes to empirical testing. As Riddell *et al.* (1999) have argued, there have also been critics who have approached the concept from counter perspectives, including Marxian critics who have focused upon the negative rather than the positive aspects of social capital. Like economic capital, social capital, according to Marxian critics, has a key role in the reproduction of unequal social relations. Those who are well endowed with capital in whichever form, can pass these advantages on to their children (although, as Riddell *et al.* go on to demonstrate, advantages arising from parental social capital may be offset by other social disadvantages such as disadvantages arising from disabilities).

In the context of this chapter the differing definitions of community empowerment and capacity-building for participation have particular relevance. Here too, there are varying and competing agendas, underpinning the differing meanings for these terms. In essence, it has been argued, 'consultation and participation are concerned with the degree of influence and control over the shaping and implementation of policy' (Brownhill, 1998: 44). Empowerment can be conceptualised in relatively consensual terms, as a process whereby those with little power can come to share in the fruits of development, alongside those who have already achieved significant power, without major challenges to the existing social order. Conversely, empowerment can be conceptualised in less consensual terms; the empowerment of the less powerful involving more significant challenges to the vested interests of the status quo (May and Craig, 1995; Atkinson and Cope, 1997). Empowerment in this sense can be a collective as well as an individual process, the empowerment of less powerful groups in society.

In relation to citizen empowerment, these differences have a history of being constructed in terms of ladders. Arnstein's (1969) eight-rung ladder of citizen participation, much cited in planning texts in North America as well as in Britain, started from the bottom rungs of 'Manipulation' and 'Therapy' moving up the ladder via 'Informing', 'Consultation' and 'Placation' to 'Partnership', 'Delegated power' and ultimately to 'Citizen control' on the top rung. A more recent twelve-rung version of 'the ladder of citizen empowerment' starts with 'Civic hype' on the bottom rung, moving up through 'Cynical consultation' and 'Poor information' towards 'Partnership', 'Delegated control' and ultimately to 'Independent control' by citizens, on the top rung (Burns *et al.*, 1994).

In a recent study carried out with colleagues in South London, 50 key stakeholders, community representatives, local professionals working in these areas and decision makers (including managers and local councillors), selected to represent a range of experiences and perspectives, were asked for their reflections on area regeneration initiatives, such as City Challenge, which had aimed to promote community participation. They were specifically invited to comment upon what the terms 'community empowerment' and 'capacity-building' meant to them, before going on to comment upon their experiences of participation in practice (Anastacio and Mayo, 1999). The replies contained a range of critical reflections, including a number of critical comments about the terms in question. 'Fashionable jargon', commented one, for example, in response to a question about 'capacity-building', 'a buzz word' for the regenerators, 'another hoop to be jumped through' said another, when asked about 'empowerment'.

Overall, the stakeholders' own meanings formed recognisable patterns. The researchers identified three types of responses, which they characterised in terms of three broad categories. The most constricted version defined empowerment in terms of the facilitation of effective consultation. Capacity-building for empowerment, according to this limited view, entailed providing stakeholders with the necessary knowledge and skills, to enable them to feed their views back to decision makers. Broadly, this view rested on the assumption of shared interests; everyone could learn to play together, just so long as they were informed of the rules of the regeneration game.

The second and more extended version defined empowerment in terms that also included the promotion of community initiatives, developing local people's abilities to ensure that their own priorities were lodged proactively on the regeneration agenda and sustained subsequently. Capacity-building, according to this version, entailed a wider range of knowledge and skills, including assertiveness and bargaining skills. It was assumed here that there would be different interests and imbalances of power to be addressed. This version was by far the most commonly held amongst community representatives and professionals and decision makers.

The third version included both of the above, together with a wider concept of power and competing political agendas. According to this version, capacity-building included developing the critical understanding to effectively challenge the vested interests of the powerful, identifying the spaces within which to promote strategies for social change. This view was held by a minority, including a minority of professionals and decision makers as well as by a minority of community representatives. As one senior officer summarised this perspective 'people without power tend to use these terms (capacity-building and empowerment) to mean the acquisition of power whilst those with power tend to mean processes that mask the withholding of power' (Anastacio and Mayo, 1999: 14).

As it will be suggested in more detail subsequently, these differing meanings have varying implications for lifelong learning in terms of the learning required *for* participation, and in terms of the learning achieved *from* participation. This is not to argue that these different approaches are necessarily mutually exclusive, however. On the contrary, in fact.

Stakeholders' views on learning *for* participation in area regeneration

There would seem to be broad agreement among policy makers, professionals and the community representatives they work with that effective training and education strategies are needed if regeneration programmes are to be effective and sustainable. This was the conclusion reached by the second research project to be referred to here, a study that was carried out jointly with the Community Development Foundation as part of the Joseph Rowntree Area Regeneration Programme (Henderson and Mayo, 1998). This was a review of training and education in urban regeneration, focusing mainly on experiences in England, with some inputs based on experiences in Wales, Scotland and Northern Ireland. This study included a literature review and a postal survey that was sent to 100 stakeholder organisations and key individuals, representing a range of interests from voluntary and community sector organisations, local and national regeneration agencies (including local authorities and training providers). While the numbers were small, 43 in total, the responses that were received included a variety of materials illustrating a range of training and learning experiences. In addition, two regeneration localities were selected for case studies (in Brixton, London and in Leeds) for face-to-face interviews with residents, local professionals and managers to provide more detailed inputs, in particular to enable the so far missing voices of black and ethnic minority participants to be heard. As Crook (1995: 1) has demonstrated, too often 'black communities have been the invisible partners'. The local case studies attempted to go some way towards redressing this bias.

From the replies to the questionnaire and from the local case studies, a number of issues were identified, and a draft summary report prepared for further discussion via four seminars/workshops in England and Scotland. Through these discussions, the initial findings were explored with individuals from a range of organisations and communities: local and national partnerships, training providers and professionals working with communities around regeneration issues. Although the numbers were small, the range of interests represented was relatively wide. Despite this breadth there was considerable agreement about the key issues that needed to be addressed. Participants' views were not readily categorisable in terms of their own positions: community representatives shared many of the same concerns as the professionals who were working with them. In particular, it emerged that there was considerable agreement that it was not only community representatives who were in need of education and training. Professionals recognised their own learning needs if they were to work with communities in more effective and empowering ways, a view that was clearly endorsed from the communities' perspectives. This added weight to the views expressed by the community representatives. There were a number of comments from professionals such as the following (Henderson and Mayo, 1998: 2):

> There needs to be more awareness among decision makers about community participation.
>
> I think that the greatest need is to educate decision makers about the voluntary sector, communities and consultation.

Professionals, it was argued, needed 'training to learn how to listen' to communities. Academic consultants, researchers and evaluators were included as being in need of training, along with the trainers themselves. Outside 'experts' should learn how to work with communities as partners in dialogue based upon mutual respect. This was the most relevant expertise of all it was suggested. There were examples of joint training that had been particularly useful in these terms. These included joint training programmes for housing officers, including tenant participation officers, tenant representatives, members of tenant management co-operatives and estate management boards.

Community representatives also considered that they were in need of education and training if they were to participate effectively in area regeneration programmes. Without this, it was extremely difficult, if not actually impossible, to act as more than a rubber stamp, legitimising decision making on the partnership boards that managed the area regeneration programmes. When community representatives attended board meetings they felt that, all too often, they were being faced with masses of paper, frequently written in what to them seemed incomprehensible jargon. There were comments too about the lack of time to seek clarification, because of the tight deadlines inherent in so many regeneration programmes. Training needed to start with a jargon-free induction process to enable them to cope. Community representatives needed to be familiarised with a range of technical information, including programme administration processes, legal frameworks and responsibilities.

In addition, both community representatives and the professionals who were working with them expressed the need for training for confidence-building. Working in new ways was challenging for both groups. Community representatives also referred to the need for basic assertiveness skills, for instance how to speak effectively in formal meetings.

There was widespread agreement, both about the importance of this type of learning, and about the reality that this was not being provided systematically across the country. The research concluded that the national picture was fragmented. While there were examples of good practice in particular areas, in relation to the education and training of decision makers and professionals and voluntary and community sector interests, overall 'there are yawning gaps' (Henderson and Mayo, 1998: v). Resources were not being provided. Even the most basic training was patchy and particular interest groups and areas were missing out almost entirely. It was, for example, difficult to find black or ethnic minority respondents with positive experiences of education and training for area regeneration (although the Brixton case study, carried out in a multi-racial area in South-east London, UK, specifically to explore this aspect, did identify some). People with disabilities were clearly missing out, and there seemed to be very few opportunities for women-only training sessions. Rural areas in Scotland and Wales also emerged as particularly disadvantaged in comparison with urban areas.

There was considerable agreement too about what constituted good practice in the provision of education and training. There was strong criticism of training programmes that failed to start from people's existing knowledge and skills, implying that people were 'empty vessels' waiting to be filled with 'capacity'. A number of the comments specifically referred to the negative impact of trainers who had been 'parachuted in' to provide particular training events, without being properly briefed about what type of learning was actually needed. For some of those who had had negative experiences of this type, the very term 'training' had become a 'turn-off', an experience that they had no wish to repeat. As one professional commented, 'people often think that training won't help. If we run "information sessions" they are often better attended.' 'Community learning might be a more appropriate term' suggested another (Henderson and Mayo, 1998: 7).

The types of experiences that were most positively valued will hardly surprise anyone familiar with adult learning debates. People appreciated learning opportunities that were specifically tailored to their requirements, especially action-based learning, reinforcing and building upon the learning that was taking place within groups. Mentoring was generally seen as valuable, including mentoring for new partnership board members. Exchanges between groups were mentioned as being useful as a source of new ideas and challenges (for example, visiting a community organisation that had already been developing a particular project that the visiting group wanted to develop in their own area, and sharing their experiences of dealing with initial challenges). Joint training opportunities were also valued; there were positive comments, for example, about joint training sessions for tenants and for tenant participation professionals.

While there was considerable emphasis upon relatively informal group learning, there was evidence of interest in course-based learning too. Where training had been experienced positively, there was also evidence of interest in accreditation and progression. In both South and West Yorkshire, for instance, there were examples of accreditation and progression systems that were cited as success stories. Once again, these were rooted in the needs of the organisations and groups in question, for example the development of accreditation to meet the specific requirements of credit unions and single parents' organisations.

There was, then, considerable agreement about the importance of training and learning for communities and for the professionals who work with them, and about the types of approaches that were most appropriate to support participation in area regeneration programmes. Broadly, these approaches were consistent with the middle rungs of the ladders of participation and empowerment. This approach was not only about providing technical information to facilitate effective consultation. There was widespread agreement that, in addition, communities needed access to the knowledge and skills to promote their own initiatives proactively, assertively bargaining for the resources for these in accordance with their own priorities – whether or not these were the regenerators' priorities.

Over and above this, there was also evidence of some interest in learning in relation to the fullest definition of empowerment, developing wider critical analysis and reflection. Safeguarding the space for this type of reflection and critical awareness of the socio-economic and policy contexts would seem to be important, if the differences of approaches towards empowerment are to be respected.

Stakeholders' views on learning *from* participation in area regeneration programmes

In the previous section the discussion focused upon the types of training needed *for* participation in area regeneration programmes. Although such training has been patchy, learning has not been confined to this less-than-adequate provision. Stakeholders have been learning informally through reflecting on their experiences in regeneration programmes, whether or not this learning has been professionally supported or formally recognised.

Although experiential learning was not the primary focus, the South-east London study (which has already been referred to) did provide illustrations of participants' learning, both learning that was facilitated (whether formally or informally) and learning that was not (Anastacio and Mayo, 1999). The following illustrate the range of comments from community participants and from the professionals who were working with them.

First, a number of comments testified to participants' increasing self-confidence, as they succeeded in coping with the new demands that they faced in these area regeneration programmes. A typical comment was that of a community representative, a woman who said that she had struggled with feelings of low self-esteem as a teenage lone parent in the past. She commented on her increased self-confidence, improved communication skills and enhanced self-esteem. She never wanted to stop learning now and she was training for employment in the community sector. There were a number of similar comments of this type.

A number of comments also referred to the value of the practical knowledge and skills that they had gained, including increased understanding of specifics such as the funding mechanisms that underpin regeneration programmes. There was widespread recognition that there were key transferable skills involved here. Area regeneration programmes represented the only realistic sources of funding – whatever reservations particular stakeholders may have expressed about this situation. A number of professionals and community representatives did express the view that these area regeneration programmes were too often being offered as substitutes, to cover for the inadequacy of the main spending programmes that were actually in place.

In addition, a number of community representatives commented upon their developing knowledge and understanding about community organising *per se* – how to build community organisations that were effective, sustainable and democratically accountable to their members. There were comments upon how community organisations had been learning collectively. The community representatives were proactively aiming to acquire the knowledge and skills to develop their own projects, and to build and sustain their own organisations, objectives that were going significantly further than simply learning how to respond effectively when consulted about official regeneration agendas. Professionals reinforced this, commenting upon the learning that was being achieved by community participants. In addition, officers expressed the view that they too had been learning.

This latter type of learning about new ways of working – amongst professionals and community representatives – has potential relevance for the third and most fully developed approach to empowerment and capacity-building, learning 'how to challenge decisions and decision-making processes – learning how to use the system and play them [decision makers] at their own game', as one community representative in South-east London summarised her view of this. Both professionals and community representatives commented on the ways in which community representatives had increased understanding of where power lay and how to organise effectively to promote community agendas.

There were also reflections on the importance of networking and building alliances for change. Professionals and community groups provided comments that demonstrated that they felt they had learnt through sharing views and experiences, and swapping strategies for coping with some of the pressures that they had been experiencing as stakeholders within these area regeneration programmes. These summaries of the lessons learnt would also be consistent with a relatively expanded approach to empowerment and active citizenship.

Clearly the comments of community representatives provide only one source of evidence. These comments may or may not be representative of wider views. The researchers were struck, however, by the parallels between the range and type of views expressed by the community representatives and the professionals who were working with them. The comments from the South-east London study were paralleled in many ways, too, by the comments emerging from the national study.

The literature on informal learning through community participation in area regeneration programmes does not appear to be extensive, although the studies that have been undertaken (albeit addressing learning in voluntary organisations more generally) would suggest that such forms of informal learning were to be anticipated (Elsdon, 1991; Elsdon *et al.*, 1993). In view of the current policy focus upon lifelong learning and active citizenship additional studies would have particular relevance here, building upon the wealth of existing literature on the connections between informal adult learning and community and social action more generally (Billett, 1998; Crowther *et al.*, 1999; Grayson, 1995; Horton and Freire, 1990; Lovett, 1995; Mayo, 1997; Jeffs and Smith, 1996).

Negative aspects too?

So far, the discussion has centred mainly on the positive aspects of learning for those directly involved, whether learning for or from participation in area regeneration programmes, with or without professional facilitation. There was, however, also evidence of more negative aspects. As has already been suggested, a number of stakeholders expressed reservations about particular approaches to training. There were, for example, specific criticisms of training provision based upon assumptions of participants' incompetence, just as there were specific criticisms of training inappropriately 'parachuted in'.

There was some evidence of negative features of experiential learning too. There were, for example, negative comments about the alienating effects of not feeling listened to. It was all too easy to conclude from such experiences that active citizenship was a waste of time. There were, in any case, comments about the time pressures inherent in becoming a community representative. Both community representatives and professionals recognised these pressures together with the pressures of potentially conflicting demands, as a community representative on a partnership board. There were references to differences of perspective here. One (official/professional) person's view of what constituted a 'responsible community representative' could be another person's view of what constituted a 'sell-out', someone who had become incorporated, effectively detached from the community interests that they were supposed to be representing. It was not only community representatives who raised this as an issue. Some of the professionals also recognised these competing pressures, reflecting upon ways in which community representatives might come to internalise official norms, through their experiences of participation. Contemporary forms of governmentability, it has been argued, are characterised by 'educating' people to govern themselves; power being exercised through seduction rather than repression (Edwards, 1997).

While active citizenship could involve learning lessons that might be characterised as negative rather than positive (depending upon the perspective in question) non-participation could also be problematic. The lessons of involuntary non-participation might be especially problematic. There were references to the potentially increasing marginalisation of particular groups if they were not effectively represented in area regeneration programmes. Each of the studies raised questions about the extent to which black and ethnic minority groups were being included at all, let alone effectively included in positive learning experiences. Similar questions emerged in relation to working-class people in mixed-class areas, women (especially single parents), people with disabilities and young people, including young women and men from black and ethnic minority communities. Missing out on potentially positive learning opportunities could effectively compound their experiences of exclusion – in sharpening contrast with the experiences of those community 'stars' who were coming to attain the knowledge, skills and status associated with community entrepreneurship.

Social capital revisited

As it has already been suggested, social capital can have negative as well as positive connotations. Far from representing an unadulterated good, critics have pointed to the role of social capital in reproducing social inequalities (Riddell *et al.*, 1999). From this perspective, social policies to strengthen social capital may be compared with economic policies to extend the holding of share capital; particular individuals and groups may indeed benefit, but the underlying structure of economic and social inequalities remains relatively undisturbed. Particular individuals and groups may even come to experience increased social exclusion as a result.

Social capital can also be undermined and even destroyed, whether or not this is actually the regenerators' intention. Community participation structures that by-pass existing organisations can lead to their further marginalisation, and subsequent decline. Participation structures that result in the detachment of community representatives from their constituencies can have similarly negative consequences. Once again, some individuals and groups may benefit – at least in some respects – while others may feel even less effectively represented and even more marginalised as a result. Strategies to strengthen social capital may pose at least as many questions as they provide answers, especially in the context of strategies to combat social exclusion and to promote social equality more generally. There are issues to be addressed here in relation to lifelong learning and active citizenship.

If missing out on learning opportunities is potentially problematic, would a more comprehensive approach to training for active citizenship provide an appropriate policy response to meet the learning needs, especially the learning needs of socially excluded groups, in area regeneration programmes? There are inherent problems here. In the conclusions of the report of 'Training and education in urban regeneration' (Henderson and Mayo, 1998) the authors argued the case for a national framework, to be negotiated with the different stakeholders, starting from the learning needs of community participants and the professionals working with them. This framework would set standards of provision, appropriately resourced, based upon experiences of best practice. The authors argued that the needs of specific interests, including women and ethnic minority communities, should be safeguarded and that there should be built-in opportunities for accreditation and progression. Adults can and do, of course, learn from their experiences without formal support: but the availability of appropriate guidance and support can facilitate this learning. As Billett (1998: 31) has argued, 'guidance during engagement in goal-directed activities also determines how social practice influences the construction of knowledge'. This implies that learning resources do need to be guaranteed, especially for those who have had least access to them. Without a national framework to ensure this the situation would continue to be fragmented and uneven – despite the appearance of so much consensus about the importance of lifelong learning for active citizenship. However, the effectiveness of such a framework would itself relate to the relative bargaining power of the different stakeholders involved.

The national framework would potentially fit in with recent and current initiatives aimed at developing a more strategic approach to training for community development work more generally. These initiatives include the proposal for a national training organisation (to bring community development together with the related areas of non-formal education to form one sector). The need for a more coherent framework for training and qualification has been recognised as being of more importance than ever, given the range of government programmes currently aimed at involving communities, including programmes that aim to promote community participation in health.

Arguing the case for a national framework, however, is not to be equated with arguing the case for uniformity of provision. On the contrary, in fact. Respondents were more or less unanimous in expressing the view that, if there were to be a national framework, this should be enabling rather than prescriptive. While there was widespread agreement about the importance of safeguarding resources to facilitate learning, there was also widespread agreement about the importance of safeguarding the space for learning strategies to be developed locally and regionally. Stakeholders should be actively involved in negotiating with providers about the most appropriate ways to meet their learning needs – as they define these, themselves. This emerged as the approach that was clearly favoured in other contexts too. To be both relevant and seen to be relevant, education for active citizenship needs to be tailored to the varying needs of the diversity of stakeholder interests, with their active involvement at every stage.

The space for diversity needs to be safeguarded, in any case, to take account of the range of conceptual and theoretical approaches involved. As it has already been suggested, debates on lifelong learning, social capital and active citizenship relate to a variety of discourses. There are competing definitions and agendas here, including competing definitions and agendas for capacity-building and empowerment. There needs to be sufficient space for the higher rungs as well as the lower rungs of the ladder of citizen empowerment.

References

Anastacio, J. and Mayo, M. (1999). 'Welfare models and approaches to empowerment: competing perspectives from area regeneration programmes', *Policy Studies*, vol. 20, no. 1, 5–21.

Arnstein, S. (1969). 'A ladder of citizen participation', *Journal of the American Institute of Planners*, vol. 35, 216–224.

Atkinson, R. and Cope, S. (1997). 'Community participation and urban regeneration in Britain', in Hoggett, P. (ed.) *Contested Communities*, Bristol: Policy Press, pp. 201–221.

Billett, S. (1998). 'Ontogeny and participation in communities of practice: a socio-cognitive view of adult education', *Studies in the Education of Adults*, vol. 30, no. 1, 21–34.

Bron, A., Field, J. and Kuratowicz, E. (eds) (1998). *Adult Education and Democratic Citizenship 11*, Cracow, Poland: Impuls Publisher.

Brownhill, S. (1998). 'From exclusion to partnership? The LDDC and community consultation and participation', *Rising East*, vol. 2, no. 2, 42–72.

Burns, D., Hambleton, R. and Hoggett, P. (1994). *The Politics of Decentralisation: Revitalisation Local Democracy*, London: Macmillan.

Crook, J. (1995). *Invisible Partners: The Impact of the SRB on Black Communities*, London: Black Training and Enterprise Group.

Crowther, J., Martin, I. and Shaw, M. (eds) (1999). *Popular Education and Social Movements in Scotland Today*, Leicester: National Institute of Adult Continuing Education.

DfEE (1998) *The Learning Age: A Renaissance for a New Britain*, London: The Stationery Office.

Edwards, R. (1997). *Changing places? Flexibility, Lifelong Learning and a Learning Society*, London: Routledge.

Elsdon, K. (1991). *Adult Learning in Voluntary Organisations*, vol. 1, Nottingham: Continuing Education Press.

Elsdon, K. with Reynolds, J. and Stewart, S. (1993) *Adult Learning in Voluntary Organisations*, vol. 3, Nottingham: Continuing Education Press.

Grayson, J. (1995). 'Training the community: the case of tenant training', in Mayo, M. and Thompson, J. (eds) *Adult Learning, Critical Intelligence and Social Change*, Leicester: National Institute of Adult Continuing Education, pp. 219–230.

Henderson, P. and Mayo, M. (1998). *Training and Education in Urban Regeneration*, Bristol: Policy Press.

Horton, M. and Freire, P. (1990). *We Make the Road by Walking*, Philadelphia, USA: Temple University Press.

Jeffs, T. and Smith, M. (1996). *Informal Education: Conversation, Democracy and Learning*, Derby: Education Now Books.

Lovett, T. (1995). 'Popular education in Northern Ireland: the Ulster people's college', in Mayo, M. and Thompson, J. (eds) *Adult Learning, Critical Intelligence and Social Change*, Leicester: National Institute of Adult Continuing Education, pp. 275–286.

Mayo, M. (1997). *Imagining Tomorrow*, Leicester: National Institute of Adult Continuing Education.

Mayo, M. and Craig, G. (1995). 'Community participation and empowerment: the human face of structural adjustment or tools for democratic transformation?', in Craig, G. and Mayo, M. (eds) *Community Empowerment*, London: Zed, pp. 1–11.

NAGCELL (1997). *Learning for the Twenty-first Century*, London: National Advisory Group for Continuing Education and Lifelong Learning.

Putnam, R. (1995). 'Bowling alone: America's declining social capital', *Journal of Democracy*, vol. 6, no. 1, 65–78.

Putnam, R. (1996). 'The strange disappearance of civic America', *The American Prospect*, no. 24, 34–48.

Riddell, S., Baron, S. and Wilson, A. (1999). 'Social capital and people with learning difficulties', *Studies in the Education of Adults*, vol. 31, no. 1, 49–65.

Schuller, T. (1997). 'The relations between human capital and social capital', in *A National Strategy for Lifelong Learning*, Newcastle: Department of Education, University of Newcastle.

Schuller, T. (1998). 'Three steps towards a learning society', *Studies in the Education of Adults*, vol. 30, no. 1, 11–20.

Tuckett, A. (1997). *Lifelong Learning in England and Wales. An Overview and Guide to Issues Arising From the European Year of Lifelong Learning*, Leicester: National Institute of Adult Continuing Education.

Index